71276

HT
169
.S82
S744

Hemdahl, Reuel G.
    Cologne and Stockholm:
urban planning and land-
use controls.

DATE	ISSUED TO

71276

HT
169
.S82
S744

Hemdahl, Reuel G.
    Cologne and Stockholm:
urban planning and land-
use controls.

COLOGNE AND STOCKHOLM:

Urban Planning and Land-Use Controls

by

Reuel G. Hemdahl

The Scarecrow Press, Inc.
Metuchen, N.J.   1971

ISBN 0-8108-0421-2

Library of Congress Catalog Card Number 77-167645

To my wife without whom ---

Table of Contents

		Page
Preface		ix

Chapter

I	Introduction: Cologne and Stockholm	15
II	Defining "Urban" and "Metropolitan"	21
III	Cologne: Results of Land-Use Control	48
IV	Cologne: Policy Formation	73
V	Cologne: Administration	93
VI	Cologne: Coordination	114
VII	Cologne: Intergovernmental Relations	126
VIII	Stockholm: Results of Land-Use Control	140
IX	Stockholm: Policy Formation	175
X	Stockholm: Administration	201
XI	Stockholm: Coordination	224
XII	Stockholm: Intergovernmental Relations	241
XIII	Comparative Analysis	264
Methodological Note		286
Appendix (Tables and Charts)		291
Index		323

Tables

1. Numbers of Metropolitan Centers in 11 Selected Countries.   x

In Appendix:
2. Cologne Metropolitan Area: Jurisdictions, Population, Area, and Density.   292

3. Stockholm Metropolitan Area: Jurisdictions, Population, Area, and Density.   294

4. Cologne: Communities and Districts showing Population, Area in Hectares, and Population Density.   296

5. Cologne: Dwelling Units by Number of Rooms, classified by Communities.   300

6. Cologne: Church Membership by Land Legislative Districts as of June 6, 1961.   301

7. Cologne: Election Returns for 1962, 1964 and 1965, by Land Legislative Districts.   302

8. Cologne: Percentage of Persons in Each Occupational Classification (Soziale Stellung), by Land Legislative Districts.   303

9. Cologne: Committees and Subcommittees of the City Council, specifying the Number of Councilmanic and Citizen Voting Members, and Party Affiliation of Members and Chairmen (September 1966).   304

10. Cologne Landkreis: Jurisdictions, Population, Area, and Density.   308

11. Stockholm: Dwelling Units by Number of Rooms, classified by Inner and Outer City, as of 1965.   309

12. Stockholm: Inner and Outer City Parishes showing Population, Area in Hectares, and Population Density, as of 1968.   310

13. Stockholm Metropolitan Area: Community Shopping
     Centers in New Towns.   312

14. Stockholm: Numbers of Establishments, Employes,
     and Median Incomes by Occupational Groupings, as of
     1965.   313

15. Stockholm Metropolitan Area: Population and Employ-
     ment in 1960.   314

16. Stockholm: Voting Participation (by Per Cent of
     Eligible Voters) in all Elections since World II.   316

17. Stockholm: Median Income per Male Income Earner,
     by Parish (1967).   317

18. Communal Blocs by Election Districts for the Pro-
     posed Stor-Stockholm Landsting, showing the Population
     in 1963 and the Estimated Population for 1975.   318

Chart 1. Number of Salaried Employees T 47 1955-1965,
          Stockholm.   320

Chart 2. Number of Workers 1955-1965, Stockholm.   321

Chart 3. Development of Salaries and Wages in Stockholm
          1955-1964.   322

Maps

Page

1. The Rhine-Ruhr Metropolitan Region   34

2. The Cologne Metropolitan Area   37

3. Metropolitan Stockholm; Greater Stockholm   40
   County, January 1, 1971.   255

4. Land Legislative (Voting) Districts in Cologne   78

5. Property acquired by the City of Stockholm
   in the City as of 1966.   150

Preface

The western world is becoming metropolitanized before its people have adequately adapted to the urban way of
life, although governmental institutions do attempt to cope
with this cultural lag. Nowhere in the United States is the
lag more evident than in land-use policy. Society and
government are reluctant to limit freewheeling private enterprise in its use of land. The pioneer spirit prevails, though
the frontier has long since disappeared, and restrictions of
a landowner's right to use his land as he sees fit are
suspect. Protected as the landowner is by the "due process"
clauses in state and federal constitutions, community benefits in most instances has to be proven beyond a reasonable
doubt before individual restrictions can be emplaced, and
the concept of community benefit itself is usually as archaic
as the concept of landowners' rights, with which it so often
conflicts.

Constantinos A. Doxiadis, the distinguished city planner from Athens, in an address to urban experts in America
surprised his audience with the proposition that not much
longer will there be cities surrounded by open countryside.
What is coming, he warned, is a situation where small
patches of open countryside are completely surrounded by
urbanization. His prediction is materializing along the East
Coast from southern New Hampshire to northern Virginia,
which area the eminent geographer Jean Gottman of the
University of Paris has analyzed in the Twentieth Century
Fund study, Megalopolis. It is likewise materializing in
the area around the southern portion of Lake Michigan from
metropolitan Milwaukee south through northeastern Illinois,
and even on through northern Indiana into the state of
Michigan. Megalopolises exist in California spreading out
from Los Angeles and San Francisco, and in a few other
parts of the U. S.

More informed attention will have to be given soon
to the planning both of urban and rural land use in order to
guide this sprawling urban development adequately and to
protect the natural resources which it threatens. Stricter

ix

Table 1. Numbers of Metropolitan Centers in 11 Selected Countries

	1. Metropolitan Areas with Population of 100,000 or over. 1955 est.	2. Municipalities with population of 300,000 or over, 1960	3. Urban Agglomerations of 400,000 population or over 1960	4. Total Population in Millions 1960	5. Area in km.	6. Population Density
United States	147	39	41	179.3	9,363,389	20
U.S.S.R.	130	51	33	208.8	22,402,200	9
United Kingdom	58	13	11	52.6	244,030	217
West Germany	40	17	14	53.9	248,454	217
France	30	4	4	46.5	551,208	83
Netherlands	14	3	3	9.6	33,612	346
Belgium	5	0	3	9.1	30,507	301
Sweden	4	2	2	7.4	449,793	17
Denmark	4	1	1	4.5	43,043	107
Finland	3	1	1	4.4	337,009	13
Norway	2	1	1	3.2	323,917	11

Sources: Column 1.   International Urban Research, The World's Metropolitan Areas.   Berkeley: The University of California Press, 1959, Appendix, pp. 39-42 and 53-60.

Columns 2 and 3.   United Nations, Demographic Yearbook, 1960.   Table 10.

Columns 4, 5, and 6.   United Nations, Ibid, 1960 and 1962, Table 1.

x

regulations will have to be initiated and enforced so that urbanization plans move from the papers on the drawing board to reality in the true interest of the community at large.

The numerous small municipal jurisdictions which now chop up our great metropolitan areas, and the numerous single-purpose governments and agencies overlapping these jurisdictions, must be coordinated as a first step in rational urban government.

Nostalgic remembrances of a past age, which cannot be resurrected nor recreated, are not prescriptions for tomorrow. Such nostalgia used as a weapon to slow or prevent urban change will not succeed. What is necessary is constructive action taken soon enough to prevent chaos.

The problems are world-wide. Cities in Germany and Sweden have struggled with the same problems that bother us. The basic question raised in this research project is: What can we in the U.S.A. learn from West German and Swedish experience? This book is focused on urban planning and land-use controls in two metropolitan areas, Cologne, in the Federal Republic of Germany, and Stockholm, the capital of Sweden.

In the final draft of a prospectus for this research, two hypotheses were established for investigation:

1. Land-use control in the interest of community development has been exerted to a degree in Cologne and Stockholm unknown in the U.S.

2. Supervision from higher levels of government has provided sufficiently successful urban coordination within the metropolitan areas of West Germany and Sweden, that it presents a worthy model for American government.

A fundamental consideration underlying this study was stated in the research prospectus as follows: Basic to urban and metropolitan development are effective urban planning and land use. Other governmental functions are conditioned by-- and the good life for the citizenry in a metropolitan area is dependent upon--the effectiveness of both.

The author's theory on effective land use is developed in his earlier book entitled Urban Renewal. This theory is supported and developed further in the present work in which

xi

attention is given to local government structure, the interrelationships of national and local governments, policy formation, and the financial and personnel policies of these two
cities.

A sabbatical and a research grant from the College
of Arts and Sciences of the University of Louisville made
this study possible. The research is based on legislation,
reports and publications in German and Swedish, numerous
interviews partially specified in the footnotes, and personal
observations while driving in and around the Cologne and
Stockholm metropolitan areas during a two-month residency
in each city in 1966. One additional month each was devoted
to interviews and observations in other cities and towns in
the two countries. The interviews should be mentioned first
as the most important source of information, since specifications concerning legislation, all of the administrative and
other reports, references to relevant publications, and
much valuable interpretation were received from the inter-
viewees.

In addition to those with officials involved in city
planning and administration of land-use controls, law,
finance, personnel, and coordination of metropolitan governmental activities, interviews were secured with members of
city councils, land and federal officials in West Germany
and national officials in Sweden, directors of and personnel
in research institutes, professors in universities and other
institutions of higher learning, representatives of the press,
representatives of the German and Swedish equivalents of
Chambers of Commerce, representatives of labor unions,
and other interested citizens.

The author is indebted for their time and ideas to all
who were interviewed, but particularly to those with whom
he was in correspondence--invaluable both in planning the
research and in analyzing the notes and materials while
writing the book. A special note of gratitude is due the
Deutschen Städtetag (German Association of Towns and Cities),
which through the personal efforts of Herr Rüdiger Robert
Beer arranged most of the interviews prior to the author's
arrival in Cologne, and similar thanks are also due the
Svenska Stadsförbundet (Swedish Association of Municipalities),
which through Herr Enar Lindquist provided an open door at
the City Hall in Stockholm. Very valuable interviews were
provided with the specialized personnel in both associations.
Grateful acknowledgment is made specifically to the Cologne
and Stockholm Statistical Offices, the Center for Local

Government Studies in West Berlin, the National Institute for Building Research in Stockholm, and the International Union of Local Authorities, in The Hague, Netherlands, for interviews and for permission to use their resources.

Prudence and custom dictate that the author accept full responsibility not only for the organization and presentation of the study, but for any errors of fact and/or judgment in it. Furthermore, there should be no assumption that the many persons who provided counsel and otherwise contributed to this study are in agreement with the judgments and conclusions herein expressed.

Gratitude is also extended to Mrs. Allen Forcht, who typed the German and Swedish correspondence as well as the manuscript.

Chapter I

INTRODUCTION: COLOGNE AND STOCKHOLM

Cologne, known among continental Europeans as "Köln,"
is situated on the Rhine, immediately north of the rugged and
castle-studded section of that famous river, which enjoys a
justified reputation for superb scenery from an indefinite
point south of Mainz to the Cologne metropolitan area. To
the north of Cologne begins the tremendous Ruhr industrial
region. Thus, the Cologne metropolitan area, located on the
flat river plain, through which winds the Rhine, bridges these
two well-known portions of the Rhine.

Incorporated by the Roman Emperor Augustus as
"Colonia Agrippina" in 50 A.D., one thousand two hundred
years before the first stone was laid for its "Dom," Cologne
is one of the oldest of German cities. Simultaneously,
Cologne is a modern city, contemporary in every respect,
where current concepts of city planning, making full use of
natural site advantages, are in evidence.

The population of Cologne is 854,000, and the metropolitan area (depending upon definition) is well over one million. The city proper covers 251.36 square kilometers (about
115.84 square miles), but the metropolitan area, the totality
of which is within North Rhine-Westphalia,[1] is substantially
larger. The city is situated midway between the northern
and southern boundaries of the Federal Republic of Germany
and within sixty kilometers (37 miles) of the Netherlands'
border. While the cities of Berlin, Hamburg and Munich are
larger, the metropolitan area of Cologne, being located on
the edge of the Ruhr complex, is part of the largest urbanized
portion of Germany, a European megalopolis, and therefore
it assumes vital importance in the German economy. Furthermore, in Cologne is located the Deutscher Städtetag (German
Association of Municipalities), servicing municipalities
throughout the Bundesrepublik. This description partially
answers the question of why Cologne was selected for this
study.

Stockholm is spread over fifteen or more islands in

Lake Mälaren and "Saltsjön" (part of the Baltic), and three
parts of the main-land. It lies about 40 kilometers (25
miles) by air from the open Baltic or a slightly longer distance by water or land depending on which of numerous
routes is taken. To the west, Lake Mälaren stretches
another 100 kilometers (62 miles). In the center of the
city, by Gamla Stan, the island on which the original city
was built in the 1250's, the waters of Lake Mälaren empty
into the channels, which by labyrinthian routes reach the
Baltic. The waterways crisscross the city and the metropolitan area, narrowing into channels and canals, and widen-
ing into bays and small lakes, which collectively are considered to be a part of Lake Mälaren and /or the Baltic. The
metropolitan area (again, depending upon definition) extends
at least 100 kilometers (60 miles) north and south, and 60
kilometers (37 miles) east and west, including the shores of
the Baltic. Throughout the area are granite projections and
a heavy growth of beech, fir and spruce trees, enhancing
the beauty of the setting, much of it mirrored in surrounding
and penetrating waters.

Metropolitan Stockholm is situated in the southern
third of Sweden geographically; but in terms of population
distribution, it is situated in the northeastern part of the
urbanized portion of the country. The Stockholm metropolitan area is the largest in population in Sweden. Urbanization is developing southwest from Stockholm to Gothenburg
on Sweden's west coast, and south from there to include
Hälsingborg and Malmö in Sweden and even Helsingør
(Elsinore) and Copenhagen, a potential megalopolis in
Denmark.

Stockholm itself is not one of the oldest cities in
Sweden; however, smaller towns within the metropolitan
area are. Sigtuna, for example, located on Lake Mälaren
between Stockholm and Uppsala, was established in the Tenth
Century and is next to the oldest municipality in the country.
The oldest is Birka, also located on Lake Mälaren. The
Stockholm metropolitan center was the first to develop in
Sweden.

Stockholm's population in the mid Sixties was 800, 000
and the metropolitan area had well over one million inhabitants. The city covers 186 square kilometers (115 square
miles), and the metropolitan area is substantially larger. [2]
Stockholm is the major manufacturing center of Sweden, but
efforts are exerted to prevent additional growth of industry

in the nation's capital, so that it can be the headquarters for decision-making in national governmental affairs, and an important decision-making center for industry, but not a production center. Here also are the headquarters for Svenska Stadsförbundet (Swedish Association of Municipalities), servicing cities throughout the country.

Cologne and Stockholm are comparable in several respects: 1) advantageous geographic location; 2) population size; 3) geographic coverage; 4) economic significance within their respective countries; 5) historic significance; 6) evidence of competent city planning; 7) headquarters site for the nation's association of municipalities.[3]

One major difference, among others, between these two cities and metropolitan centers is the circumstances behind their redevelopments. Cologne has been in the path of military invasions from the beginning of its history and has suffered numerous destructions by military conquest. Current German literature about Cologne merely mentions the devastation from bombing during World War II as one more of a lengthy list. Cologne, however, never was exterminated. Always after the military ravages, the citizens who had sought temporary refuge elsewhere and those who were still alive within the city rebuilt Cologne.

Stockholm, on the other hand, has never suffered military destruction or even attack. In 1471, Danish troops laid siege, and in 1719, Russian troops; however on both occasions, the attacking forces were defeated before any damage was done to the city. In 1520, Danish troops entered the city by subterfuge and slew 80 to 100 of Stockholm's leading citizens. Again there was no physical damage to the city. The only destruction ever suffered in Stockholm occurred in the Middle Ages from an ancient enemy of cities and towns: fire. Since 1751 there has been no seriously dangerous conflagration in Stockholm. In brief, the redevelopment of modern Stockholm has been by the peaceful processes of land acquisition, land clearance, and redevelopment.

Rebuilding a city after destruction by war and the peaceful process of land development are both expensive. The destruction of Cologne in World War II did provide that city an opportunity to rebuild according to contemporary needs and planning ideas; however, this had to be done at a terrible cost, far greater than any peacetime process of redevelopment.

Why select two metropolitan areas instead of concentrating on two municipalities, which would be a far simpler research problem? A basic premise of this research is the proposition that cities no longer function in isolation, but are more and more becoming integral parts of larger urban complexes; therefore to be realistic, municipal government must be investigated only in the larger setting.

Since over-all metropolitan governments in American metropolitan centers do not seem to be "in the cards" in the foreseeable future, the problem of effective coordination of existing governments within each of the metropolitan centers needs to be solved, either as the best remaining alternative, or as a step towards eventual formation of real metropolitan government, which some people fear today as "monster government."

Why select metropolitan centers in Germany and Sweden? No systematic study of German municipal government or metropolitan development has been published in English since World War II although noteworthy changes have taken place since the termination of hostilities. Even though numerous magazine articles and portions of larger publications in English have dealt with city planning and with the administration of the so-called welfare programs at the local level in Sweden, very few systematic studies of Swedish metropolitan development have been published in English. In general, European governments faced with limited land resources have inaugurated land-use controls much earlier than in the U.S.A. and have had more experience with this kind of control. We in America, therefore, may profit from European experience.

The problems facing German and Swedish municipal governments are very similar to those facing U.S. municipalities. The techniques of city planning are also very similar. The major differences concern the land-use policies themselves, the process of their formation, and the nature of their administration. In this book the organization of findings will be given in terms of problem areas well known in U.S. metropolitan centers:

1.   The Central Business District--the old city.

2.   The Gray Area--the areas surrounding the central business district.

3.   The Growing Edge--the suburbs and the urban

fringe (new towns in both Cologne and Stockholm).

4. Circulation--movement of people and material throughout the city and the metropolitan area.

The chapters on how this was accomplished will raise questions about and present analyses of:

1. The procedure of policy formation.

2. The opportunities for citizens to participate in policy formation.

3. The legal power of government to control land use and related matters.

4. The rights of affected private property owners.

5. The bureaucratic structure of policy administration.

6. The inter-relationships of the national government, the Länder (in West Germany), the municipal governments, and other local and intrametropolitan governments as regards land use.

The chapter on the comparative analysis and evaluation will be presented in terms of:

1. Problems.

2. Policy.

3. Programs of action.

4. Opportunities for popular participation in policy formation and program development.

5. Administrative structures and procedures.

6. Coordinative devices and techniques both within the core city and within the metropolitan area.

Even though the above schema may not seem to show emphasis on "coordination," the efforts and accomplishments as well as failures in this direction are presented. Coordination is a difficult problem in the Cologne and Stockholm centers as it is in metropolitan centers in the United States.

The coordination of land-use controls is no simple
matter, and research analysis of it necessitates the inclusion
of much that may seem relatively unrelated in order to provide a useful frame of reference.

Notes

1. Estimate for 1965 vom Das Statistischen Amt der Stadt
   Köln, February 9, 1966.

2. Statistiska Centralbyrån, Statistisk Årsbok for Sverige,
   1965, p. 5 and 6.

3. The term "city planning" is used to designate planning
   by the personnel of an incorporated municipality. The
   term "urban planning" is used to designate that planning, joint or otherwise, done by several jurisdictions
   for the larger urbanized area.

Chapter II

DEFINING "URBAN" AND "METROPOLITAN"

A study of urban problems that reaches across national boundaries raises questions of definition--what is "urban"? what is "metropolitan"?--that have baffled students of
comparative urban affairs since 1895 when Adna Ferrin Weber courageously initiated research for his Ph. D. disserta-
tion on the Growth of Cities in the Nineteenth Century. [1]
Even studies within one country leave much to be desired
in the way of adequate definitions. A series of questions
face the researcher: 1) Is the definition basically valid?
2) Having a reasonably valid definition, does it enable him
to measure what he wants to measure? 3) Is it possible
for him to secure data that are comparable?

Since comparisons will be made among Cologne,
Stockholm, and cities in the U. S. , and observations will be
made as regards cities in other North European countries,
the concept of urbanization will be examined in the general
setting of selected North European countries and the U. S. A.

"Urbanization" is defined largely in terms of political boundaries and population. West Germany and France
specify as urban those communes (Germeinde in West Germany) that have 2, 000 or more inhabitants, qualified in
France with the phrase "in the administrative center."
Scanning the map of North Europe, variations immediately
become evident. Denmark reports as "urban" all agglomerations of 250 or more inhabitants. Norway reports all incorporated urban centers. In contrast Austria and Belgium
report as "urban" only communes of 5, 000 or more inhabitants; Switzerland, only communes of 10, 000 or more population; and the Netherlands only communes of 20, 000 or
more. [2]

In a report on Growing Space Needs in the Urbanized
Region, prepared at the International Conference of the International Federation for Housing and Planning, held in

Örebro, Sweden, in June and July 1965, the following unofficial statement appears:

> It should be noted that the lower statistical limit
> for an urban settlement varies enormously. In the
> Nordic countries the boundary is set at 200 per-
> sons. [3]

The United Kingdom and Sweden have included cities, boroughs and urban districts as urban. The term "city" has no legal significance in England, Wales, and North Ireland. All incorporated places are either boroughs or county boroughs. In Scotland, cities and boroughs (burghs) with a population of 1,000 or more inhabitants are included as urban. In England and North Ireland, both "urban" and "rural" districts have the same population spread: from under 1,000 to over 100,000, differing in size from 2 to 40 square miles in the case of urban districts and 3 to 450 square miles in the case of rural districts, and with this an obvious difference in land use and building density. [4]

In a reply, dated April 3, 1967, to an inquiry concerning the distinction between urban and rural districts, the following statement was given:

> The present law sets no exact criterion by which
> a rural area can claim to be renamed urban. Un-
> der the Local Government Act, 1933, a county
> council must institute an inquiry for any proposed
> change of status within its jurisdiction if "a prima
> facie case exists."

> In the future however we can expect more precise
> criteria. Population is to be one of the factors
> which the Royal Commission of Local Government
> will take into account when formulating their pro-
> posals for submission to the Minister for Housing
> and Local Government. The Royal Commission
> was set up in February 1966, held its first meet-
> ing at the end of May, 1966, and is expected to
> complete its work in about two years. [5]

Throughout the decades, Sweden has made several changes in its definition of "urban." In the 1940 and 1945 census, cities (städer), boroughs (köpingar) and communes (kommuner) were included; however, during the 1920-1935 period and again in the 1950's, only cities were included in

the official statistics. [6] As of the present, there is very
little difference between cities, boroughs and other communes.
As Per Langenfelt describes the situation:

> It cannot be denied that these historical names
> have now lost their real sense. There are rural
> communes which have about 30,000 inhabitants and
> are completely urbanized, while on the other hand
> there are small towns of historical importance
> with scarcely one thousand people. [7]

On June 6, 1966, Secretary Lundh, Kommunalförbundet (Association of Communes) in an interview in the offices
of the Kommunalförbundet, commented:

> Originally a commune (landskommun) was a small
> village; a borough, a moderate-sized market town;
> and a city, a substantial urban center. Now,
> there is virtually no difference legally or in popu-
> lation. For example, Öregrund, which is a city,
> has 2,000 inhabitants; Täby, which is a borough,
> has 28,000; and Häddinge, which is a landskommun,
> has 41,000. [8]

Taking cognizance of this, the Swedish Satistiska Centralbyrån has during the past decade distinguished "urban"
and "rural" not in terms of political subdivision, but in
terms of "densely populated areas" and "sparsely populated
areas," and the population in urban and rural areas is reported in this way in the Swedish 1960 and 1965 census reports.

Densely populated areas are defined to include all
house groupings with at least 200 inhabitants provided the
distance between the houses normally does not exceed 200
meters. If the distance between the houses exceeds 200
meters, this shall not be considered as a break in the house
grouping when the space between the houses is used for public benefit, such as street or highway right of way, parking
area, park recreation area or church yard. The same applies to such unbuilt areas as are used for storage space,
railroad right of way, and embankment. [9]

The 200 meters distance between houses makes possible the inclusion in a "densely populated area" of parcels
9.8 acres in size, or in effect parcels of ten acres. On
the assumption of three persons per family, this would mean

only about 200 inhabitants per square mile. One may seriously question whether this openness of development, or lack
of density, can properly be classified as urban; nevertheless,
avoiding the use of governmental entities, such as "city,"
"borough," and "commune," which have less and less significance within countries as well as in international comparisons, and using instead a measure involving building
density, an improvement in reporting has resulted. If the
statistical agencies of all the countries would report urbanization to the United Nations Statistical Office in terms of
housing density, population density, or both, within larger
administrative, record-keeping districts, such as counties,
or their equivalent, significant comparisons could more
readily be made.

For the 1960 census, the U. S. Bureau of the Census
defined as "urban population" all persons living in: a) incorporated places of 2, 500 inhabitants or more; b) the
densely settled urban fringe, whether incorporated or unincorporated, of urbanized areas; c) counties that have no incorporated municipalities within their boundaries and have
a density of 1, 500 persons or more per square mile; d)
unincorporated places of 2, 500 inhabitants or more. [10]

"Urbanized areas" are defined in another connection
as "enumeration districts with a population density of 1, 000
inhabitants or more per square mile." [11]

The above specified population densities seem to be
more realistic for the determination of the "urban condition" than the criteria specified by the Statistiska Centralbyrån in Sweden; nevertheless the implications of the criteria, established by the U. S. Bureau of the Census, need
to be examined. These U. S. criteria actually mean 2. 34
persons per acre in the case of 1, 500 persons per square
mile, and 1. 56 persons per acre in the case of the 1, 000
persons per square mile, both of which are less than the
statistically average family. The actual average density in
incorporated places of less than 2, 500 population and "other
urban" areas, which are unincorporated, happens to be
1, 781 per square mile, or 2. 78 persons per acre. Utilities
in the midwest of the U. S. A. have for years used the rule
of thumb policy that it is normally not economically feasible
to extend utilities through areas with less than five persons
per acre. [12] This means a population density of 3, 200 persons per square mile, which is almost equal to the current
population density in North Rhineland-Westphalia, which is

partly agricultural and partly urban with adequate open space
for the amenities of life. [13]

So far as a population density minimum for the definition "urban" is concerned, the 1,000 persons per square
mile of residentially used land, roughly the U.S. Bureau of
the Census minimum specification, seems to be a more reasonable minimum than various other criteria currently used.
This equals 620 persons per square kilometer or 31% of the
current density in all of Rhineland-Wesphalia.   Since utilities are undergoing continuous technical improvement with
resultant reductions in cost of extensions, and other modern
factors as well enter the pattern of urban growth outside of
municipal boundaries, service to a lower density of population
than that formerly considered economically feasible comes
within the realm of the reasonable.   Furthermore, in order
to provide comparability with U.S. statistics on "urbanized
areas," the minimum of 1,000 persons per square mile is
accepted for application in the Cologne and Stockholm areas.
This means 620 persons per square kilometer.

The relative similarity in definition of "urban" in
West Germany, France, England, United States, Sweden, Denmark, Finland, and Norway (despite the various areas containing a minimum of 200 persons that are called "urban" in
Nordic countries) seems to justify comparison of the degree
of urbanization in these countries on the explicit understanding that this is a very rough comparison of over-all urbanization, based upon reports to the United Nations Statistical
Office for the years specified.

Per Cent of Population in Urban Areas[14]

Year	England and Wales	Year	Germany 1937 Area	Year	U.S.A.
1921	79.3	1925	64.6	1920	51.2
1931	80.0	1930	67.3	1930	56.2
1951	80.8	1939	69.9	1940	56.5
1961	80.8	West Germany only		1950	64.0
		1939	70.5	1960	69.9
		1946	68.6		
		1950	71.1		
		1960	76.8 [15]		

Year	France	Year	Sweden	Year	Denmark
1921	46.4	1920	29.5	1921	43.2
1931	51.2	1930	32.5	1930	58.9
1936	52.4	1935	34.2	1940	63.9
1946	53.0	1940	44.4	1950	67.3
1954	55.9	1945	49.5	1960	74.0
1961	(no report)	1950	47.5		
		1960	(51.9)		
			72.8		

Year	Finland	Year	Norway
1920	13.9	1920	29.6
1930	18.6	1930	28.4
1940	23.3	1946	28.0
1950	32.3	1950	32.2
1960	55.9	1961	32.1

The first of the two percentage figures for 1960 in Sweden is on the 1950 basis of including "städer" only. The second percentage figure represents the urbanization in accordance with the 1960 formula, which includes cities, boroughs, and communes with the required building density. The first percentage is obviously an understatement. Without questioning the validity of the formula used in the 1960 census determination of urban population, notice needs to be taken of the change in formula, and the resultant exaggeration of the urbanization increase in Sweden, also the affect of this on comparisons with the other countries in which no changes were made in the definitions of "urban," except for very minor changes in the U.S.A.

It is evident from United Nations Demographic Yearbook data that the United Kingdom has the highest degree of urbanization, with West Germany second, in Europe. The percentages for the Netherlands and Belgium as reported by the United Nations are not included in the above table because of comparative understatement due to dissimilar notions in these two countries of what constitutes an urban area. It is reasonable to rank the Netherlands with the United Kingdom, and Belgium between West Germany and France, as regards urbanization. Southern England, the Netherlands, Belgium and southern Germany are situated in one of the densest population concentration belts of the planet. Within the U.S. a comparable high population density belt extends from Boston to Washington, D.C., for which specific area Jean Gottmann coined the term "megalopolis"; however, the over-all urbanization of population in the United States is at a lower level than in any of the countries mentioned above.

Another observation from the United Nations census reports is the greater rate of urbanization in the formerly less urbanized countries, except in the case of Norway, indicating the possibility of an eventual high level of urbanization throughout Western Europe; particularly in the middle and northern portions. In spite of the probable exaggeration of urbanization reports from Sweden due to the low population minimum for qualification statistically as urban settlements, it is noteworthy that the speed of urbanization is of concern to the Swedish public.

At a session of the twelfth congress of the Swedish Farm Association, held in Stockholm on June 21, 1966, a report was submitted that the membership had diminished one third in five years. In connection with this report, Stockholm's Dagens Nyheter, published (on the same day) the following first page headline: "No Farmers Left in Future Agriculture." The article analyzed the proposition that the acquisition of the less productive agricultural land for forestry, the mechanization and "rationalization" of agriculture, and the increasing demands for more skilled labor in industry, continue to decrease the need for manpower in agriculture and have caused a sharp increase during the past ten years in urbanization in Sweden.

A study by Sven Godlund estimates that the urban settlements' share of the population in Sweden by 1975 will be around 85 percent. [16] As highlighted at the International Conference of the International Federation for Housing and Planning, held in Örebro, Sweden, in 1965:

> One of the most important problems is the shortage
> of building land near the expanding cities. With the
> present and expected pace of growth this problem
> will be difficult to surmount. This agitates the im-
> portant task of harmonizing to a smoothly running
> unit the varying competing claims on space within the
> limited areas of concentration. [17]

The human dimension of this problem was provided by

a Mr. Ramsten, Ombudsman for Lands Organizationen Av Arbetare (the Confederation of Swedish Trade Unions), in an interview in Stockholm, June 9, 1966: The worker in a small
town finds no market for his home, but must sell at a low
price and compete in a high priced market for a residence in
order to accept a job in the metropolitan center.

Housing is equally difficult to secure in the metropolitan centers of West Germany, yet the migration to these centers continues unabated. The three officially recognized metropolitan centers in Sweden contain over 26 per cent of the total
population and the percentage is increasing each year.[18] In
West Germany, the 69 officially recognized "Stadtregionen"
(metropolitan centers) contain over 58 per cent of the total population and the percentage is increasing each year.[19]

What is the definition of "metropolitan"? The full
meaning of this word is much more complex than that of "urban," yet it may be more useful and significant for purposes
of international comparisons. A brief digression may be helpful here in understanding the present-day significance of "metropolitan."

In 1956 the Ford Foundation granted the University of
California the principal funds for a five-year research
program on cities and urbanization throughout the
world. With these funds the International Urban Research Center was established on the Berkeley cam-
pus, under the aegis of the University's Institute of
International Studies.[20]

As far as "cities and urbanization throughout the world"
is concerned, the I. U. R. Center staff soon discovered that:

The available data on cities, although often used and
cited, suffer from serious defects. Among these the
most important is the lack of comparability from one
country to another in the way cities are deliniated.
A second important defect is the lack of correspondence between cities, so-called, and the actual urban
aggregates. The International Urban Research Center therefore tried to establish greater international
comparability in the delimitation of urban populations,
and to do this in terms of a unit, the metropolitan
area, which would embrace the actual urban aggregates.[21]

The definition adopted for a metropolitan area is: Any administrative division which is considered a county-equivalent with a total of more than 100,000 inhabitants and with at least 65 per cent of its labor force working in economic activities other than agriculture. [22]   This is a modification of the U.S. Bureau of the Census 1950 definition of the Standard Metropolitan Statistical Area (SMSA).

For the 1960 census, the Census Bureau specified that in order to be "metropolitan," there must be at least one central city with a population of 50,000 or more.   Included also is the county in which this city is situated and the contiguous counties provided: a) at least three quarters of the labor force in that county is engaged in non-agricultural employment; b) at least half or more of its population lives in contigious minor civil divisions with a density of at least 150 persons per square mile in an unbroken chain, if minor civil divisions with such density radiate from the central city in the area; (an alternative to this criterion is the requirement that the number of non-agricultural employees in the county in question must equal 10 percent or more of the non-agricultural workers in the county containing the central city); c) social and economic integration with the central city is established by means of evidence from records of newspaper circulation and delivery service from the central city, telephone calls and public transport to and from the central city, maintenance of charge accounts in retail stores of the central city, and cooperation by civil groups and planning organizations in the central city and the county concerned. [23]

Dr. John C. Bollens of the University of California specified in 1965:

> At the world level, the closest widely used concept to metropolitan area is "the great city," which is applied to urban concentrations of at least 100,000 population.   However, it should be noted that different criteria are employed in various countries to determine the boundaries of urban concentration.   Data for great cities, therefore are not fully comparable on a world-wide basis, but they do represent useful information. [24]

Dr. William A. Robson of the University of London takes the position that the concept of "metropolitan" must be variable, depending on the total population of the country and the size and nature of its economy.   In 1954, he expressed the opinion:

> In our view, in a country as large and highly de-
> veloped as the U. S. A. , only metropolitan areas with
> a central city of not less than 300, 000 and a total
> population of at least 400, 000 should be regarded. [25]

In this connection, notice should be taken of comments
by Dr. Olaf Boustedt, Direktor des Statischen Landesamtes
Hamburg, who prepared the section entitled, "Stadtregionen
1961" for the Statisches Jahrbuch Deutscher Gemeinden:

> Among the great number of varying possibilities of
> setting boundaries for the metropolitan agglomera-
> tions of space, in Germany it was decided to pro-
> ceed in accordance with the concept of socioeconom-
> ic space arrangement which approximates most
> closely the American "Metropolitan Area." [26]

For each of the "Stadtregionen," listed in the Statistisches Jahrbuch, the population of the core city, of each of
the suburbs, the total population of the "urbanized zone," and
the total population of the "border zone" surrounding the urbanized zone, are specified, also the grand total for each
"Stadtregion." Of the 69 "Stadtregionen," six had core cities
with populations in the 40, 000 category, and ten Stadtregionen
had total populations under 100, 000: one in the 70, 000 category, six in 80, 000 category, and three in the 90, 000 category. Simultaneously, the Statistisches Jahrbuch classified
only cities with 100, 000 population or more as "Gross-
städte." [27]

It is also of interest that boroughs in England become
county-boroughs, comparable to city-county consolidations in
the U. S. when the borough has reached a population of 100, 000.
The 100, 000 population factor seems to carry weight in European statistical considerations as regards the "great city," or
what statisticians in the U. S. A. describe as "metropolitan
city."

The criticisms leveled at the definition of "metropolitan" as used in America are worth consideration by the Office of Management and Budget (formerly Bureau of the Budget), which defines the Standard Statistical Metropolitan Area
concept for the Census Bureau; nevertheless it is true that a
serious effort has been made in this country to provide a
precise definition. Of particular significance are the criteria

of non-agricultural employment and social and economic integration with a "core city," or "core cities." In a metropolitan area, open spaces may well reduce the population
density in parts of the metropolitan area below the 1.56 persons per acre level without making those parts "rural." At
this point, the qualifications specified above by the Office of
Management and Budget and the Swedish statistical practice
of excluding land use for public benefit, are relevant.

Drawing upon the specifications presented above as
regards metropolitan centers, the number of urban agglomerations of 100,000 population or over, recognized by the International Urban Research Center, University of California,
as metropolitan areas, (populations estimated in 1955); the
number of municipalities with populations of 300,000 or over;
and the number of urban agglomerations of 400,000 population or over (as of 1960), are presented for the several
countries concerned below in Table 1 in the Appendix. The
U.S.S.R. is included for the sake of super-power comparı-
son.

Accepting William A. Robson's thesis about metropoli-
tanization, the U.S. and the U.S.S.R., the two super-powers,
are obviously in a classification by themselves. West Germany and the United Kingdom, which are comparable, are
highly metropolitanized; so also are the smaller neighbors,
the Netherlands and Belgium. The southern portion of Sweden is becoming metropolitanized though not yet on a similar
scale.

In a Seminar on Metropolitan Planning, held July 17
to 21, 1964, at Ditchley Park in Oxfordshire, England, at
which British and American planners, professors and government officials participated, Professor Donald Foley, Associate Professor of City Planning and of Architecture, University of California, issued this caution:

> The urban regions (more commonly termed "metro-
> politan region" in America) represents more than
> an enlarged scale of city or town, and more even
> than an amalgam of cities. It involves no less than
> a fundamental reorganization of social and economic
> life so that most of such life is centered on the
> metrolpolis . . . .
>
> Urban regions, as they are emerging, are neither
> separate nor clearly definable, for they, in turn,

are interlocked in an even larger urban system
of amazing complexity. In the United States, at
least, it no longer makes sense to try to ascertain
exactly how many urban regions we have or exactly what hierarchical position each region's center
holds with respect to the larger system. The fundamental fact is that urban and non-urban can no
longer be meaningfully differentiated, nor can precise geographic community boundaries be validly
identified. 28

    While accepting Professor Foley's caveat, it neverthe-
less remains basically valid that social and economic life is
centered on the metropolis and therefore it is necessary to
determine, or attempt to determine, in any particular area,
towards what metropolis is social and economic life center-
ing. This requires a measurement of the push and the pull
towards the various metropolitan centers. Furthermore, in
order to gain the necessary data and information, collected
and supplied by public agencies and in order to implement
the plans through public agencies, metropolitan centers must
be delineated by administrative boundary lines. For example,
the metropolitan areas of Cologne and Stockholm can be
briefly so delinated.

    Cologne is a part of the largest metropolitan region
in Germany, known as the Rhein-Ruhr Stadtregion, extending
north along the Rhine 60 miles from Bad Godesberg through
Duisburg and east-west 60 miles from Dortmund to Mönchen-
gladbach near the Dutch border. In 1961, this region encom-
passed five cities with over a half million population each,
five cities with populations ranging from 200,000 to 500,000,
ten cities with populations from 100,000 to 200,000, and nine
cities ranging in population from 50,000 to 100,000. Including the core cities, suburbs, the urbanized zones, and border zones, the total population in 1961 was well over ten
million. 29

    Several of the Rhine cities were established during
the First Century A.D., and were important trade centers
before there was a Berlin. Ever since the industrial revolu-
tion, the Rhine-Ruhr area has been vital to Germany because
of its hard coal resources and steel production, producing in
the early 1960s over four-fifths of West Germany's hard coal
and three-fifths of its steel. In spite of this, however, the
Rhine-Ruhr was not central to Bismarck's or Hitler's thinking. Berlin was. Since World War II, Berlin has lost pop-

ulation, its industrial production has increased at a slower
rate than the remainder of West Germany, and numerous
significant headquarters for public and semi-public agencies
have moved away. The national capitol is now at Bonn, also in the Rhine-Ruhr sector. With this shift have come many
others. Insurance company headquarters have moved to Cologne; other financial institutions to Cologne and Düsseldorf;
several federal departmental headquarters to Cologne; the
headquarters of many of the powerful industrial enterprises
to Düsseldorf; and the headquarters of many mining and steel
firms to Essen. Headquarters for workers', employers',
and technical organizations are also in Essen. As Peter Hall
expressed it:

> . . . this is evidently the region of postwar Feder-
> al Germany in which the distinctively metropolitan
> functions are concentrated. The Rhine-Ruhr cities
> are to modern Germany what the Randstad is to the
> Netherlands, Paris to France, London to Britain:
> it is post-1945 Germany's world city. [30]

The Rhine-Ruhr megalopolis is actually a polycentric
metropolitan region, comprising seven distinct metropolitan
areas, as shown in Map #1. Commencing from the north:

1. Essen-Dortmund-Duisburg metropolitan area (MA),
   known as the Inner Ruhr, which comprises seven-
   teen core cities, whose total population was
   4,225,798 (1963).

2. Hamm MA, includes one core city, which has developed separately from the Inner Ruhr on the
   northeast edge of the Rhine-Ruhr complex. The
   population of this core city was 72,088 (1963).
   The MA, which can be distinctly delineated, has
   a total population of 154,000.

3. Düsseldorf-Neus MA, includes two core cities,
   immediately south of the Inner-Ruhr. Total population of the core cities was 808,089 (1963).

4. Wuppertal-Solingen-Remscheid MA includes three
   core cities, situated east of the Dusseldorf-Neuss
   MA. Total population of the core cities was
   724,258 (1963).

5. Mönchengladbach-Rheydt-Viersen MA includes

Map 1. Rhine-Ruhr Metropolitan Region.

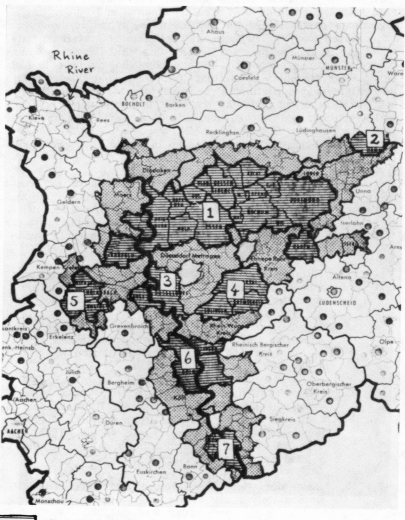

 Core Urban Areas.

Surrounding Urban Areas.

Source: Innenminister des Landes Nordrhein-Westfalen, Staatsburgerliche Bildungstelle.

three core cities, situated west of the Düsseldorf-
Neuss MA.   Total population of the three core
cities was 293, 622 (1963).

6.   Köln-Leverkusen MA includes two core cities,
situated south of the Düsseldorf-Neuss MA.   Total population of the two core cities was 935, 857
(1963).

7.   Bonn-Siegburg MA includes two core cities, situated at the southern terminus of the Rhine-Ruhr
complex.   Total population of the two core cities
was 177, 706 (1963). [31]

The core cities of the specified metropolitan areas
above contained 7, 170, 330 persons (1963).   An additional population totalling over three million inhabit the suburbs and
the surrounding urbanized zone.

The population, area in square kilometer, and population per square kilometer are given for all of the jurisdictions in the Cologne metropolitan area in Table 2 in the Appendix.

The delineation shown on Map 2 is the official North
Rhine-Westphalian census presentation, which follows in
principle the U.S. Bureau of the Census criteria for standard metropolitan areas.

To the north, the Düsseldorf MA crowds in and to the
south the Bonn MA sets a limit.   Urbanization is clearly
spreading westward in Landkreis Bergheim and eastward
in Rheinisch Bergischer Kreis.   The delineation as shown in
Map 2 follows in principle the SMSA specification of the U.S.
Census Bureau.   It is in accordance with the delineation by
the International Urban Research Center in 1955, which was
based largely on commuter flows.   The population of the
Cologne MA was then given as 1, 243, 900. [32]   Peter Hall in
1966 for his study, The World Cities, used the same delineation and specified a population of 1.4 million. [33]

Donald Foley's caution as regards urban regions being "neither separate nor clearly definable" is well substan-
tiated in the Rhine-Ruhr complex of metropolitan areas.
Even though there may be a levelling of population growth
during the 1967-1969 period in the Rhine-Ruhr Stadt Region
due to the economic stabilization in West Germany, this is

Cologne Metropolitan Area

Jurisdiction	Population 1966	Area in sq. km.	Population per sq. km.
Kreisfrei Stadt Köln	859,830	251.38	3,420.4
Kreisfrei Stadt Leverkusen	106,347	46.16	2,303.8
Landkreis Köln	237,543	292.61	811.8
Eastern Portion of Landkreis Bergheim	13,161	25.36	518.9
Western Portion of Rheinisch Bergischer Kreis	198,452	345.02	575.2
Northern Portion of Landkreis Euskirchen	16,174	34.00	475.7
Southern Portion of Landkreis Grevenbroich	33,269	69.96	475.5
Southern Portion of Rhein Wupper Kreis	86,079	93.78	917.8
Total	1,550,855	1,158.27	1,138.9

Map 2.   The Cologne Metropolitan Area.

Arbeitsplatzbilanzen der Gemeinden in der Stadtregion Köln
− Volkszählung 1961 −

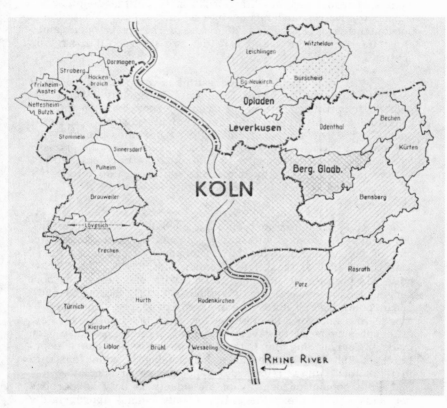

```
⊢⊣⊢⊣    County Boundary
·⊢·⊣·⊣·  Regierungs District Boundary
─────    Commune Boundary
```

```
├──┼──┼──┼──┼──┤
0   2   4   6   8   10 km
```

Source: Statistisches Jahrbuch der Stadt Köln, 1964, p. 106.

considered to be temporary, the slowing down of the West
German economy (in relative terms) from its previous
heated production.   Peter Hall's projection, therefore, war-
rants serious consideration: the danger is that the Randstad
in the Netherlands, including the cities of Amsterdam, Rotterdam, The Hague, Leiden, Haarlem and Utrecht, will expand eastwards and the Rhine-Ruhr metropolitan complex will
expand westwards and merge into a colossal stretch of metro-
politanization.   Only about 70 miles of relatively open land
along the frontier now separate the two metropolitan agglomerations. [34]

     With the continued, successful development of econom-
ic ties within the European Economic Community, the pros-
pect of urbanization within the frontier zone between the
Randstad and the Rhein-Ruhr Stadtregion, causing a coales-
cence of the two metropolitan regions, becomes probable.
Not only are larger geographic areas needed for the proper
organization and governance of metropolitan developments,
as has been suggested by numerous writers, also international cooperation is becoming a necessity.

     The Stockholm metropolitan area is without question
the largest in Sweden with a total population more than twice
that of the second ranking MA, Gothenburg, and more than
four times that of the third ranking, Malmö. [35]   The Stockholm MA follows the normal pattern with one large city core,
surrounded by several small suburban cities, boroughs and
urban communes.   Since one metropolitan area does not
merge into another, the delineation of it is simplified.   For
different purposes, however, different delineations have been
made.   Surrounding the City of Stockholm which has a population of 793,714, is the County of Stockholm which has within it 52 local jurisdictions and a population of 566,235.
Since the population density of the county is only 76 persons
per square kilometer, the entire county cannot appropriately
be included in the Stockholm metropolitan area.   The Greater
Stockholm Planning Region includes 48 jurisdictions, excluding a few obviously rural communes in the County of Stockholm and including a few urban communes from the neighboring Upsalla County, and extends north to Väddö on the Baltic
Coast.   This Region has a population of 1.7 million. [36]

     On December 17, 1964, a Greater Stockholm Local
Traffic Association was formed and officially recognized by
the City and County Stockholm.   This Association encom-

passes 33 units of local government in addition to the City of
Stockholm. [37]   A Greater Stockholm Planning District in-
cludes 18 units of local government in addition to the City of
Stockholm.   This last is officially recognized in the Statistisk
Årsbok 1965 as the metropolitan Stockholm. [38]

On Map 3, the Stockholm suburban delineation includes
all the communes which belong to the Greater Stockholm Local Traffic Association except Sigtuna, northwest of Stockholm; Södertälje, southwest; and Sorunda and Nynäshamm,
south of Stockholm.   Table #3 in the Appendix lists the 33
units of local government, which signed the Greater Stockholm Local Traffic Association Agreement, geographically
north, east, south and west around the City of Stockholm.
The 18 units of local government, which have been and continue to be part of the Greater Stockholm Planning District,
are shown by asterisks.   Totals for the two districts follow:

The Greater Stockholm Local Traffic Association

Jurisdiction	Population 1965	Area in sq. km.	Pop. per sq. km.
Total for Suburbs	498,016	2,877.71	173
City of Stockholm	793,714	186.03	4,267
Grand Total	1,291,730	3,063.74	

The Greater Stockholm Planning District

	Population	Area in sq. km.	Pop. per sq. km.
Total for Suburbs Asterisked	385,626	1,168.49	330
City of Stockholm	793,714	186.03	4,267
Grand Total	1,179,340	1,354.52	

From a population density point of view, the 18 local
governmental units which comprise the Stockholm Planning
District seem to be the more realistic delineation of metropolitan Stockholm, with the possible further addition of the
City of Södertälje, which is connected with the City of Stockholm by a limited access highway passing through Botkyrka
which in turn is included in the Planning District and has a

Map 3. Metropolitan Stockholm; Greater Stockholm County,
January 1, 1971.

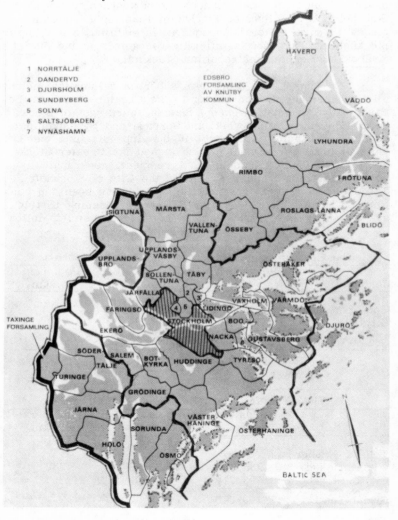

1 NORRTÄLJE
2 DANDERYD
3 DJURSHOLM
4 SUNDBYBERG
5 SOLNA
6 SALTSJÖBADEN
7 NYNÄSHAMN

EDSBRO
FÖRSAMLING
AV KNUTBY
KOMMUN

HAVERÖ
VÄDDÖ
LYHUNDRA
RIMBO
FRÖTUNA
SIGTUNA
MÄRSTA
ROSLAGS-LÄNNA
VALLEN-TUNA
ÖSSEBY
BLIDÖ
UPPLANDS-BRO
UPPLANDS-VÄSBY
ÖSTERÅKER
SOLLEN-TUNA
TÄBY
JÄRFÄLLA
VAXHOLM
VÄRMDÖ
FARINGSÖ
LIDINGÖ
TAXINGE
FÖRSAMLING
STOCKHOLM
BOO
DJURÖ
EKERÖ
NACKA
GUSTAVSBERG
SÖDER-TÄLJE
SALEM
BOT-KYRKA
HUDDINGE
TYRESÖ
TURINGE
GRÖDINGE
JÄRNA
VÄSTER-HANINGE
SORUNDA
ÖSTERHANINGE
HÖLÖ
ÖSMO
BALTIC SEA

▥ City of Stockholm
⌇ Stockholm suburbs limit
▬ Greater Stockholm boundary

Source: Storlandstingskommittens kansli och landstingets informationssektion, Information om det nya landstinget (Tiden-
Barnängen tryckerier ab 1970)

population density of 187 persons per square kilometer.
Furthermore, Södertälje has a population density of 417 per
square kilometer. The City of Nynäshamn is also connected
with the City of Stockholm by an excellent highway, the Eu-
ropaväg, and has a population density of 367 per square kilometer; however, at least 30 kilometers of the distance between Nynäshamn and the City of Stockholm passes through
Västerhaninge Commune, which has a population density of
no more than 60 persons per square kilometer. The population break in this case is too great for inclusion insofar as
the current study is concerned.

Inclusion of the City of Södertälje as part of metropolitan Stockholm will provide the following totals:

Stockholm Metropolitan Area (Revised)			
	Population	Area in sq. km.	Pop. per sq. km.
City of Stockholm	793, 914	186. 03	4, 267
Suburban Stockholm	429, 098	1, 272. 86	337
Grand Total	1, 223, 012	1, 458. 89	

Negotiations are in process for the formation of a
Stor- Stockholm Län (Greater Stockholm County), which would
obviously be the recognized metropolitan Stockholm. The
due date for the establishment of an official government agency covering all of Metropolitan Stockholm is 1971. The drawing of boundary lines for a metropolitan government will require the inclusion of currently non-urban territory in the direction of probable urban expansion, in order to avoid the
immediate necessity after 1971 of geographical extension of
the official metropolitan jurisdiction. From this point of
view, taking into account the influence of transport and transit on urban extension, the 33 governmental units which are involved in the Stockholm Local Traffic Association should very
likely be included in the future official metropolitan Stockholm.

The professional planners project continued urbanization west from Stockholm around Lake Mälaren, connecting
several cities and extending on southwest to Örebro on the
western tip of Lake Hjälmaren southwest of Lake Mälaren.
Furthermore, continued urbanization is anticipated south by

west from Stockholm along route E4, which is part of a European highway network, through Norrköping, Linnköping and
on to Jönköping at the southern tip of Lake Vättern; thereafter west through Borås to the Gothenburg metropolitan area.
The Kattegatt coast from Gothenburg to Hälsingborg is becoming increasingly non-rural, land use is largely recreational,
and the Öresund coast from Hälsingborg to the Mälmö metropolitan area is becoming increasingly urban. This latter
phenomenon is attracting attention because of the existing urbanization and non-agricultural developments on the Danish
side of Öresund from the Copenhagen metropolitan area, opposite the Malmö metropolitan area on the Swedish shore, to
Helsingør (Elsinore), opposite Halsingborg in Sweden. [39]

    Currently, ferries carry the continuously heavy traffic
across Öresund at the two termini of these urbanization belts
on both coasts. A debate is in progress as to whether Copenhagen and Malmö at the southern end of Öresund, an Helsingør and Hälsingborg at the other end should be connected
by bridges, tunnels, or both. Here again an international
megalopolis is emerging. Increasingly, Swedes and Danes
have their residences on one side of the sound and their summer cottages on the other side. Increasingly, they cross the
sound for the evening, or weekend, entertainment. With
bridge, or tunnel, connections, the two coasts of the sound
will speedily become one international metropolitan area, the
beginning of one more megalopolis. [40]

    In Ide '65, which was found on a table in a waiting
room of the Department of Planning, Nämndehuset, Stockholm, appeared the following:

> Efforts to anticipate the future land requirements
> for city building have shown that we should calcu-
> late with a doubling of land area per inhabitant dur-
> ing the remainder of this century.

> We accept concentration as a prerequisite for a
> large employment and commercial market, which
> gives the individual great freedom of choice with
> regard to employment, service and recreational
> facilities.

> We do not accept the injurious effect of concentra-
> tion--production reducing, crowding, and a hygieni-
> cally unsuitable environment.

The new city, the regional community, is planned
for rapid transportation and is therefore spacious.
It encompasses many people and is therefore a
large employment market.

We have passed the age of poverty when our chief
goal was to increase production and thereby our
economic security. Our resources now permit us
new choices. We can build a new community where
our security and our freedom of choice with regard
to residential, working and recreational environments is greater than in the existing concentrated
cities, a community, which by its spaciousness and
flexibility, is in harmony with the dynamics which
characterize our culture. [41]

This policy spells rapid geographic expansion of urbanization along transportation and transit routes--urbaniza-
tion, in general, from Stockholm to Jönköping and on to Gothenburg, thereafter south to Mälmö.

Concerned about the probable results of this urban
expansion (former) Communications Minister Olaf Palme,
speaking for the national government, stressed before the Society for Local Planning at its annual meeting in Stockholm
the absolute need for national planning in order to avoid chaos in local planning. [42]

This also indicates continued urbanization along the
routes described above but under national guidance. In his
address, Mr. Palme cautioned against the danger of local
communities engaging in unhealthy competition for industry
and the local harboring of unrealistic expectations.

Notes

1. Weber, Adna Ferrin, The Growth of Cities in the Nine-
    teenth Century (Cornell Reprints in Urban Studies,
    Cornell University Press, 1963). Originally pub-
    lished in 1899 for Columbia University by Macmillan.

2. United Nations Demographic Yearbook, 1960. Defini-
    tions of "urban" are given on p. 394-395.

3. International Conference of the International Federation
    for Housing and Planning, "Growing Space Needs in

the Urbanized Region" (Stockholm: National Swedish
Board of Building and Planning, 1965-   Mimeographed),
p. 3, footnote a.

4. Stones, P., Local Government for Students (London:
   MacDonald & Evans Ltd., 1964), p. 34.

5. Letter from Mr. M. Ratcliffe, Reference Section, British Information Services, April 3, 1967.

6. United Nations, Loc. cit.

7. Langenfelt, Per, Local Government in Sweden (Stockholm: The Swedish Institute, 1964), p. 5. Mr. Langenfelt is a Secretary of the Swedish Association of
   Communes.   The term "commune" in Sweden has the
   same significance that it has in France and Germany
   (Germeinde). All the land in Sweden, France and Germany, with the exception of forest and military reservations, is organized into communes, which may be
   urban, rural, or a mixture of the two. Some communes in Sweden have been officially designated as
   "köpingar" and others as "städer," just as some "Gemeinde" in Germany are officially designated as
   "städte."

8. Interview with Secretary Lundh in his office in Kommunalförbundet, June 6, 1966.   Population data verified in
   Statistiska Centralbyrån, Statistisk Arsbok, 1965, Table
   13, p. 10.

9. Statistiska Centralbyrån, Statistisk Årsbok, 1965,
   "Sources and Notes," following the Table of Contents.

10. 1960 Census of Population, Vol. I, Part A, Introduc-
    tion, p. XII. Special provisions are made for towns
    in New England, New York and Wisconsin, also for
    "townships" in New Jersey and Pennsylvania, all of
    which are in effect 'urban.' "

11. Ibid, p. XIX.

12. Harland Bartholomew and Associate Reports in numer-
    ous Midwest cities of the U.S.A. during the 1950's.

13. Press and information Office of the German Federal
    Government, The Bulletin, June 28, 1966, p. 2.

> The most recent figure on the population density in
> North Rhineland Westphalia is about 2000 residents
> per square kilometer. This equals 3,225 persons per
> square mile.

14. United Nations Demographic Yearbook, 1960 and 1962,
    Table 9, except as otherwise specified.

15. No report was given in the United Nations Demographic
    Yearbook 1962; used here was Peter Hall, The World
    Cities, (London: Weidenfeld and Nicholson, 1966),
    Table 3, p. 18.

16. Godlund, Sven, Urbanisering i Sverige (Göteborg, 1961).
    Reported in the International Conference of the Inter-
    national Federation for Housing and Planning, loc. cit.

17. Ibid.

18. Statistiska Centralbyrån, Statistisk Årsbok, 1965,
    Table 7.

19. Deutscher Städtetag, Statistisches Jahrbuch Deutscher
    Germeinden, 1964. (Bearbeitet vom Verband Deutscher
    Städtestatisker), p. 39. West Berlin is included.

20. International Urban Research, The World's Metropoli-
    tan Areas (Berkeley: The University of California
    Press, 1959), Preface, p. V.

21. Ibid.

22. International Urban Research, Ibid., p. 26 & 27.

23. 1960 Census of Population, Vol. I, Part A, "Introduc-
    tion," p. XXIV.

24. Bollens, John C. and Schmandt, Henry J., The Me-
    tropolis, (New York: Harper & Row, 1965), p. 25
    & 26.

25. Robson, W. A., Great Cities of the World, (London:
    George Allen and Unwin Ltd., 2d ed., 1957), p. 31.

26. Deutscher Städtetag, Op. cit., p. 34.

27. Deutscher Städtetag, Ibid, p. XI and p. 40-44.

28. Senior, Derek (editor), The Regional City, An Anglo-
American Discussion of Metropolitan Planning, (London: Longmans, Green and Co. Ltd., 1966), p. 11.

29. Deutscher Städtetag, Op. cit., p. 43.

30. Hall, Peter, The World Cities (Verona: Officine Gra-
fische Arnoldo Mondadori, 1966), p. 126.

31. International Urban Research, Op. cit., Appendix, p.
95 and 96.

32. International Urban Research, Ibid., Appendix, p. 54.

33. Hall, Peter, Op. cit., p. 129.

34. Hall, Peter, Ibid., p. 196.

35. Statistiska Centralbyrån, Loc. cit.

36. Interview with Mr. Gösta Carlestam, architect (planner),
Stockholmtraktens Regionplanekontor, May 12, 1966.

37. Principöverenskommelse om Samordning, Utbyggnad och
Drift av Det Kollektiva Traffiksystemet i Stor-Stockholm, December 17, 1964. Mimeographed copy received from Mr. Nils Hörjel, Communications Coordinator in the Stockholm metropolitan area, June 7,
1966.

38. Statistiska Centralbyrån, Loc. cit.

39. Interviews with Mr. Thomas Atmer, architect (planner),
Stockholm Stadsbyggnadskontor, May 10, 1966; Mr.
Gösta Carlestam; and Mr. K. Borseng, Boligminis-
teriets Kommitterde, Copenhagen, July 19, 1966.

40. Interview with Mr. K. Borseng. The writer drove
around Lake Mälaren and on E4 from Stockholm to
Jönköping several times, also west to Gothenburg and
south along the coast to Malmö, as well as several
times between Copenhagen and Helsingør. The planners' projections are not daydreams. These are the
urbanized portions of Sweden and Denmark, and
the expectations for their growth are realistic.

41. E. Norberg, "The Planned Region," Ide 65.

42. Address by Mr. Olaf Palme before Föreningen för
     Sämhällsplanering in Kongress-salen, Stockholm, May
     23, 1966. (See Stockholms Dagens Nyheter, May 24,
     1966: news article entitled "Riksplanering av marken
     lovar Palme"; and editorial entitled, "Riksplaner-
     ingen. ")

Chapter III

COLOGNE: RESULTS OF LAND-USE CONTROL

        Lewis Mumford in a critique of Le Corbusier has
written:

> In short, he ignored the main office of the city,
> which is to enrich the future by maintaining in the
> midst of change visible structural links with the
> past in all its cultural richness and variety. [1]

        This Cologne has done, despite numerous destructive
military invasions throughout the 2000 years of its existence,
including the devastation by air attacks during World War II.
These multiple military destructions have provided the people
of Cologne little opportunity to select what they should preserve.   They have preserved what was left and ingeniously
rebuilt so as to have an harmonious ensemble, in terms of
architecture, land use and social value.   Illustrations of
this follow:

        The Center of Cologne, of course, is the "Dom," the
magnificent cathedral which was carefully avoided by attacking air forces during World War II.   This is the center of
interest for most tourists, most of whom are aware that
construction of it began in 1248.   Amazing to a foreigner is
the location, following post-war reconstruction, of the Hauptbanhoff (central railway station) virtually at the feet of the
cathedral.   The inappropriateness of the site is mitigated by
several factors, however.   It is placed at the rear of the
cathedral; and with the towering height of the cathedral, the
railway station seems to be grovelling at its feet.   Furthermore, the architecture of the railway station is not ostenta-
tious nor distracting.   One might expect, however, that with
the opportunity to provide a wide, sweeping vista on all sides
of the cathedral, this would have been done.   On the contrary, the intent seems to have been the provision of as
much activity as possible on all sides, no isolation from the
daily life of the citizenry.   Cologne has protected its cathe-

dral in another way.   There are no other towering structures
in the Altstadt (Old City).   No building in Cologne is taller
than the cathedral spires, which soar 160 meters (546 feet)
from the street level.   There is no legal prohibition on this;
however, public pressure has prevented more than one attempt to construct a building as tall as the cathedral in Cologne.   On the skyline and in the heights, the cathedral
reigns supreme.

Less well known is the history of Hohestrasse, which
extends south from the cathedral square approximately one
kilometer.   This was the original main business street when
Colonia was incorporated as a municipality by Emperor Augustus in 50 A. D. , and had then been in existence since the
First Century B. C.   This area was destroyed in World War
II, but the reconstructed street follows exactly the former
route at exactly the same width.   Hohestrasse has given the
citizens of Cologne a continual link with the year one throughout the city's two thousand years of history, and the citizens
of Cologne are proud of it.   It is now a pedestrian street
crowded at all times by shoppers, amusement seekers, and
people who want to be where other people are.   At the southern end of Hohestrasse, another pedestrian street intersects,
Schildergasse, which extends westwards approximately one
kilometer to Neumarkt, a pedestrian plaza, around which
trams for all parts of the city circulate.

The air attacks destroyed much of modern and medieval Cologne, but also made possible the discovery of ancient remains below the ground.   For example, a part of
the Medieval Rathaus was destroyed.   In the process of reconstruction, large scale excavations in 1953 revealed the
ruins of the ancient Roman Praetorium underneath the destroyed portion of the Medieval City Hall, over which the
new addition was built.

> In the light of the impressive ruins which were
> gradually being uncovered, the City Council and Ad-
> ministration decided to suspend the work of build-
> ing for six months, in order to render possible a
> thorough excavation for which considerable funds
> were made available.   The profusion of walls
> throughout the whole area, in part dovetailing, in
> part sunken and overlapping, of different centuries,
> and of which even today only the most typical and
> impressive part is visible, rendered the task of
> clarification and explanation seemingly hopeless.

But by accurate measurement, photography and the
leveling out of all details, it has been possible to ob-
tain a general history of this area which is so significant for the development of the town and the
western world. [2]

The contemporary architecture of the new portion of
the Rathaus harmonized with the so-called "Spanish-style" of
the old, and covers the remains of the Roman Praetorium below the surface. Thus, the historical remains of the municipal governmental center is preserved from the first century
to the present in one building. In a large entrance lobby are
displayed models of the Rathaus reconstruction, subway construction plans, autobahn plans, and other city plans. In this
same lobby is a handsome, two-story, contemporary-design,
stained glass window, which sets the tone for the interior.

Excavations for the subway have revealed portions of
the Roman wall previously covered by the debris of the centuries. It is now known that the Roman wall extended from
the site of the Dom west along the present Komödien and
Zeughaus Strasse about one kilometer. On Zeughaus Strasse
immediately west of the Roman-Germanic Museum a portion
of the Roman wall is visible above ground, serving as a demarcation wall for the museum parking lot, where modern,
motorized chariots can now be parked. A few rods beyond,
the Römerturm projects above the ground; this was the northwest corner of Roman Colonia. In excavation, the base of
the Roman tower was found six meters (approximately 20
feet) below the present ground level. From this tower, the
wall is known to extend one and one quarter kilometers
south, passing between Neumarkt, the pedestrian plaza mentioned above, and the tenth-century Apostelen Cathedral, to
the Alte Mauer; and from this intersection it extends eastwards to a point southeast of the Kirche St. Maria i Kapitol.[3]
Within these boundaries was situated Colonia Claudia Ara
Agrippinensium, which came to be known as "Colonia;" in
German, "Köln," and in English, "Cologne."

During World War II in 1942, the Dionysius-Mosaic,
the floor of a wealthy Roman's banquet hall, was discovered
directly south of the Dom. The Cologne City Council ordered the construction of a museum over it, in order to a-
void the danger of irreplacable damage in removing it to an
existing museum.

In the middle of the Thirteenth Century, when work

commenced on the great cathedral, a new town wall with numerous towers was constructed around Cologne on the west side of the Rhine about two kilometers distance from the site of the Dom. Following World War II a multiple-lane boulevard, called the "Ring," was constructed following the exterior side of the remains of the thirteenth-century wall and towers. Now, between the remains of the wall and the boulevard, a continuous park area is provided. Against the inside of portions of the wall, contemporary apartment buildings have been built and are rented by the city. Thus the city, as owner of the ancient wall, gains a continuous income from it. Furthermore, delightful housing is provided within easy access of the central business area in a city afflicted by a housing shortage, and the medieval wall is assured preservation.

From Neumarkt, Hahnen Strasse extends less than one kilometer west to Rudolf Plaz on the Ring. At this point a substantial arch has been built over Hahnen Strasse from a modern office building on the southside to a medieval tower, part of the thirteenth century wall, on the northside. In the arch is a restaurant, from which one can watch the flow of traffic into and out of Rudolf Plaz, also on Hahnen Strasse, Aachner Strasse beyond Rudolf Plaz, and on the Ring. The restaurant permit is, of course, a source of revenue for the city and maintenance of the tower, in itself a museum, is also provided.

Within the area, encircled by the Ring and the medieval wall, are to be found cathedrals from every century beginning with the Tenth. Before the World War II destruction, there were 140 cathedrals, churches and chapels. Eighty-one were totally destroyed. Only seven were undamaged. Of the 52 partially destroyed, 20 were more than 15 per cent destroyed and many of these remain in partial ruins.[4] Within the Ring is also the central business district (CBD), where is to be found the major business and governmental headquarters, the cultural and entertainment centers, points of historic interest, and multiple-story residential facilities.

Along the Rhine, except for space reserved for harbor purposes, most of the river front is preserved for public use: parks, pedestrian walks, benches, greensward, and parking spaces; in back of these lands are driveways; and overlooking these public lands are multiple-story commercial and residential structures in the heart of the city, and multiple-story residential beyond the CBD.

Along the left bank of the Rhine there are 19 kilometers of land; along the right bank, about 17, totalling 36
kilometers.   Eighty to 90 per cent of this is municipally
owned.   On the right bank, low-lying meadows are federal
property, due to their susceptibility to flooding.   The Bunde
has legal jurisdiction over all rivers and adjacent land liable to flooding.   The overwhelming proportion of the land
along the Rhine is thus public property for public use.   Not
all of it is publicly managed.   For example, a promontory
on the left bank of the Rhine at the northern terminus of the
Ring, which provides an excellent view both up and down-
stream, and also a clear view of the Dom, has been leased
to a private restaurateur for De Bastei, a public restaurant,
one of the best in the city. [5]

Messrs. Meinel and Schwendy of the Neue Rhein-
Zeitung, Social Democrat newspaper with headquarters in
Köln-Kalk, on the east side of the Rhine, contend that inadequate public use has been made of the right bank of the
Rhine.   They advocate the preparation of a new general plan
for the entire right bank, the development of a new skyline. [6]
The Rheinpark is on the right bank, but more kilometers of
promenadoes have been provided on the left bank, where
there are more historic structures and thus less latitude for
development.

Throughout the year, even in the winter season, Cologne residents crowd onto the banks of the Rhine during
week-ends, enjoying the river view, and meeting friends and
fellow citizens.   During the week, people parade along the
banks of the Rhine, watching the busy river traffic.   The
Rhine, with the Dom visible up and down it, is the heart of
the city.

In most categories of land use, German and Swedish
municipalities are willing to accept municipal ownership and
management more readily than are American cities.   One example to the contrary as regards municipal management that
may be worthy of notice by officers of American cities is
the Cologne Zoo.   Situated within easy walking distance north
of the Ring, on the left bank of the Rhine, and blessed with
excellent public transport, the zoo property is leased to a
"private Gesellschaft" for development and management, thus
relieving the City of Cologne of the financial problems of zoo
administration that have plagued many American cities.   The

Cologne Zoo Corporation charges 2 DM per person for admission, and subleases property for a restaurant, which is adjacent to the zoo, but not within the zoo proper; that persons
who may not wish to visit the zoo can use the restaurant facilities without paying the admission fee.   The zoo corporation meets all expenses and pays the City for the leasehold.
The City is a minority stockholder in the corporation, thus
it has a voice in policy formation; however the corporation
is not an official part of the municipal government, and is
directly responsible to the municipal government only insofar
as the lease requires it.   Hardly anyone can recall whether
the zoo has ever been a public issue, and currently it is not
a problem for the city.   The Cologne Zoo is now over one
hundred years old, and apparently from everyone's point of
view has been and is a success. [7]

The area within the Ring known as "Alstadt" has the
heaviest population density in Cologne.   The multiple-story
residences are well maintained and are occupied.   The residents live in the center of affairs where there is constant
activity.   At a variable distance of 300 to 600 meters out
from the ring a greenbelt about 400 meters in depth circles
most of the city west of the Rhine.   About three kilometers
further out another greenbelt from one to two kilometers in
depth circles the southern half of Cologne west of the Rhine.
Finally, five kilometers from the inner greenbelt, a third
green area circles the northern half of Cologne west of the
Rhine.   East of the Rhine, from one to four kilometers from
the river a string of parks, woodlands and open spaces penetrate through the city from the southern to the northern city
limits; and from one to five kilometers further east, open
space and woodlands extend along the eastern city limits.
In addition, small parks, playgrounds and open spaces are
scattered throughout the city.   These open spaces obviously
provide opportunities for outdoor recreation, but also firebreak safety, as well as an improved environment for urban
living.

A quick review of Cologne history is necessary to understand its development.   Until the Fourth Century A. D.,
the Rhine was the boundary between the Roman and the "barbarian" lands.   In 310 A. D., Emperor Augustine ordered the
construction of the first bridge across the Rhine.   Settlements were thereafter made on the right bank.   About 800
A. D., the bridge was destroyed, not to be rebuilt for one
thousand years, except for occasional pontoon bridges that
were usable for relatively brief periods.   Main reliance was

placed on ferries for river crossings until the early part of
the Nineteenth Century when a new permanent bridge was
constructed.   For this reason, Cologne developed largely on
the west side of the Rhine.

During the thousand years of Cologne history with no
permanent bridge across the Rhine, the city spread in a
semi-circle on the left bank.   The remains of the Roman
wall and the remains of the medieval wall mark two stages
of development.   A third stage of development is shown by
the second greenbelt out from the center, which marks the
location of defenses in the Napoleonic Wars.   Geographic expansion thereafter has taken place northwards on the west
side and eastwards from the river on the east side.   Such
geographic additions can be made only by legislative action
of the Landrat.

As regards overall land use, only one quarter of the
Cologne area is composed of "bebaute Flächen," built areas,
as is evidenced by the following tabulation from the 1965
census by the Statisches Amt:

Generalized Land Use by Hectare and Per Cent of Total[8]

Land Use	Number of Hectares	Per Cent of Total
Agriculture & Gardening	8, 201	32. 6
Built Areas	6, 354	25. 3
Street & Railway Rights-of-Way, Harbors, & Docks	3, 267	13. 0
Forests	3, 077	12. 2
Public Greens, Athletic Fields, & Cemeteries	1, 823	7. 3
Other (desolate)	1, 469	5. 8
Water	946	3. 8
Total	25, 137	100. 0

The Landrat has provided Cologne ample space for
growth, the most recent additions being in the northern, relatively undeveloped stretch along the left bank of the Rhine.
The substantial amount of land, almost one third of the total,
that is devoted to agriculture and gardening is explainable by
two factors: 1) the Landesbauordnung (building law) prohibits
any land from lying idle or unused (if nothing else, land must
be used for gardening purposes);[9] 2) this land has not, to
date, been needed for urban purposes.

Eliminating the 32.6 per cent of the land used for agriculture and gardening, a more normal land-use pattern
emerges:

Land Use, Excluding Agriculture and Gardening, by Per Cent of New Total[10]	
Land Use	Per Cent of New Total
Built Areas	37. 6
Street & Railway Rights-of-Way, Harbors, & Docks	19. 2
Forest	18. 1
Public Greens, Athletic Fields, & Cemeteries	10. 8
Other	8. 7
Water	5. 6
Total	100. 0

In comparison with American cities, however, this
shows a smaller portion of the total area devoted to street
and transport rights-of-way, in spite of the fact that in the
new total are included the percentages of rights-of-way for
agricultural and gardening lands, which are excluded in the
calculation.   The above table also highlights the substantial
amounts of land within the city limits reserved for forests,
public greens, athletic fields and other open-space uses.

The North Rhineland-Westphalia Landesbauordnung
has strict regulations concerning open space, setbacks,
spaces for carpet cleaning, playground space and other amenities for decent living, parking space, and prohibition of
overcrowding. [11] Sixty per cent of existing construction is
new. Overcrowding, however, has been prohibited since
1918 by Prussian law, governing the Cologne area until after
World War II. The current legal definition of overcrowding
is anything less than eight square meters per person (about
26 square feet). [12] The size of an apartment is not regulated by law. In the event of the proposed conversion of a
building, it is necessary to prove to the Bauaufsichtsamt
that the structure can satisfactorily (legally) sustain the conversion. The technical requirements are high and maintenance is satisfactory; however, the stretches of multi-family
housing from the Ring out on the west side of the Rhine, and
beyond Deutz on the east side, are architecturally uninterest-
ing, greatly lacking in variety. This may be called the gray
area of Cologne.

A noteworthy precaution, which is applicable to the
entire municipal area, but particularly relevant to the CBD
and the area described above, is the Landesbauordnung requirement that each Hochhaus (high house) shall have an
emergency electric power supply installed that automatically
starts when the public supply breaks down, and will maintain
the minimum requirement of light, ventilation, and other
electrical needs. [13]

The overwhelming proportion of the residential development is multiple-family; single-family residences are the
exception to be found in exceptional districts such as Marienburg. This situation is partially due to the serious need
for housing since the World War II destruction. Virtually
all of the post-war residential construction has been multiple-
family. With the average income ranging from 800 to 1700
DM (about $200 to $425) per month, the need for single-
family residences has been severely limited. Likewise, Cologne was still classified in 1966 as a "black," meaning
"serious housing shortage," area, the criteria being a housing deficit of 3 per cent or greater, as determined by the
Regierungsbezirke (administrative district of the Land). Behind the predominance of multiple-family dwellings there are
furthermore the planning desiderata of the most effective
land use and the minimization of the cost of the extension of
municipal services. Single-family housing however is being
encouraged east of the Rhine, in Mulheim (northeast of

Deutz), Humboldt-Gremberg (southeast of Deutz), Merheim, and Holweide. [14]

The population densities per hectare in the Stadtbezirke range from 1.4 in Roggendorf Thenhoven in the Northwest corner of Cologne to 174.5 in Altstadt-Süd. In addition to Altstadt-Süd and Altstadt-Nord, seven other Bezirke have more than 100 per hectare; Klettenberg and Sülz, southwest of Altstadt; Ehrenfeld, directly west; Nippes and Mauenheim, northwest; Vingst, east of Deutz; and Buchforst, northeast of Deutz. Of the remaining 43 bezirke, 32 have 50 or less per hectare and eleven have between 50 and 100 per hectare. The overall population density for Cologne is 34.8 persons per hectare; west of the Rhine it is 38.1, and east of the Rhine, 29.7. [15] This means an overall density of 14 persons per acre with the heaviest density in Altstadt-Nord at 70.6 per acre. Dwelling unit density is now approximately what it was at the beginning of World War II. The following tabulation shows the changes:[16]

Date	Avg. No. of Persons per Dwelling Unit	Avg. No. of Persons per Room
1939	3.04	.78
1950	4.84	1.28
1964	3.01	.89

The size of dwelling units is shown by the following tabulation:[17]

No. of Rooms Per D. U.	No. of D. U.
4	3,750
3	2,615
1	1,196
5	1,194
2	1,129
6	503
7	151
8	35
9	12
10 or more	9

Taking into account a total of 233, 771 single persons
over the age of 18, 71, 863 widowed, and 23, 386 divorced
persons in Cologne, [18] the total of 1, 196 one-room dwelling
units does not seem excessive. Furthermore, the overwhelming proportion of families have no more than one or
two children and therefore the dwelling-unit size in terms of
number of rooms seems adequate. [19] Although there is a
shortage of dwelling units in Cologne, the persons who now
have accommodations are by and large not crowded and are
not poorly housed. There is, however, little or no choice
in housing. As was emphasized by Meiner and Schwendy at
the Neue Rhein-Zeitung there are two kinds of deficiencies:
1) statistical, and 2) actual. The 3 per cent statistical
shortage becomes a 5 per cent actual shortage due to the absence of choice. The city has provided housing for its tramway employees. An apartment building for the police was
under construction in 1966 and the provision of housing for
teachers was under consideration. Trade unions do not approve of this linking of housing with job. The policy tends
to freeze the worker to the job. The government, however,
has found the policy necessary, as has private enterprise,
as an inducement to employment.

Relevant to the housing shortage is, of course, the
new town planning, which began in 1952-54. Four new towns
are recognized by the Cologne Stadtplannungsamt:

1.   Neu Stadt in Chlorweiler--north 14 kilometers
from der Dom. Population planned: 100, 000.

2.   Garten Stadt Nord--north 7-1/2 kilometers.
Population planned: 18, 000.

3.   Ostheim--east 7-1/2 kilometers. Population
planned: 10, 000.

4.   Bockelmünd--west 12 kilometers. Population
planned: 10, 000.

The newest is Neu Stadt in Chlorweiler, on which construction commenced in 1960. It is reputed to be the largest
in the Bunde. This is also the one true new city in that it
includes an industrial area and with the service requirements
for a substantial population will provide employment opportunities for the residents. A two and a half square kilometer
lake will also provide recreational opportunities. [20] The other so-called new towns are dormitory towns.

Mindful of the tendency towards dormitory town development, a Mr. Willings, director of the new Department of Development Planning, refuses to speak in terms of "new towns."[21] They do not long remain "new." Furthermore, they are all too quickly absorbed by the surrounding urbanization.

The Neue Rhein-Zeitung representatives, Meinel and Schwendy, advocate the building of new towns. They are thinking in terms of real new towns, claiming that the traffic problem in Cologne would be relieved thereby. They also claim that only by the construction of new towns can the dwelling shortage be solved. Cologne has not reached the number of dwelling units that it had before World War II, and the number then was below that of an earlier period.[22]

Director Willings sees possibilities for Neu Stadt. Now employees of industry in north Cologne live all over the city. The plan for Neu Stadt will make it possible for industrial employees to live near the job. Industrial parks for light industry requiring highly skilled workers are planned. Coordinating committees between the chemical industry and the Cologne municipal government have been formed and are facilitating the effectuation of the plan.

The plan contemplates ten groups of 10,000 population each in 6,600 hectares (15 square miles of 9,708 acres) with a population density of 100 persons per acre. Multiple-story apartment building will be constructed in the middle of each housing group and lower apartment buildings and single-family residences along the edges. The multiple-story structures will be cooperatives; the single-family residences, private development. Parking garages will be provided under the housing. Schools, churches and community buildings are planned for each housing group. It is anticipated that the total population will eventually expand to 160,000.[23] Neu Stadt will have one Hauptzentrum, four or five Nebenzentrum, and several Kleinezentrum in the commercial development.

Neu Stadt in Chlorweiler is the most completely and imaginatively planned of the new towns in Cologne. Three new towns have been developed and one is being planned within the city limits of Cologne. From this point of view, they are more properly to be considered very large scale subdivisions, or urban renewal projects within the American concept. All four so-called towns are within the jurisdiction of the City of Cologne.

The city is currently organized into eight Stadtteile
(communities), five on the west side of the Rhine in addition
to Altstadt, and two on the east side in addition to Deutz,
which is part of the old city community. The number of
Stadtbezirke (neighborhoods) per Stadtteile range from three
in the old city to nine each in the northernmost Stadtteile on
the west side and in the two full Stadtteile on the east side,
totalling 52 Stadtbezirke in the city. The Stadtteile and
Stadtbezirke are used for administrative purposes to facilitate administrative decentralization.

In addition to serving as administrative districts, the
Stadtbezirke tend to be real sociological entities. One no-
tices a marked change in driving from Marienburg--a high
level, well-established single-family residential neighborhood
at the southern extreme of the city--northwest in a circle at
the same distance from the Ring through Zollstock, Sülz,
Lindenthal, and into Ehrenfeld, an industrialized area; and
likewise the change is apparent if one drives northeast from
Ehrenfeld through Bickendorf, partially industrial, through
Vogelsang into Bocklemünd along the western city limits,
which is spoken of as a "Neu Stadt" of 10, 000 population,
situated 12 kilometers from the Dom. Mulheim, immediately northwest of Deutz on the right bank of the Rhine is spok-
en of as a district that has most clearly retained its identity
as a separate area, or community. In terms of citizen a-
wareness and action, north of Ehrenfeld was mentioned as an
area in which the residents arose in strong opposition to proposed urban renewal, which was blocked by organized citizen
opposition. The continued existence of community feeling and
spirit through the centuries is partially explained by the
workers' custom of returning after a day's work to their
home community to join their neighbors in the local bierstube,
kellar or restaurant for a sociable drink and discussion of
community affairs before returning home for dinner, a phenomenon worthy of sociological research. [24]

The Bezirke and Teile have been delineated by the
municipal Statisches Amt. Hereafter, sociological data in
Cologne will be gathered by blocks, of which there are 5000
for computer purposes. The first step is a census on apartment buildings by city blocks in 1967. From the annual census, population pyramids are prepared; studies are made of
specific areas, and comparative studies made of different
types of communities. Furthermore, research is conducted
into economic trends, which is available for city planning and
is used by individual industrial plants. In addition, Statisti-

cal Yearbooks are published for general use. [25]

Professor Dr. Heinz Mohnen in assuming office as
Oberstadtdirektor in 1966 emphasized having a close working
relationship with the University of Cologne. The City has a
contract with sociology Professor König Scheuch for community studies, starting with short-range and gradually working
into long-range studies. Instead of contracting with private
planning firms, the City will hire university students to make
the community surveys and studies, thus enabling the City to
get exactly what it wants and needs at less cost, simultaneously interesting and preparing university students for municipal service and helping the students finance themselves
through their university education. [26] This will provide a
solid research base for the recently created Development
Planning Agency.

Cologne leads the nation in wages and salaries paid to
personnel engaged in the production of motor vehicles and
machinery. In overall industry, Cologne ranks fifth national-
ly in the number of employees and wages and salaries paid,
and sixth in the number of types of industries. Cologne has
the fourth largest population. The three cities ranking ahead
of Cologne in population are: West Berlin, Hamburg and
Munich. The ranking of industry in Cologne follows:

Financial Operations of Industrial Groups
in Cologne in 1966 [27]

Type of Industry	Annual Turnover (in thousands of DM)
Motor Vehicle	2, 264
Machine	1, 350
Chemical	1, 201
Electrotechnical	1, 017

If in the above table the Farbenfabriken Bayer Aktien-
gesellschaft in Leverkusen (which is adjacent to Cologne on
the east side of the Rhine to the north and is included in the
Cologne metropolitan area) is included, the chemical industrial group becomes by far the largest financially with a total annual turnover of 4,501,000 DM. The Bayer firm is the
largest in the Cologne MA with an annual turnover of

3, 300, 000 DM, greater than that of any other industrial
group in the Cologne MA. [28]

    In addition, Cologne is a national major center for in-
surance headquarters, and ranks high in headquarters for
other financial institutions.

    Industry is situated in three substantial sites west of
the Rhine: 1) in Ehrenfeld beginning two kilometers west of
the Ring, and extending about two kilometers west between
the first and second greenbelts; 2) in Niehl and Weidenpesch
beginning five kilometers north of the Ring with two kilometers along the Rhine, extending north three kilometers;
and 3) in Worringen in the northern tip of Cologne, beginning more than 15 kilometers north of the Ring, and extending north one and one-half kilometers along the Rhine. East
of the Rhine, there are several smaller industrial sites,
none larger than one square kilometer: 1) two sites in Kalk,
west of Deutz; 2) two sites in Mulheim, north of Deutz;
and 3) one site in Flittard, the same distance north as the
Niehl site west of the Rhine. In addition, small industrial
sites are scattered throughout the city. According to Baurat
Riedel, industry is authorized for sites planned in terms of
traffic, providing short connections with railway rights-of-
way, main thoroughfares, or the autobahn. [29] With the light
industry characteristic of Cologne, such availability of workers' transportation is not an unreasonable criterion.

    The scatter of light industry throughout Cologne is
shown by Table 4 in the Appendix, giving the number of hectares in each district with subtotals for each community and
the grand total for the city. Many of the industrial sites
are very small handicraft sites, yet only 17 of the 51 districts have no such sites. Each of the 8 communities
(Stadtteile) have industry ranging in total hectares per community from 16. 4 hectares out of a total of 1, 856 in Lindenthal Stadtteile in the southwestern portion of the city, to
660. 5 hectares out of a total of 3, 044 in Stadtteil Nippes in
the near north close to the autobahn. Both communities are
west of the Rhine. The number of hectares devoted to industry in Cologne is 1, 926. 6 out of the grand total of
25, 136; in other words 7. 6 per cent of the total city area
is given over to industry. Excluding from the city total the
8. 201 hectares devoted to agriculture and gardening, which
is non-urban land-use reserved for future development, the
amount of land used for industry is 11. 4 per cent of the total. Another useful measure of the amount of land devoted

to industry, including handicraft operations in Cologne is secured by making the additional exclusions of forest land, public greens, athletic fields, street and railway rights-of-way,
harbors, and docks, which then leaves the number of hectares classified in Cologne as "built areas." Of this total,
industry in all its forms has 30.3 per cent, or roughly one-
third of the total. Modifying the breakdown in the table giving "Generalized Land Use by Hectare," which shows 25.3
per cent of the land in the "built areas" category, the percentage of the total for the city devoted to residential and
commercial will be 17.7 and the percentage devoted to industry 7.6.

No agency in Cologne attempts to keep a record of the
number of hectares devoted to business. Residential and
business land-uses are mixed. This does not mean that such
land-uses are uncontrolled. Business property use is approved in the interest of customer convenience, is considered as a supporting facility for residential use and therefore is classified with residential use.

There are special units of government regulating
water and air pollution and providing noise control. In North
Rhineland-Westphalia, land law sets the standards and supervises the Kreisfreistadt, or the Kreis, in enforcement. Air
pollution is still a problem. In every square kilometer of
industrial development, a testing box is placed which is
checked every month. If an industrial plant is found polluting the air and does not take corrective action it loses its
permit, which it secures from the Kreisfreistadt, before
commencing operations. Noise control is still in the experi-
mental stages of development. [30] Neither air nor noise pollution however is the problem in the Cologne MA that both
are in the inner Ruhr area.

Circulation of men and material is well planned and
managed. [31] Cologne is a part of the network of railways
and highways provided for the Rhine-Ruhr industrial complex,
and is situated at the southern end of the Rhine-Ruhr autobahn configuration, which from Cologne continues southwest
to Aachen and Liege, also northeast to Bonn, and continuing
beyond the Rhine to Frankfort, Nuremberg, or Munich.
Cologne is the one city in Germany fortunate enough to have
an autobahn by-pass completely circling the city. [32]

Four automobile bridges and two railway bridges now
cross the Rhine in the city. Another automobile bridge

crosses immediately south of the city limits. A suspension
bridge from the Zoo to Rheinpark, called "Zoobrücke," which
served recreational rather than commercial purposes, was in
need of repair in 1966 and was not in use. All eight bridges
have been constructed since World War II.

While the war destruction necessitated painful and expensive reconstruction under adverse circumstances, indirect
advantages have accrued to the city. Cologne has rebuilt for
the automobile age. Sixty per cent of the tram service is
independent of automobile traffic. The trams are connected
two or three together. In the first tram only, a conductor
is available to sell tickets. The other one or two are used
only by tramriders who have tickets, which they deposit in
a machine, or have stamped for the next transfer. Movement is possible from car to car within the two- or three-
car tram. During two months of tram riding, the author
never saw anyone neglect to deposit his ticket or have it
punched. The self-service system works. With trams running
on the Ring and other main thoroughfares every few minutes,
and no automobile traffic slowing tram movement over the
main routes, transport was both speedy and convenient. Bus
service supplements the tram service over different routes.

There are 21 parking buildings in the CBD with 6,500
parking places. Research has shown that three-fourths of
the central business district would have to be torn down to
take care of all the automobiles, if all the motorists who
wanted to bring their cars into the central business district
were encouraged to do so. Immediately prior to Christmas,
Easter, and a few other holiday seasons, all automobiles,
except fire trucks and taxis, are forbidden entry into the
CBD.[33] Furthermore, the two kilometers of pedestrian-only
streets at all times provide the reasonable opportunity of
movement unhampered by motor vehicles.

Since street rights-of-way have many effects, including enhancement or ruination of the appearance of the city,
mention will be made in this connection of the strict regulation of billboards and other forms of advertising in German
cities. In North Rhineland Wesphalia, the Landesbauordnang
prohibits a "heaping up" of advertisements in open spaces
or on vacant buildings. The following are permitted: 1) a
combined list of agencies and firms on one placard at the
entrance to a city; 2) announcements with information at the
juncture of streets outside the city limits to help move traffic; 3) announcements at airports, sportsgrounds and assem-

bly places insofar as the landscape is not disturbed thereby;
4) announcements at fairgrounds and exhibition grounds; and
5) advertising on the building in which the commodity advertised is produced.   Announcements on sheets of paper are
permitted on kiosks, in shops where news is sold, and in
windows of shops, exhibiting what the owner is selling. [34]

Similar regulation of advertising is apparently prevalent throughout West Germany.   The author and his wife
drove through every land in West Germany, except the Saar.
At the entrance to each city were two placards, one listing
the businesses in the city, the other listing the churches.
No billboards cluttered the countryside or cityscape or blocked
the view of surrounding scenery, rural or urban.   The limitations specified above were enforced.

Subway construction commenced in the center of the
Cologne CBD in 1965.   The plans specify seven and one-
half kilometers by 1971.   Trams will travel underground.
Stations will be located near pedestrian streets.   According
to two newspapermen there, there are over 100,000 too
many automobiles in Cologne. [35]   In brief, Cologne has rebuilt for the automobile age, and has problems with motor
vehicles similar to other cities in kind but not in degree.
Cologne is not dominated by the car as American cities are.
Travel by rapid-mass transit will be encouraged more in
the CBD, and travel by automobile discouraged.

Berlin has had elevated train and subway service since
the beginning of the century, and currently has more than 70
miles of subway track in operation.   Hamburg has had subways since 1912, and currently has about 50 miles of subway track.   Hamburg and Munich, in addition to Cologne,
are engaged in extending their subway systems.   Hamburg
began in 1966 tunneling four parallel tubes, 100 feet below
the surface, directly under the Hauptbanhoff and its 20 railway tracks, using "shield tunneling" techniques, by means
of which structures on the ground are not disturbed and the
underground tubes are constructed much as tunnels are dug
under rivers.   This costs $15 million per mile, or almost
twice the cost of normal construction from top down by tear-
ing up streets.   Hamburg plans four levels of tunnels: 1)
pedestrian; 2) high-speed motorized traffic; 3) train tunnel;
and 4) subway.   Seven subway lines are being built at the
rate of one and one quarter miles per year.   This is a heavy
burden on the municipal budget, but Hamburg officials claim
that this subway program is "saving the life of the central

city." Out of necessity, Hamburg plans to proceed further
with it than the other German cities. The Hamburg Plan
specifies about 90 miles of subway.

"Parking garages are being built--but not downtown.
Most are in outlying areas, convenient to subway stops, so
that drivers may park and take public transportation into the
city."36

Munich is introducing the subway by tunneling under
the "Stachus" and "Karlsplatz," just east of the Hauptbahnoff,
said to be the most traffic-ridden city square in Germany.
There are to be at least five subterranean levels: 1) pedestrian passageway, lined with shops; 2) motorized traffic;
3) parking garages for 800 cars; 4) railway; and 5) local
transport.

"During most of the construction period, residents
will not even be aware of what is going on beneath the surface; there will be a 'hole in the ground' for only one
year." 37

In Munich also, it is believed that the subway program
will save the central city from traffic paralysis caused by
private cars.

Cologne is currently planning one level only of subway
construction, which is tunneled by the simpler open-cut method. Cologne, however, has faced a problem that apparently
has not seriously bothered Munich and has not caused Hamburg difficulty. Virtually every scoopful of dirt dug out for
the subway in the CBD of Cologne unearths anthropological
and Roman artifacts, which immediately brings the professional archaeologists into action. The ensuing conflict continues: the archaeologists have their professional interests
to protect, supported by portions of the citizenry, and engineers involved have their interests--a time schedule--which
is also supported by portions of the citizenry. Cologne is
likewise convinced that rapid-mass transit is necessary "to
save the old city."

Because of several years of interest in the monorail
among long-range urban planners in America, it may be
worthy of notice that a monorail is in the planning stage, not
for intra-municipal rapid mass transit, but for inter-munici-
pal transportation, connecting Düsseldorf with Cologne and
Bonn. The director of the Department of Development in

Cologne, recalled that the first experiments with the monorail took place in Fühlingen Bezirke (now Chorweiler), Cologne, and in Wüppertal, north of Cologne, in the 1950s under the direction of the Swedish scientist and engineer, Axel
Wennergren.   He implied clearly that planners in Cologne
know the appropriate use of the monorail. [38]

Following World War II, a goodly proportion of the
population in Cologne wanted to rebuild the city as it was
prior to destruction. [39]   The professional planners, however,
convinced the Stadtdirektor, the Mayor, and the City Council
that here was an opportunity to rebuild in accordance with
current needs, but in the process retain links with the past.
Thus, the historically and culturally significant was preserved, and variety in development was encouraged.   Businessmen on Hohestrasse and Schildergasse objected to the
prohibition of motorized traffic from these streets; however,
they agreed to a trial closing.   Now, they would not consider returning to the "mixed traffic."   Furthermore, in the
reconstruction, satisfactory residential redevelopment was
permitted in the Altstadt with the highest residential density
in the city, so that there would be crowds of people in the
old city at all times night and day.   On this note, observations from Hamburg are in order.

"Doubts have risen lately, however, among experts
and laymen as to whether the Hamburg development plan of
1960, based on the 'Charta of Athens'--that is to say with
the greatest possible areas of green and the separation of
dwellings and businesses, pedestrians and traffic--is still
valid today.   Warnings from prominent German city planners
and also the trip through the United States of the Mayor of
Hamburg, Paul Nevermann, will lead to changes.   Following
a decision by the Senate, new guidelines for city-planning
are being worked out, according to which building will be
denser and higher, at least in the city center.   In addition,
ways and means are being sought to bring more people into
the city center so that after business hours and at week-
ends, Hamburg will still retain its former atmosphere and
bustle." [40]

With the exception of the separation of pedestrian
and motorized traffic on the banks of the Rhine and in the
pedestrian streets, Cologne has applied these planning principles in the Altstadt.   One problem, which is a development problem rather than a planning problem, is the provision of more housing to relieve the definite housing shortage.

There is agreement on the goal.   The problem is how to ac-
complish the goal, how to provide more housing more rapidly
than the increase in population.   One likely planning problem is the improvement of the right bank of the Rhine to
equal the supposed advantages of the left bank.   There is apparently not sufficient public sentiment on this to make it a
public issue, nor has it emerged sufficiently to make it a political problem.   One can properly question the need for planning action on this.   The claim can be considered part of a
running competition for additional public improvements between the two banks of the Rhine, plus a probable fear on the
right bank that somehow they have not "caught up" with the
development on the left.   Interviews with representatives of
the DGB (overall trade union), Handelskammer (Chamber of
Commerce), CDU and SPD (the two political parties), Stadt-
vertreter (City Council), Deutschen Städtetag (German Municipal Association), University of Cologne faculty, professional
planners, municipal officials, and various of the citizenry in
their homes yields the conclusion that aside from the housing
shortage there seems to be general satisfaction.

To an American, accustomed to urban sprawl on the
outskirts of cities, the neat orientation of all activity outside
the city limits is a pleasant surprise.   This is due in large
part to the fact that planning and land-use control do not end
at the city limits, nor at the kreis (county) limits.   The governmental units in the Cologne metropolitan area plan and administer land use in accordance with the Nordrhein-Westfalen
Landesplannungsgesetz (state planning law), and Landesbauordnung (state building law), but also within the broad principles
established by the Federal Republic in a Raumordnungsgesetz
(Space Ordering Law).

This last law specifies: "local planning shall fit into
national patterns and national patterns into local planning."[41]

Particularly relevant illustrations of principles in the
Federal Law are:

> Such land as is specially suited for agricultural use
> shall be planned for other use only when absolutely
> needed for other purposes.
>
> Landscapes adjoining population concentration areas
> shall be preserved.   Respect shall be paid to the
> characteristically historical and cultural associa-
> tions.

Gemeinden (communes) and Gemeindeverbände (Associations of Communes) shall work together in regional planning. [42]

There is also the specification that Federal interests shall be respected. These include the military, railway, long-distance highway traffic, air traffic, and telegraphy.

The key principle for the Raumordnungsgesetz, which appears in the first paragraph, may sound unduly idealistic to American readers, yet it sets the tone for what follows:

The Federal Republic has to be led, in its utilization of public space, towards such a development as will best serve the free development of personality in society.   Thereby the natural realities as well as the economic, social and cultural needs have to be observed. [43]

The same respect for and preservation of historical landmarks is in evidence in adjoining areas outside Cologne as within.   Furthermore, the state legal requirement that if land is used for no other constructive purpose, it must be devoted to gardening plots, is applicable in every commune, rural or urban.   In addition, the personnel of the planning and building departments of every commune function under the supervision of Land (state) planning personnel.   As a matter of fact, since the smaller communes lack the finances to hire the caliber of personnel that the larger cities can attract, the Land (state) supervision is closer in the case of the smaller communes.   Thus, land development around the borders of the Cologne city limits is orderly and in harmony with the land development within the city.

Notes

1.   Mumford, Lewis, "The Future of the City," Architectural Record, Part II, November 1962.

2.   Doppelfeld, O. , "Brochure," distributed in the Rathaus, 1966.   Among the Roman remains in the Praetorium was a monument, on which the Cologne aldermen of the 17th century had carved their names.

3.   Interview with Dr. Droege, Assistant to the Rector, University of Cologne, in the Office of the Depart-

ment of Development Planning, Stadthaus, Room 97,
March 10, 1966.

4. Robson, W. A. (editor), Great Cities of the World,
    (London: George Allen and Unwin Ltd., 2d ed., 1957),
    p. 655. The Chapter on Cologne was prepared by
    Lorenz Fischer, one-time Director of the Statistical
    Office of the City of Cologne, and Peter Van Hauten,
    also one-time Director of that office.

5. Interview with Mr. Stemmler, Direktor, Liegenschafts
    Amt (Real Estate Office), Dischhaus, Bruckenstrasse
    19, Room 224, March 4, 1966.

6. Interview with Messrs. Meinel and Schwendy, Neue
    Rhein-Zeitung, Deutzer Druckhaus, 5 Köln-Kalk,
    March 16, 1966.

7. Interview with Mr. Stemmler.

8. Des Statistischen Amt der Stadt Köln, Johannisstrasse
    72/80, February 9, 1966.

9. Bauordnung für das Nordrhein-Westfalen, 1962. Teil
    I Allgemeine Vorschriften, Section 8: "Open Space
    and Distance."

10. Der Statistisches Amt der Stadt Köln, Ibid.

11. Bauordnung für das Land Nordrhein-Westfalen, 1962.
    Teil II: "Die Grundstücke und ihre Bebauung."

12. Interview with Baurat Pohl, Planungsamt, Stadthaus,
    Room 369, February 9, 1966.

13. Bauordnung für das Land Nordrhein-Westfalen, 1962.
    Teil VI, Unterabschnitt 7: "Elektrische Anlagen und
    Antennen."

14. Verwaltungsbericht Der Stadt Köln, 1964. (Bearbeitet
    und Herausgegeben vom Statistischen Amt Der Köln,
    p. 160.

15. See Table 4, Appendix.

16. Statistischen Amt der Stadt Köln, Statistisches Jahrbuch
    der Stadt Köln, 1964, Table 106 "Wohnungen, Wohn-

räume and Wohndichte."

17. See Table 5, Appendix.

18. Statistischen Amt der Stadt Köln, Op. cit., Table 11,
     "Wohnbevolkerung und Familienstand."

19. Statistischen Amt der Stadt Köln, Op. cit., Table 38,
     "Ehelich Lebendgeborne nach Ehedauer und Geburten-
     folge."

20. Interview with Baurat Pohl.

21. Interview with Baurat Willings, Direktor, Abteilung für
     Kommunale Entwicklungsplannung (Office of the Devel-
     opment Planning Agency), March 10, 1966.

22. Interview with Messrs. Meinel and Schwendy.

23. Interview with Mr. Willings.

24. Interviews March 10, 1966 with Mr. Willings, Dr.
     Droege, and Mr. Brown, Fulbright Research Grant
     recipient in Cologne in the Office of the Development
     Planning Agency.

25. Interviews with Direktor Bamberger and Mr. Sirp,
     Diplom-Volkswirt, Das Statistischen Amt, Johannis-
     haus, Room 194, February 9, 1966.

26. Interview with Mr. Willings.

27. Deutschen Stadtetag, Statistisches Jahrbuch Deutscher
     Gemeinden, 1964, "Industriebrechte 1963," p. 72-86.

28. Press and Information Office of the German Federal
     Government, The Bulletin, August 13, 1963.

29. Interview with Baurat Riedel, Direktor, Planungsamt,
     Stadthaus, February-March, 1966.

30. Interview with Dr. Wagener, Landkreistag Nordrhein
     Westfalen, Schafterstrasse 10, Dusseldorf, March 15,
     1966. In the Ruhr Valley, water-resource associa-
     tions (Genossenschaften), which include municipal,
     rural and private water users, manage the waters of
     the Ruhr River and several tributaries of the Rhine.

They have the power to enact regulations and exercise control, so that the water returned to the river is of the same quality as that originally removed.

31. See Generalverkehrsplan der Stadt Köln, 1956; 275 pages of excellent street maps and descriptive material.

32. See Planung einer Stadtautobahn in Koln, 1962; 65 pages of well prepared designs and maps.

33. Interview with Baurat Klose, (Bauaufsichtsabt), February 9, 1966, Stadthaus, Room 367.

34. Bauordnung für das Land Nordrhein-Westfalen, 1962, Teil V: "Anlagen der Aussenwerbung."

35. Interview with Messrs. Held and Falter, Kölner Stadt-anzeiger, February 24, 1966.

36. "One Way to Beat the Traffic - Hamburg Goes Under-ground," U. S. News and World Report, October 3, 1966, p. 112.

37. Press and Information Office of the German Federal Government, The Bulletin, January 18, 1966.

38. Interview with Mr. Willings, March 17, 1966.

39. Interview with Mr. Blomeier, Kölner Stadtanzeiger, February 24, 1966.

40. Press and Information Office of the German Federal Government, The Bulletin, February 2, 1965.

41. Raumordnungsgesetz 8 April 1965 (B. G. B. I. I. S. 306), Sec. 1.

42. Ibid., sec. 5.

43. Ibid., sec. 1.

Chapter IV

COLOGNE: POLICY FORMATION

Following World War II, the occupying powers granted
self-government to the local governments first, then to the
Länder (states), and thereafter to the Bunde (federation).
Thus, immediately after the war, the best qualified and most
capable political leaders and administrators were brought into the local government level.   Finding reliable non-Nazi personnel presented a problem; however, since the occupying
powers gradually released authority to German officials, the
opportunity to screen carefully was available and was used;
and the local level received first attention.   This provided
a solid base for a reactivation of the federal system, which
Germany has continuously had since its inception as a nation-
state, except for the National Socialist period of the Third
Reich.

Germany, furthermore, has had a tradition of local
self-government.   This can be traced back to the free cities
of the Middle Ages, and in the Rhineland to earlier times.
Particularly since the days of Baron von Stein in the early
part of the Nineteenth Century have the ideas of local self-
government in a more meaningful sense been present. Baron
von Stein advocated the concept of representative democracy,
which placed authority over municipal affairs in elected town
councilors, who in turn selected the mayor and other officials.   His proposals called for the elimination of local oli-
garchies, the exclusion of civil servants from election to the
municipal council, and a reduction of higher-level supervision.   While these ideas were radical in his day, they were
not lost; and local self-government in German materialized
before any semblance of it appeared in whole or in part, at
the higher levels.   This tradition survived the Nazi regime,
and helped in the rebuilding of a new West Germany.

In North Rhineland-Westphalia, British occupation authorities in 1945 eliminated those civic regulations that had
a Nazi character, and introduced a municipal frame of gov-

ernment, patterned on British experience. The council of
elected representatives once again gained control of the administration. This was not at variance with German experience. The council selected a chairman, who became the
Lord Mayor and official representative of the city, and a full-
time Chief Town Clerk, who was responsible to the council
for administration. These changes were finally incorporated
into a municipal code for North Rhineland-Westphalia on October 28, 1952. [1]

Each of the occupation authorities attempted to influence the formation of local government. Simultaneously, traditional, pre-Nazi, German patterns emerged. Furthermore,
as in the United States, regulation of local and municipal
government came within the jurisdiction of the Länder
(states), so that determination of the forms of municipal government is made by each of the eleven Länder. As a result
West Germany has almost as much variety of municipal patterns of government as does the United States; these patterns
are as admittedly confusing to the German as they are to the
American. In all the varied forms of local government,
however, the elected council forms basic policy and legally
controls the administration.

North Rhine-Westphalia and Lower Saxony have required that all municipal governments within their jurisdictions shall have the form of government described above
(council, lord mayor, chief clerk). In practice throughout
the two Länder, the chief clerk has developed into a city
manager, sufficiently so that the International City Managers'
Association recognizes the cities in these two Länder of Germany as council-manager cities. [2] It is worthy of notice
that the German title for the Chief Clerk is "Oberstadtdirektor." At the same time, the Lord Mayor of these cities, as
chairman of the council, which exercises closer supervision
over the administration than does the council of the council-
manager form of government in the United States, has gained
some of the characteristics of the regular German Ober-
bürgermeister; and he, in fact, has this title.

One variation among several between the federal system of West Germany and the federal system in the United
States is the inclusion in the Basic Law of the Federal Republic of Germany of two articles dealing with local governments. [3] Article 28 specifies:

1) The Constitutional order in the Länder must

conform to the principles of republican, democratic
and social government based on the rule of law,
within the meaning of this Basic Law. In each of
the Länder, counties and communes, the people
must be represented by a body chosen in universal,
direct, free, equal, and secret elections. In the
communes, the assembly of the commune may take
the place of an elected body.

2) The communes must be guaranteed the right to
regulate on their own responsibility all the affairs
of the local commune within the limits set by law.
The associations of communes also have the right
of self-government in accordance with the law within the limits of the functions given them by law.

3) The Federation guarantees that the constitutional
order of the Länder conforms to the basic rights
and to the provisions of paragraphs (1) and (2). [4]

This is known in Germany as the principle of "universality of competence," and is akin to the principle of "home
rule" in the United States, which is effective as a constitutional principle in about half of the states. Distinguishing
that which is primarily of local concern from that which is
primarily of state-wide concern is a problem in West Germany as it is in the U.S.A.; however, the administrative
courts are available in case of a contested jurisdiction.
Furthermore, in the event of a serious question of constitu-
tionality, the Federal Constitutional Court can settle the question. One characteristic of the West German federalism
that makes the principle of "universality of competence" particularly difficult is the interrelated nature of all the levels
of the West German Federal system, whereby most of the
federal laws are administered by Land (state) officials, who
in turn delegate much to local administrative personnel.
Even with "universality of competence," municipal personnel
are functioning simultaneously as agents of the state and of
the federal governments; in so doing, the municipal corporation lacks true universality of competence.

Article 106, section 7, specifies that the Federation,
if it establishes special institutions in the Länder or communes which cause immediate higher expenditures or lower
receipts to those Länder or communes, and the Länder or
communes are financially handicapped thereby, the Federation shall grant the necessary financial equalization. [5]

The two provisions in the federal constitution dealing
with local governments are thus protective rather than regulatory. Insofar as city planning and land use is concerned,
the Gemeinde have the power of initiation, but must function
within the framework of principles enunciated in the Federal
Raumordnungsgesets, and in accordance with the Land Planning Law, which is procedural, and the Land Building Law,
which is regulatory.

As in all other West German cities, the basic policy
forming body in Cologne is the council, which is elected by
general, direct and secret ballot for a five-year term of office. The number of councilors is dependent upon the population of the city. Since September 27, 1964, the Cologne
Council has had 67 members. [6] According to the municipal
electoral law of North Rhineland-Westphalia, all citizens of
the Federal Republic of Germany who are twenty-one years
of age and have resided in the city for three months are en-
franchised. Each voter has two ballots. The first ballot is
for the election of a representative from the councilmanic
district, of which there are 33 in Cologne; the second ballot
is cast for a party, which is totalled city-wide, providing
each party with the number of seats to which it is entitled
on a proportionate basis. The council has 34 seats to be
filled by the list proportional representation system. The
candidates, listed on the second ballot, are elected from the
top down, depending on the number of seats won in the election, the party having decided the listing of the candidates on
the ballot. [7]

At a recent municipal election, of the total population
of 835, 832, the Statistical Bureau showed that 589, 332, or
70. 5 per cent, were eligible to vote. Of this total 381, 828,
or 64. 8 per cent, voted in the municipal election. [8] With the
exception of the 1948 municipal election, when only 54. 7 per
cent of those eligible voted, since World War II, more than
60 per cent of the eligible electorate in Cologne have voted
in each municipal election.

Freedom of political parties is guaranteed by Article
21 of the Basic Law as follows:

> 1) The political parties participate in the forming
> of the political will of the people. They may be
> freely formed. Their internal organization must
> conform to democratic principles. They must pub-
> licly account for the sources of their funds.

2) Parties which by reason of their aims or the be-
havior of their adherents, seek to impair or de-
stroy the free democratic basic order or to endanger
the existence of the Federal Republic of Germany
are unconstitutional. The Federal Constitutional
Court decides on the question of unconstitutionality.

3) Details will be regulated by Federal legislation. [9]

In 1952 the Federal Constitutional Court declared the
Socialist Reich Party (SRP), an extreme rightist party, unconstitutional. The Communist Party (KPD) was similarly
proscribed in 1956. The German Reich Party (ARP), established to continue the propagandizing of the SRP, gained no
seats in the parliamentary election of 1953 and thereafter,
but it was particularly active in Rhineland-Palatinate and had
been declared illegal in that Land. [10] Prior to this, the Communist Party in Cologne failed to meet the minimum requirement of 5 per cent of the total vote necessary for representation in the council by the municipal electoral law in the
1952 municipal election. The German Party, the Free
Peoples Party, the United German Block, and the German
Centrum Party also failed to meet the 5 per cent requirement in the same election.

Municipal councilors are elected by plurality vote.
From 1948 to 1956, the Christian Democratic Union (CDU)
was the governing party in the council. Since 1956, the Social Democratic Party (SPD) has been the governing party.
The 1956 municipal election resulted in 32 seats for the SPD,
29 seats for the CDU and 5 seats for the Free Democratic
Party (FDP). The 1961 election resulted in an even closer
margin with 31 SPD seats, 30 CDU seats, and 5 FDP seats.
A change came in the 1964 elections with a clear majority
for the SDP which gained 40 seats to 27 for the CDU. The
FDP gained only 16,880 votes, or 4.5 per cent of the votes
cast, therefore failing to meet the minimum requirement for
recognition as a party for representation in the council. An
"Arbeiterpartei" also campaigned in 1964 and polled 96
votes. [11] At the local level in Cologne as well as at the Federal level, a two-party system seems to be emerging. The
1964 party change in the council was noteworthy for at least
two reasons; the CDU had been the governing party in Cologne since World War II and Cologne had been Konrad Adenauer's home base.

Map 4. Land Legislative (Voting) Districts in Cologne.

——— Voting District Boundaries.

Source: Statische Mitteilungen der Stadt Köln, 1965, p. 111.

The overwhelming proportion of the population was
and is Roman Catholic, averaging 66 per cent for the city
and not less than 63.8 per cent in any of the seven legislative districts. [12]

Comparison of the 1962 Landtagswahl (election of state
legislators), the 1964 Stadtvertreterwahl (election of city
councilmen), the 1965 Bundestagswahl (election of Federal
legislators) and the 1966 state legislative election in Cologne
is illuminating. [13] Overall for the City of Cologne, 62.4 per
cent of the eligible electorate voted in the 1962 State Legislative elections; 64.8 per cent, in the 1964 city councilmanic
elections; and 81.0 per cent in the 1965 Federal elections.
In the 1962 state and 1965 Federal elections, the CDU gained
a plurality; in the 1964 municipal and the 1966 state elections the SPD won a majority.

The Statistical Bureau has tabulated the election returns from the 612 election precincts for 1962, 1964, and
1965 by the seven state legislative districts in Cologne. In
the 1962 state legislative election, the SPD carried three of
the seven districts: the 14th, 19th, and 20th, which include
all of Cologne east of the Rhine plus Altstadt-Süd west of
the Rhine.   District 20, which Map #4 shows is inclusive
of most of the southern portion of Cologne east of the Rhine,
gave the only majority vote to the SPD.   The CDU carried
the other four legislative districts, but none of them by a
majority vote.   In the 1964 municipal election, the SPD
gained a clear majority of the vote in all of seven legislative districts, the largest majority vote being registered in
the 20th.   The 1965 election is by and large a repetition of
the 1962 election with the SPD carrying three of the seven
districts: the 14th, 19th and 20th, the latter by a majority
vote.   The CDU, as in 1962, carried the other four legislative districts, but none by a majority vote.   In the 1966
state legislative election, however, the SPD won in all seven
legislative districts.   Except for the 1964 municipal election
and the 1966 legislative election, the two major parties have
been fairly evenly balanced in Cologne.   With the exception
of Altstadt-Süd, the area west of the Rhine has been normally CDU, and east of the Rhine, plus Altstadt-Süd, SPD.
This has been the political topography of Cologne. [14]

The economic and sociological background of Cologne
is significant in this trend.   Table 8 in the Appendix provides the percentage of persons in each "Soziale Stellung,"
which terminology gives the impression that the classifica-

tion is by social status. A footnote to the table in the report, published by the Statistical Office in Cologne, explains
that the classification is made by the predominant means of
livelihood of the supporter of the family, including members
of the family helping in the household. The impression,
nevertheless, remains that this is both an occupational and
social status classification. It is worthy of note that District 20 (southern half, east of the Rhine) has half the percentage of self-employed persons recorded for District 15
(southern end, west of the Rhine), and that Districts 19 and
20, which include all of Cologne east of the river, plus District 18, the northern portion of Cologne west of the river,
have a below-average percentage in this category, while the
remaining four districts, all west of the river, have an
above-average percentage. A similar geographical generalization applies to the second category, "Family Members
Helping in the Household." The lowest proportion of "officials" (Beamte) live in Districts 19 and 20, and the highest
proportion live in Districts 15 and 17, which include the
central business district west of the river and the area immediately northwest of it. Office employees are fairly evenly distributed through all of Cologne. Laborers, while distributed all through the city, are clearly in an above-average concentration east of the Rhine and in District 18. Pensioners are fairly evenly distributed through all of Cologne.
In the "Other" category, however, which includes largely
students and military personnel, the area east of the Rhine
is definitely under-represented, and over-represented west
of the Rhine, except in District 18. The political topography of Cologne is thus partially clarified. [15] Table 8 does
show, on balance, that all the population classifications are
fairly well scattered throughout the entire city with no sharp
differences from district to district.

It is a matter of speculation whether this pattern is
now in the process of being changed. The conclusive 1964
municipal victory for the SPD is attributable more to the
popularity of Mayor Theo Burauen, who is a Roman Catholic
and an active SPD leader, than the political programs of the
two major parties, which did not differ substantially. Both
promised more town-developing, modernization, housing, and
public transport. Other factors entered the 1966 legislative
election: the closing of coal mines in the Ruhr district and
the economic impact of this on Cologne, plus the general
slowing of the economic growth, which always hurts a party
in power, then the CDU in North Rhineland-Westphalia and
in the Federal Republic. Furthermore, the retirement of

Konrad Adenauer, former Mayor of Cologne, and the difficulties that Ludwig Erhard experienced as chancellor in 1966
also hurt the CDU in Cologne.   Instead of small right-wing
parties gaining from the current dissatisfactions, as has
happened in a few other parts of West Germany, the SPD in
Cologne has definitely benefited. [16]

     While the trade unions have historically been close to
the SPD throughout Germany, in Cologne, Mr. Lehman,
President of the Cologne DGB, (Deutsche Gewerkschaft Bund),
overall industrial union, admits that the SPD and the CDU
differ very little in policy.   There are no issues, according
to Mr. Lehman, in the fields of city planning and land-use
control.   This is partially due to the fact that the one area
in which there could have been an issue, the policy of the
city purchasing land and determining its use before development, was initiated by Dr. Konrad Adenauer when he was
mayor in the 1920s and was reactivated by him when he became mayor again after World War II.   Thereafter, when
the elder Adenauer became chancellor, Dr. Max Adenauer,
his son, as Oberstadtdirektor through the 1950s to 1965,
pursued the same policy.   This has been a CDU platform
which the SPD wishes it had originated and so there has
been no difference between the two major parties on this
question.   Dr. Werner Bockelmann, former SPD mayor of
Frankfurt, in speaking of this policy, refused to recognize
that Dr. Adenauer demonstrated vision on this policy, and
claimed instead that Adenauer was "clever." [17]

     The Free Democratic Party has made an issue of
government intrusion on private property rights, but in the
1964 municipal election this political party failed to gain
representation in the council; and the SPD, which is known
to be favorable to planning and land-use powers, gained
substantially in strength.

     Industry and business can exercise influence on civic
affairs through the Industrie und Handelskammern (Chamber
of Commerce), which is closely integrated with the municipal government.   Its legal status is based on a public contract.   Every enterprise whose business is over a specified
amount must legally be a member.   This requirement does
not extend to agricultural enterprises, the free professions,
or crafts.   Membership fees, based on trade taxes, are
collected for the Chamber by the municipality, and the municipality supervises the budget.   Certain "delegated tasks"
are performed by the Chamber on behalf of the municipality:

for example, the examining and accrediting of applicants to
a trade.   The Chamber also provides education for apprentices.   According to Dr. Schoser, Industrie und Handelskammern official, the British and Americans after World
War II attempted to change this relationship between government and the Chamber, and attempted to change the Chamber to the Anglo-Saxon pattern; however, said Dr. Schoser,
"We successfully avoided this." [18]

Mr. Lehman, the overall industrial union president,
was questioned about this close relationship between the
Chamber and the municipal government.   He analyzed it as
follows:

> The Industrie und Handelskammern have a legal
> basis, therefore they are supervised.   The trade
> unions are non-registered societies, do not have
> a legal basis.   If we did, it would mean govern-
> ment regulation.   We do not want it. [19]

Mr. Lehman mentioned one conflict between the DGB
(the union) and the Chamber: the training of apprentices by
the Chamber.   Other interests of the unions are housing for
workers, schools, and playgrounds.

According to Dr. Schoser, the major interests of the
Chamber are:

1.   Transportation and traffic

2.   The municipal budget

3.   City planning for industry

4.   New towns

5.   Shopping centers

6.   Water and air pollution

The only controversial issue in this list of interests
is the tax question in connection with the municipal budget.
Seventy per cent of all tax revenue comes from business;
therefore, the Chamber feels that it has much at stake.
All of the interests listed are directly involved in city planning, and all are at least indirectly involved in land-use
control.

Political pressure at the local level seems to consist largely of "contacting a friendly member of the Council," a telephone call, a conference over the luncheon table in a restaurant, or a club, not too different from local pressure action in American cities. Of particular significance in this connection is the wide range of occupational interests represented by membership in the Cologne City Council. The vocational classifications given below are listed according to the number per group.

Vocations of the Members of the Cologne City Council[20]

1.	Business Managers (incl. 1 manufacturer and 1 contractor)	11
2.	Angestellte (office employees)	11
3.	Professionals (not incl. lawyers)	8
4.	Craftsmen	6
5.	Lawyers	5
6.	Business Secretaries & Chief Clerks	5
7.	Union Secretaries	4
8.	Tradesmen	4
9.	Government and Political Party administrators (Overregierungrat, Staatssekretär, Fraktionsgeschäftsfuhrer, Parteisekretär)	4
10.	Salesmen	3
11.	Housewives	3
12.	Misc.: farmer, railway, 1 not spec.	3
	Total	67

Thirty are trade union members: 20 SPD and ten CDU.[21] The professional category includes two architects, two economists, and one each of the following: physician, public school principal, science assistant, and statistician. Six of the council members are women.

Council committees provide a structure by means of which the council can secure citizen opinion. The Cologne Council has the seemingly phenomenal number of 48 committees of which two have subcommittees: 1) Youth Welfare, three subcommittees; 2) Art and Culture, four subcommittees.[22]

All of the committees contain a majority of the majority party (SPD), except two which have an equal number from each of the two parties. The first, the "Working Committee for Questions of Social, Cultural, and Health Care of Foreign Workers situated in Cologne," in addition to two council members from each party serving, has thirteen representatives from organizations interested in the welfare of workers from abroad serving the committee with voting rights.   The second, the "Transfer Committee," which is a technical committee concerned with the transfer of parcel ownership in the interest of more feasible and effective land use, has one member from each party, plus three administrative technical experts with voting rights.

        Nineteen of the 48 committees, however, have CDU chairmen.   Several of these committees are worth notice: 1) Committee for the Retrenchment of Expenditure;   2) Auditing Committee;   3) Expenditure Committee for Above and Underground Facilities;   4) Real Estate Committee;   5) Committee on Public Facilities; and 6) Special Committee on Completed Construction.

        The Committees vary in size from two to 17 councilmanic members with party distribution as follows:

Numbers of Committees by Size and Party Distribution of Councilmanic Members. [23]

No.'s of Committees	No. of Councilmanic Members	SPD mbrs.	CDU mbrs.
3	17	10	7
3	15	9	6
13	13	8	5
8	9	5	4
5	7	4	3
1	6	4	2
13	5	3	2
1	4	2	2
1	2	1	1
48	78	46	32

        Eleven members of the Council serve on two committees: six SPD members and five CDU, thus keeping party membership on the committees relatively equal to voting strength in the Council.

In the light of practice in other countries, a unique feature in Cologne is the voting membership on councilmanic committees of persons who are not members of the council: 41 representatives of organizations and 26 other citizen representatives, some of whom are administrative experts and represent government agencies.

Four committees have representatives from citizen organizations:

1.   The Social Committee, which has 13 councilmanic members, has an additional six voting members representing six welfare organizations.

2.   The Committee for Questions of Traffic Safety, which has 13 councilmanic members, has an additional seven voting members representing four private agencies and three governmental agencies concerned with traffic safety (magistrate court, police, and public schools).

3.   Youth Welfare Committee, which has nine councilmanic members, has an additional 12 voting members representing youth and welfare societies, and three advisory members with no vote.

4.   The Working Committee for Questions of Social, Cultural, and Health Care of Foreign Workers, which has four councilmanic members, has an additional 13 voting members representing five welfare societies, three labor organizations, three youth organizations, one employer's union, and the police.

Seven committees have citizen representatives who are in large part expert in their respective fields of interest:

1.   City Planning Committee, which has 15 councilmanic members, has an additional three voting members, who are Architects.

2.   The Advisory Council for Questions concerning Building Design, which has five councilmanic members, has an additional three voting members, who are Architects.

3.   The School Committee, which has 15 councilmanic members, has an additional four voting members who are educators, plus three non-voting church representatives.

4.   The Subcommittee on Theater and Music, of the Committee on Art and Culture, has in addition to seven councilmanic members two voting citizen members with no specification as to vocation.

5.   The Committee on Jurists, which has six councilmanic members, has an additional four voting members who are lawyers.   Two of the citizen members are specified as SPD and two as CDU.

6.   The Resolutions Committee, which has five councilmanic members, has in addition two voting citizen members, one each from the two major parties.

7.   The Transfer Committee, which has two councilmanic members, has an additional three voting non-council members, one of whom is an architect, and the other two, government officials competent as regards property questions.

One committee, the Committee on Traffic Signs, which has five councilmanic members, has an additional three voting members, representing the municipal administration (two Beigeordneter and one Oberverwaltungsrat) and two voting members representing the police.   Another committee, the Transfer Committee, has in addition to two councilmanic members a Ministerialrat as chairman and specifies that one citizen voting member shall be a competent surveyor from the higher ranks of civil service and one shall be an expert in real estate.

For all committee members, citizens as well as councilmanic, a substitute is appointed to serve when the regular member is unable to attend.

Of special interest as regards city planning, land use, and urban development, in addition to some of the committees mentioned above, which are obviously involved, are the committees on:

1.   Real Estate.
2.   Residential Construction.
3.   Multiple-Story Housing.
4.   Design of the Cathedral Neighborhood.
5.   Custody of Ancient Monuments and Natural Beauty.
6.   Gardens, Greenspaces, and Forests.
7.   Federal Garden Appearance.
8.   Inns and Restaurants.

9. Industrial Developments - New City, Worker Concern.
10. Neu Stadt.
11. City Hall, New Construction.
12. Public Facilities.
13. Water and Bridge Construction.
14. Underground Construction.
15. Subway
16. Stadtautobahn.
17. Completed Construction.
18. Expenditure for Above and Underground Construction.

The broad range of municipal interests, extending from the very practical to the amenities, is worthy of notice. Special notice needs to be taken of attention paid in Cologne beyond the strictly urban development area: 1) the Committee for Questions of Traffic Safety; 2) Committee for Cooperation with Displaced Persons and Refugee Organizations; 3) Youth Welfare Committee; and 4) Committee on Law and Security.

Land law requires a Chief Committee, which has the responsibility of coordinating the other 47 councilmanic committees, and is available to consider for councilmanic action emergency matters which allow no delay. Land law also requires a Finance Committee and an Audit Committee. Another committee of a generic nature, but not required by Land Law, is the General Administrative Committee.

In general, committee sessions of the council are not open to the public. The press is admitted to sessions of the following committees: Schools, Social Affairs, Sports, Youth Welfare, and Questions of Traffic Safety.[24]

If the public is admitted to a committee meeting, protests and other reactions or opinions may be submitted by mail, and are considered by the committee. According to Mr. Lehman, a member of the council, an attempt was being made to develop a real public hearing process, in which interested citizens could question committee members and express their own views before the committee.[25]

Each committee selects its own chairman, except the coordinating Chief Committee, of which the Oberburgermeister is chairman automatically. The minutes of the various committee meetings are submitted to the Obserstadtdirektor, so that he is kept informed and he can provide whatever information or advice a committee may need or desire.

The Council elects the mayor (Oberburgermeister) and
three deputy mayors from the Council membership, all for
five year terms of office.   The Council also selects for a
12-year term, the Oberstadtdirektor, the Stadtdirektor, the
Director of Finance, and nine Beigeordneter.   All of these
officials, except the Oberstadtdirektor, serve as heads of
groups of municipal "Ämter," or agencies.   These officials
may not simultaneously be members of the Council.

Below the Beigeordneter, the higher administrative officials, the "Beamte," who are professionally educated, have
life tenures.   Approval of a council committee is necessary
for the promotion of anyone to the Beamte classification. [26]
Thus the elected representatives have a voice in personnel
up through the Beamte level.   The Oberstadtdirektor, however, has weekly meetings with the top administrators, and
represents the administration in dealing with the Council. [27]

Throughout, there was evidence of deep respect for
professional education and experience, and for the expert and
the expert's opinion, both within and outside the administration, in council committees and in the Council.   The current
Oberstadtdirektor, Professor Mohnan, (prior to 1966, Stadtdirektor) was orginally secured from the faculty of the University of Cologne.   The Director of Finance, Dr. Linpinsel,
and six of nine Beigeordneter have the Ph. D. degree and use
the title (a far more widespread custom in Germany than in
America).   There is a continued emphasis from times past
on a legal education for administrative responsibility and
advancement.   A slow change is coming in that more attention is paid to higher education in the field of public administration, which will be noted in Chapter 6; nevertheless
greater weight is given to professional experience and expert
opinion in all areas in local government in the Cologne area
than is generally given in local government in the United
States.   The question may be raised whether this attitude
places an undue limit on democracy in action.   Some may say
that this is not democracy; however, in a technological age,
particularly in an industrialized and highly metropolitanized
area, where government requires expertise to perform its
duties satisfactorily, respect for professional experience and
expert opinion may be not a limitation of popular government but a necessary guidance for it.

Land law requires the Council to meet at least once
every two months. In practice, the Council normally meets
once a month, depending on the volume of business and these
sessions are open to the public, but in addition executive
sessions may be held to which the public are not invited.
The Oberburgermeister presides. The Oberstadtdirektor and
the administrative agency heads, appointed by the council,
attend the meetings; they provide through the Oberstadtdirektor any information, reports, or records that may have been
requested. The councilors are seated at tables, two to a
table, set in nine rows, four tables in each of eight rows,
two in a ninth row. The Oberburgermeister has a table in
front from which he presides. A tribune to his left is used
for the delivery of any report or speech; also to the left
and above, the entire length of the hall, is the public gallery
with ten rows of seats. Adjoining the Council Chamber are
caucus rooms, offices for the Oberburgermeister, the Bur-
germeister, the Oberstadtdirektor, and several for administrative agency heads.

Public attendance leaves much to be desired. The City
Council Office reports that the citizenry have made relatively little use of the opportunity to attend official meetings of
the City Council. Classes from the schools attend sessions
of the Council regularly in order to learn parliamentary procedure, and may as a by-product gain some interest in municipal affairs. The representatives of the press are always
present and report amply on the sessions.[28]

Dr. Elmer Pliscke, University of Maryland, ob-
serves:

> One of the serious weaknesses in the present situ-
> ation--not necessarily unique to West Germany--
> is the widespread indifference of the average citi-
> zen toward the affairs of local government. To
> some extent this has been caused by the intensi-
> fied tempo of everyday life and the concomitantly
> increased complexity of local governmental prob-
> lems, on the one hand, and to the tendency to
> focus public and political attention on national and
> international issues on the other.[29]

There is without question a continuously increased
competition for the attention of the citizen, every citizen,
so that he develops a thick hide against requests for his
time. Greater and more effective use of television by mu-

nicipal governments may be necessary to catch local public
interest.   Otherwise, only highly controversial issues, such
as "open housing" in the U.S. will attract public attendance
at city council meetings.

In Cologne, policy making is the responsibility of the
City Council.   The participation of the electorate in the
councilmanic elections has been sufficiently high to hold the
council on general policy responsive to a popular majority.
On specific policies, the wide range of vocational and other
special interest representation on the council has given special interest groups ample opportunity to have their special
points of view heard.   Furthermore, the councilmanic committee structure with non-councilmanic voting membership
ensures a wide range of supplementary special interest voting representation.   This ranges through a wide spectrum of
social, cultural, economic and other public interest areas.
There is also sufficient non-councilmanic voting representation of professional experts on the committees to ensure
competent consideration of specialized issues.

For these reasons, political pressure activity, which
in the United States normally takes place outside of the
council--frequently resulting in decision-making outside of
the council chamber--has been built into the council structure in Germany, where outside political pressure activity is
at a minimum.

Notes

1.   Gesetz und Verordnungsblatt für das Land NRW, 1952,
     no. 57, p. 23 ff.

2.   International City Managers' Association, Directory of
     Council-Manager Municipalities in Europe, August
     1960 and January 1966.   Both issues of the Directory
     list those municipalities recognized as having Council-
     manager systems in Finland, Germany, Ireland, Nor-
     way and Sweden.   The 1966 Directory gives a total of
     1,042 such municipalities in these countries, over
     half of which are in West Germany.   In North Rhine-
     land-Westphalia the total number of "cities" is 220,
     "small towns" 56, and "counties" 57.

3.   The Basic Law of the Federal Republic of Germany,
     which became effective September 21, 1949.

4. The Basic Law of the Federal Republic of Germany
    (Amendments as of December 31, 1961), as prepared
    by the German Information Center, Article 28.

5. Ibid., Article 106, section 7, as amended by Federal
    Law of December 23, 1955 (Federal Law Gazette 1,
    p. 817).

6. Statistisches Amt der Stadt Köln, Verwaltungsbericht
    der Stadt Köln, 1964, p. 30.

7. Robson, W. A. (editor), Great Cities of the World,
    (London: George Allen and Unwin Ltd., 2d ed., 1957),
    p. 663.

8. Statistisches Amt der Stadt Köln, op. cit.

9. The Basic Law of the Federal Republic of Germany,
    Article 21.

10. Plischke, Elmer, Contemporary Government of Germany,
    (Boston: Houghton Mifflin Co., 1961), p. 152-153;
    and Heidenheimer, Arnold J., The Government of
    Germany, (N.Y.: Thomas Y. Crowell Co., 1966), p.
    166-168. Both Plischke and Heidenheimer provide an
    analysis of the situations leading to the Federal Con-
    stitutional Court decisions.

11. Statistisches Amt der Stadt Köln, op. cit.

12. See Table 6, Appendix.

13. See Table 7, Appendix.

14. The 1966 state elections results were received from the
    Deutsche Welle (broadcasting station) and the Kölner
    Stadtanzeiger (newspaper).

15. See Table 8, Appendix.

16. Assistance in the analysis of the 1964 and 1966 election
    victories for the SPD was received from Deutsch
    Welle and the Kölner Stadtanzeiger; also from the CDU
    and SPD party headquarters in Cologne.

17. Interview with Dr. Werner Bockelmann, Business Man-
    ager, Deutscher Städtetag, Deutscher-Städtetag Head-

quarters, Köln-Marienburg, February 18, 1966.

18. Interview with Dr. Schoser, Industrie und Handelskammern, Unter Sachenhausen 19, March 11, 1966.

19. Interview with Mr. Lehman, President, Cologne Branch, DGB, Hansbockler Platz 9, Room 301, March 3, 1966.

20. Alphabetical Register of the City Council Members from the Office of the Oberstadtdirektor, March 1, 1967.

21. Interview with Mr. Lehman.

22. Public Committees and Subcommittees from the Office of the Oberstadtdirektor, September 1966.

23. Ibid.

24. Letter from Mr. Peter Fuchs, Pressechef der Stadt Köln, Stadt Köln Nachrichtenamt, August 11, 1967.

25. Interview with Mr. Lehman.

26. Interview with Mr. Stolberger, Stadtamtmann (Personnel Department), Stadthaus, Room 22, February 8, 1966.

27. Interview with Mr. Stratmann, Verwaltungsrat, Stadthaus, February 8, 1966.

28. Interview with Mr. Fuchs.

29. Plischke, Elmer, op. cit., p. 180.

Chapter V

COLOGNE: ADMINISTRATION

The responsibilities and activities relevant to land use, with two exceptions, are concentrated in one Department: Building Administration (Bauverwaltung). According to the official administrative chart, dated February 22, 1964, this department is organized into seven offices (Ämter), and 19 divisions (Abteilung); also several divisions are subdivided into sections.

The seven offices in the Department of Building Administration include: 1) the Administrative Headquarters (Bauverwaltungsamt); 2) the City Planning Office (Stadsplanungsamt); 3) the Building Inspection Office (Bauaufsichtsamt); 4) the Office for Residential Housing Promotion (Amt für Wohnungsbauförderung); 5) the Office for Above-Ground Construction and Maintenance (Hochbauamt); 6) the Office for Below-Ground Construction and Maintenance (Tiefbauamt), which actually includes surface as well as below surface operations; and 7) the Garden and Cemeteries Office (Garten- und Friedhofsamt), which also has responsibility for the administration of parks and open spaces.

The two agencies having responsibilities over land use, which are not placed within the Department of Building Administration, are the Real Estate Office (Liegenschaftsamt) and the Division for Municipal Development Planning (Abteilung für Kommunale Entwicklungplanung). The Real Estate Office has responsibility for all municipal real estate transactions and for this purpose was placed under Stadtdirektor Berge. The Division for Municipal Development Planning was recently created and was placed for an indefinite period in the Oberstadtdirektor's office. One other agency, which may be considered related to land use and which performs a planning function, is the Conservation Office (Konservator), which has responsibility for the conservation of historical monuments and architecture. In order to provide this office a proper orientation and the necessary

technical supervision, it is located in the Department of Arts
and Adult Education. [1]

    While the entire municipal administration will be sur-
veyed, this study will center on the agencies listed above.

    Dr. Kleppe, Beigeordneter for the Department of
Building Administration, had in the administrative headquarters eighty persons (1965 budget): 14 officers (Beamte), 30
employees (Angestellte), 22 students from technical schools
in training and serving without pay, and 14 laborers. [2] Even
though the Department of Building Administration is a very
large department, according to American standards, the a-
bove 80 persons are adequate for running it.

    The City Planning Office is organized into a Planning
Division and an Implementation Division (Durchfuhrungsabteil-
ung), more properly translated a "leading through" or "put-
ting into practice" division. The Planning Office was budgeted 1,723,700 DM, of which 1,376,000 DM were allocated
to salaries. The staff of 60 persons included 16 Beamte
and 54 Angestellte. In 1966, fifteen persons were assigned
at the time of the interview to advance planning and 45 to
current planning. The advance plan, which is in large part
a land-use plan, prepared in 1952-53, projects land-use
needs and requirements for a 30-year period. Since the office is updating the land-use plan, staff are being shifted
from current planning to advance planning assignments as
needed. When the advance planning is updated, the staff so
shifted will be returned to their former assignments. It is
the intention of the office to update the long-range plan each
decade.

    The advance planning is performed entirely by Stad-
planungsamt personnel. Contracts with outside experts are
negotiated only for advisory services, which in addition to
providing expert counsel, also provides excellent training
and valuable experience for the permanent city planning personnel.

    Having determined land use, street planning follows.
Simultaneously with street planning comes the planning of
housing and the necessary accessory land uses, such as
parks, recreation, schools and commercial. The development plans (subdivison plans) are prepared by the city planning staff. Land law requires that all municipal services
be available before actual development takes place. This in-

cludes drainage, sewage disposal, water, and utilities, as well as parks, recreation facilities and schools.

The development plan is submitted by the Beigeordne- ter to the Building and Planning Committee of the City Coun- cil, where it is considered by the councilmanic committee with non-council experts present.   After this committee con- sideration, the committee holds a public meeting, at which occasion the proposed development plan is publicly presented. Citizen's and/or property owners' protests or objections may be presented by mail.   The committee thereafter holds an executive session to consider the objections or protests.   The Building and Planning Committee proposal is thereafter sub- mitted to the City Council where it is also considered at two sessions, normally open to the public. [3]

In the event that specified parcels of land are too small for economic development, or are so oddly shaped as to be relatively unusable, which occurs in the older portions of the city where parcels of land have been handed down through the centuries, it is necessary for the property owner, or owners, to appeal to the City Council for action.   The Council submits the appeal to a special councilmanic commit- tee (Umlegungsausschuss), which can be translated loosely in- to English as "Transfer Committee."   This committee is composed of two members of the City Council, one lawyer representing the city, and three specialists.   There is a sec- tion of the Transfer Committee, which has the superb Ger- man title of "Geschäftsstelle des Umlegungsausschusses," placed in the Real Estate Office, to which such an appeal is referred for investigation.   On the basis of the findings of the investigation, the committee can recommend a redrawing of property lines, if this seems advisable, to the Council. This may involve a mere transfer of property.   If the Coun- cil approves the proposal, it is legally effective.   This pro- cedure, "is designed to cut parcels of land into more usable parts." [4]

Only the City Council can initiate this action, which was established in 1951, by which time Cologne was beginning to rebuild and there was both a need and an opportunity to do something about the many very small and oddly shaped par- cels which had outlived their usefulness from centuries past. It should be noted, however, that it is a strictly controlled process and is available to the Planning Office in the devel- opment of land cut into unusable parcels, as well as to prop- erty owners handicapped in land use.

The Implementation Division concentrates on the legal aspects of planning control, checking on the individual building applications to see that they do not conflict with the city plan. Both the city plan and the implementation thereof, or the "Operational Plan," are subject to decisions of the City Council.

The legal aspects of urban planning and land-use control are a large enough area to be a separate study by someone competent in West German law. A few explanatory comments, however, are advisable. [5]

The municipality prepares what is known as the "Bauleitplän," the closest definition of which might be "basic principles for planning."

Within this framework the municipality prepares the preliminary "Flächennutzungsplan," which is in effect a land-use plan; the "Bebauungsplan," a building development plan; and the "Bauordnung," which is the building law and only it has a legally binding effect. Furthermore, the Bauleitpläne must conform to the Federal "Raumordnungsegesetez" (space-ordering law), which specifies principles concerning land-use, prohibits certain misuses of land, and provides guidelines for planning land use; and the Bauleitpläne must also conform with the "Bundesbaugesetz," which provides the broad legal authorization for planning and building laws. Both the Raumordnungsgesetz and the Bundesbaugesetz are legal frames for further laws at lower levels.

The local planning must also conform to the Land Planning Law, which is procedural, providing assurance that the local planning fits into the Land planning and area development plans, and providing "due process" protection to property owners. It is likewise necessary that the local building law conform to the Land Building Law, which details much of the building requirements in the interest of safety, health and decent living.

Each of the laws and the plans is expected to fit into every other as a coordinated planning and land-use whole. This is possible because Land officials represent the Land in the Bundesrat and participate in legislating for the Bunde; and there is provision by Land law for the coordination of planning officials from the Bunde, the Land, and the Stadt in the planning process.

It is this complex of principles, laws and regulations that the Implementation Division of the Planning Office within the Department of Building Administration checks and enforces. [6]

Another organizational point for American administrators to notice is the concentration of all inspections concerning land and buildings in one office, the Building Inspection Office. This office is organized into two divisions: 1) the Building Inspection Division (Bauaufsichtsabteilung) and 2) the Electrical Inspection Division (Statische Abteilung), which in addition to all electrical and electrically-related inspections also has responsibility for others such as drainage inspections. The entire Building Inspection Office had a total of 171 persons: 83 Beamte, 85 Angestellte, and three laborers.

The field inspections involve examination of the structures, the land use, and the neighborhood, but disapproval can be registered only on legal grounds. In the event of a violation, a notice is mailed to the responsible person with an order to make a change according to specified legal requirements. If compliance is not forthcoming, a penalty (Zwangsgelt) is imposed and a new order to pay the penalty (Fetzsetzung) is issued. If the accused contests the order in court, he is obliged to pay the penalty anyway but if the court rules in his favor the penalty payment is refunded. In actual practice, the penalty payment is frequently waived, depending on the circumstances of the specific situation. Legally, the city has the authority to tear down the structure and charge the demolition to the owner.

To illustrate the inspectional activity of the Building Inspection Office, the 1964 report in the Verwaltungsbericht der Stadt Köln (p. 160) states

> The building activity brought an increasing influx of 3727 applications. The final result was 2,860 buildings with 10,594 dwellings reported finished. That is 526 buildings with 2085 dwellings more than last year. Including the heating and drainage, electrical computations and supplements as well as applications for advertizing signs and boarding around building sites, a total of 15,700 applications were processed. Furthermore, 1042 preliminary inquiries and building notifications were processed. In addition 1,522 applications for licenses and ap-

plications for property separations were received
for review and recommendation and were processed.

In addition to all private building electrical inspections,
the Electrical Inspection Division has a section for inspecting
communal buildings.   This section provides such inspections
for the Administrative Districts of Cologne and Aachen.   A
second section inspects electrical installations used in advertising, and a third inspects those in assembly rooms.   A
separate section provides drainage inspections of residential,
commercial and industrial districts, including special inspections of radioactive refuse disposal at research institutions. [7]

The 1965 Budget authorized an expenditure of 3,807,500
DM, of which 3,285,000 covered salaries and wages.   It is
noteworthy, however, that 3,213,600 DM in receipts were
anticipated, so that only a 593,900 DM subsidy requirement
(Zuschussbedarf) was considered necessary.   In brief, the Inspection Office almost pays for itself.   A breakdown on the
anticipated receipts, which is, of course, based on past experience follows:

Inspection charges and fees	3,150,000 DM
Refinds to cover cost of safety measures required to maintain safety of habitable buildings	40,000 DM
Fines	20,000 DM
Sale of forms	3,000 DM
Miscellaneous	600 DM
Total Receipts	3,213,600 DM

Special notice should be taken of the absence of any
land-use control similar to American zoning.   Large industrial developments are encouraged where they seem to be
most suitable for the entire urban area.   The site of any
industrial enterprise is approved, or disapproved, on the
basis of its compatability with surrounding land-use.

Residential and business land use is mixed; however
the mixture is not uncontrolled.   Since 40 per cent of land in
the city is municipally owned, large scale development usually takes place on municipally owned property, the land use
of which is carefully planned before development, and the
contract of sale, or the lease, whichever is used, requires

meticulous observance of the official land-use plan for the area to be developed. In the case of redevelopment, official approval must be secured by the redeveloper, regardless whether one or several parcels of land are involved, for the contemplated land-use. Likewise, in the event of a proposed change of the use of an existing building, official approval must be secured from the Bauaufsichtsamt. For change from residential to commercial use, approval is normally secured, unless the change of function is considered to be objectionable to the neighborhood. [8] Grocery stores, apothecaries, and other businesses meeting the daily needs of the residents (convenience shopping) are widely and conveniently scattered. Each application is considered by, and the decision is made by, the professional staff on the basis of merit alone. The procedure is simple, speedy, and there is no expense involved.

The Stadtplannungsamt for a decade and a half has been thinking and planning in terms of shopping centers. According to Baurat Riedel, who is in charge of planning, Cologne is now following the Swedish thinking and practice with four categories of business centers:[9]

A. Stadtzentrum (Central Business District).
B. Hauptzentrum--main center in a suburban community serving a radius of four to eight kilometers with 100,000 population.
C. Nebenzentrum--four in one suburban area, serving about 20,000 population.
D. Kleinezentrum--6 or 8 stores with a coffee house or restaurant serving 5,000 population.

For the new shopping centers, the Land Bauordnung requires one parking space for every 25 square meters (269 square feet) of store space. The shopping center development with parking space requirements is a reflection of the rapid increase of the automobile population, which makes unnecessary widely scattered stores within walking distance and makes feasible the convenience of commerical groupings in shopping centers.

With the type of land-use control described above, single-family, two-family, and multiple-dwelling residential developments are possible and are permitted within one neighborhood, and each is approved, or disapproved, on the basis of its effect on surrounding properties. This does not imply any lack of interest in residential developments. Quite the contrary is evidenced by the fourth office in the Department of Building Administration: the Office for Residential Housing Promotion.

        This office (Amt für Wohnungsforderung) administers Land and Stadt grants and loans for housing.   The Federal Government participates by means of a complex formula.   In brief, it guarantees housing loans (similar to the FHA in the U. S.), provides direct Federal loans for anticipatory and interim credits for the construction of family homes under publicly-assisted house-building, and administers the Equalization Burdens Fund.   This is so-called "social housing" in West Germany, and is frequently compared with public housing in America.   Many differences, however, will be noticed in the following analysis.

        The Office was administered by a staff of 110:   57 Beamte and 53 Angestellte.   In this case, salaries accounted for a small portion of the operating budget: 1, 931, 000 DM out of a total of 18, 852, 400 DM.   The two major expenditures were 6, 826, 100 DM payment of interest on housing loans, and 8, 968, 500 DM payment of principal on loans.   Receipts of 4, 515, 300 DM were anticipated.   These consisted of interest payments on loans by recipients thereof and repayment of principal on loans, plus investment earnings.

        While the amounts for housing vary slightly from year to year, the figures specified in the 1964 Municipal Administrative Report are indicative of the amounts involved.   The Land provided Cologne 70 million DM for housing, of which 60 million was for housing loans, 5 million for aid to savings for construction, and the remainder for scattered housing purposes.

        Cologne matched this with 44 million DM largely for supplementary housing loans.   The municipality also provided housing loans to municipal employees in order to secure their employment.   In addition, municipal financial sources were used for a variety of housing purposes: relocation for planning reasons, promotion of housing for the elderly and young families, and social housing for people in need of assistance.   In total, 41. 72 million DM of municipal funds were spent on contracts for housing construction. [10]

        Social housing is built and administered by non-profit societies.   Complete tax exemption is provided; also under certain circumstances, grants, or loans, and rent control

can be effected. Private firms may also build social housing on the basis of grants from the municipality and under
the same conditions. Aside from the above specified rent
control in social housing, rent control was eliminated during
the years 1963-65.

Social housing may be rented only to persons below
a specified income level, and the rent may cover only capital cost and maintenance. This rent, even though controlled
and held to a minimum, is partially subsidized if the tenant
is able to establish inability to pay it.

The upper income limit for social housing is an annual income by the head-of-household of 9,000 DM, plus 1,500
DM for each additional member of the family. There are
also legal limits on the size of apartment that may be rented
with subsidized rentals in social housing: 30 square meters
for one person, 50 square meters for two persons, and so
on. The average annual income for all families in Cologne
ranged from 9,600 to 20,400 DM in 1966. About 10 to 12
per cent of income was normally spent for housing. In the
"old housing," which was built before 1948, during the overall serious housing shortage, rent rarely took over 20 per
cent. For a small family, 60-65 square meters has been
considered sufficient, and at a normal rent rate of 4 to 6 DM
per square meter, the rent for such apartments would thus
be 240 to 390 DM per month; 2,880 to 4,680 DM per year,
indicating a continued need for subsidized housing in Cologne
within the income limit above specified. There is concern,
however, at the Bunde level for the continued occupancy of
social housing by people whose incomes have risen above the
legal limits. [11]

The share of public funds in the total housing expenditures throughout the Bunde, including the Federal Equalization of Burdens Funds, the expenditures of the Länder and
the communes, totaled about 22 per cent. Even though the
Bunde has not been directly involved in housing construction,
it has influenced policy. Priority has been given to home
ownership. The proportion of home-owned dwellings has increased, partially due to government promotion of home-
ownership and partially to the easing of the housing shortage.
In 1957, every second single-family house contained two
dwelling units, while in the period from 1961 to 1962 this
applied to only every third single-family house. If the second dwelling, which is generally rented, is not taken into
consideration, this means that in 1963, 36 per cent of all

newly built and reconstructed dwellings were owner occupied.[12]

The promotion of housing for young couples and young
families is stressed. Reduced rates of interest (6 per cent)
is granted provided neither spouse is over 40 years of age,
and provided that the annual income is not over the income
limit for publicly-assisted house building. A similar arrangement is made for loans to young couples for rented apartments.

This is all finally administered at the local level. In
Cologne, it is the responsibility of the Office for Residential
Housing Promotion.

The office for Above-Ground Construction of Public
Buildings (Hochbauamt) has responsibility for the construction and maintenance of all municpal buildings in the city, except in the parks, gardens, cemeteries and open spaces.
The scope and emphasis is shown by the 1964 report:[13]

	DM in thousands
Administration	1, 918
Schools	27, 776
Cultivation of Culture	6, 138
Correctional Education for Youth	8, 591
Health for Youth	6, 245
Public Equipment & Furnishings (incl. upkeep)	9, 136
Management Undertakings	5, 104
Structural and Installation Technical Maintenance of City Buildings	10, 960
	75, 868

The last three generalized categories includes service
to municipal buildings not classified above with "education,"
"culture," and "health." Approximately half of the architectural work and a substantial proportion of the construction
are contracted with private firms, who are very closely su-
pervised. To administer this responsibility, the Hochbauamt
is organized into four divisions: 1) Design; 2) Construction;
3) Maintenance; and 4) Machinery and Installations. [14]

The Machinery and Installations Division is further subdivided into three sections: 1) Design for New Construction; 2) Operations and Maintenance; and 3) Utilities.

The Office had 385 persons employed: 42 Beamte, 259 Angestellte, and 86 Arbeiter. The total amount of the budget for the operating expenses was 7,705,600 DM, of which approximately one half, it was anticipated, would be repaid through a revolving fund arrangement. Salaries and wages accounted for 5,403,000 DM. The next largest expenditure covered the cost of supervision of construction. Through the supervision of this Office, all municipal buildings above ground in Cologne are built, maintained and manged with the exception, again, of structures in the parks, cemeteries, and open spaces.

The Office for Below-Ground Construction of Public Facilities (Tiefbauamt) actually has both surface and below-ground responsibilities. It is organized into the following divisions and sections:[15]

1. Street Construction Division
   a) Design
   b) Construction
   c) Materials
   d) Traffic Installations
   e) Statistics and Street Planning
2. Drainage Division
   a) Design
   b) New Construction
   c) Operations and Maintenance
3. Water and Bridges Division
   a) Bridge Construction
   b) Maintenance of Bridges
   c) Water and Harbors
   d) Subways
4. Traffic Planning Division
5. Materials Testing Division
6. Rubble Clearance Division

The Street Construction Division and the Drainage Division are self-explanatory. Of unusual interest is the placement of responsibility for subway construction in the Water and Bridges Division. Along with this responsibility, the U-Strassenbahn Section also has responsibility for tunnels, and under- and over-passes, both pedestrian and vehicular. The Traffic Planning Division engages in continuous traffic counts

and continuous traffic planning.   The Materials Testing Division gives quality tests of materials purchased and charges
a fee for the tests.   In 1964, fees totalling 545,000 DM were
received for 8500 tests.   The Rubble Clearance Division dis-
poses of rubble from private properties. [16]

The 1965 Budget maintained accounts for the Drainage
Division, the Water and Bridges Division, and the Rubble
Clearance Division separate from the account for the re-
mainder of the Below-Ground Construction office.

The Drainage Division account showed anticipated receipts almost equal to authorized expenditures: receipts,
30,696,00 DM; and expenditures, 31,056,600 DM.   The receipts were from a variety of sources.   The major portion,
however, came from channel fees.   Expenditures consisted
largely of construction and repair costs, and interest payments.   Salaries and wages totalled only 3,910,000 DM

The account for the Water and Bridges Division authorized 1,005,800 DM expenditures, of which 431,000 covered salaries and wages.   Anticipated receipts totalled
204,100 DM, of which 100,000 DM were received from the
Land Government and 100,000 from fees.

The Rubble Clearance Division account authorized expenditures totalling 5,533,800 DM, of which 469,000 DM
covered salaries and wages.   Almost all of the receipts totalling 4,003,400 DM, were received from the Land.

The remainder of the Tiefbauamt was budgeted for
55,006,100 DM, of which 7,072,000 covered salaries and
wages.   A major portion of the expenditures involve street
construction.   The receipts, which total 16,000,000 DM,
were anticipated largely from developers, who pay a portion
of the cost.

The following table shows the distribution of personnel through the Tiebfauamt:

		Beamte	Ange-stellte	Arbei-ter	Total
1.	Headquarters	23	25	1	49
2.	Street Construction	45	98	235	378
3.	Drainage	30	66	179	275
4.	Water and Bridges	7	41	10	58

	Beamte	Ange-stellte	Arbei-ter	Total
5. Traffic Planning	3	17	0	20
6. Materials Testing	1	20	6	27
7. Rubble Clearance	2	19	5	26
	111	286	436	833

The Verwaltungsbericht der Stadt Köln 1964 on the Office of Garden and Cemeteries devotes the major portion of the report to "Green and Recreation Areas." The first paragraph (p. 174) reads as follows:

> The significance of a well-planned and purposeful "green politics" in a great city of the class of Cologne is undisputed. Every great city knows the danger of the growth of industry and commerce collected in the city center until constantly increasing numbers of motor vehicles, the reaching back and merging of dwelling and settlement space, and many other concomitant [understandable] circumstances of modern urban development have all been brought in as well.

Thereafter the report elaborates on recreation areas, large gardens, green belts and open spaces, and the cemeteries.

The Garden and Cemetery Office, which is responsible for the physical maintenance of parks as well as gardens and cemeteries, had a total of 1,037 personnel distributed as follows:

	Beamte	Ange-stellte	Arbeiter	Garden Apprentices	Total
Parks & Gardens	30	83	739	6	858
Cemeteries	1	38	140	0	179
	31	121	879	6	1037

The Budget for the Cemeteries totalled 7,037,400 DM authorized expenditures, of which 4,482,000 DM covered salaries and wages. Anticipated receipts totalled 4,114,300 DM, half of which consisted of receipts from fees. The Budget for Parks and Gardens totalled 11,380,900 DM authorized

expenditures, of which 7, 890, 000 DM covered salaries and
wages. Anticipated receipts totalled 507, 900 DM, more than
half of which was expected from the produce of nurseries.

The recreation program, which ranges from sports
and recreation to financial aid for supervized recuperation,
is placed in the Department of Social and Health Administration, with which close cooperation is necessarily maintained.

The Department of Building Administration (Bauverwaltung) thus has a broad range of responsibilities over urban
development within the confines of the Kreisfrei Stadt Köln
(Countyfree City of Cologne), or in American terminology
"the City-County of Cologne." The amount budgeted for all
the activities of the Department of Building Administration,
as shown on the official outline of the municipal administration, including the drainage, cemetery, park and garden
maintenance functions, totals 144, 157, 700 DM. [17] This responsibility under the supervision of one Beigeordneter includes overall city planning, legal control over the implementation thereof, all inspections over private and public construction, supervision over publicly assisted housing, direct
control over all public construction above and below ground,
physical management of green belts, open spaces, parks,
gardens and recreation areas, and overseeing specialized
planning of all the areas of responsibility, including traffic
planning and the circulation of men and material in general.

One of the major problems from the point of view of
the professional planners is the time and difficulties involved
in land acquisition by the city. A six to eight months' delay
in the administrative courts may be anticipated. This is obviously in the interest of the private property rights of the
person whose property the city wishes to acquire. Five years
may be consumed in appeals in the rather complex judicial
system. Another year may be needed for property-line
changes, a non-judicial procedure.

In the best cases, four months are involved in land
acquisition. If the development of a substantial portion of
land and public acquisition is involved, two and a half to three
years is considered good. [18]

The above explains the advocacy of municipal lease instead of sale of publicly-owned undeveloped land, and why the
Bocklemund community was developed on a leasehold basis
with the city retaining ownership of the land. When a change

in land use seems advisable, it can more readily be accomplished.

One advantage for the Cologne planning staff (but simultaneously a weakness) is the wealth of data available from the Statistischen Amt, of which adequate use is not made. This weakness may be cured by the new Development Planning Agency (Abteilung für Kommunale Entwicklungsplanung). The man in charge of this new municipal agency was taken from the Statistischen Amt, and has a working knowledge of the rich resources of the Statistical Office as well as being research-minded, which fills another gap in the Stadtplanungsamt.

As was mentioned in the beginning of this chapter, the new Abteilung für Kommunale Entwicklungsplanung is directly under the Oberstadtdirektor along with the News Office, which is in effect a Public Relations Office. As long as the new Development Planning Agency is situated within the top management orbit, there is little danger of a lack of coordination with the planning in the Stadtplanungsamt. This new planning agency may remain in the Büro des Oberstadtdirektor as the Oberstadtdirektor sees the vital importance of having close to him a purely staff-composed, land-use planning agency whose personnel are qualified to conduct research and to guide him in top policy decisions concerning the urban development. This is a splitting of a portion of the city planning function from the Planning Office in the Building Administration, and it may be well justified. Perhaps the entire Stadtplanungsamt should be moved into the Oberstadtdirektors Büro, or the current arrangement should be retained: there are advantages and disadvantages to either arrangement. Retaining the new Development Planning Agency in the Oberstadtdirektors Büro will obviously require very close coordination with the City Planning Office in the Building Administration. Another consideration is that the Development Planning Agency in its present position will be close to Real Estate Office, the land acquisition and sale agency of the City.

The Real Estate Office is placed under the Stadtdirektor along with the Statistical Office and the Registration Office. Concentrated in the Real Estate Office are the following responsibilities:

1.   The measurement of all real estate.

2.   The registry of all real estate.

3.   The valuation of all real estate.

4.   The negotiations for the purchase, sale, transfer, or lease of all real estate for the City.

Each function is performed by a separate division within the Real Estate Office. [19]   Of special interest here is the land evaluation system.   The Director of the Real Estate Office (Liegenschaftsamt) has 50 employees making property evaluations.   Three methods of valuation, which differ from the method of evaluating improvements on the land, are used: [20]

1.   Analysis of comparables.   The basic question is: how can the property be used by the owner?

2.   Valuation of the land on the basis of comparables. The improvements are valuated on the basis of construction price minus depreciation.   The cost of construction is se-cured per cubic meter on the basis of the material used, the price index at the time of construction, and the equipment and facilities in the building.

3.   Another type of land-evaluation on the basis of comparables.   The improvements are valued on the basis of building profit minus current costs, which is a capitalizing of the net income.   The interest at 6 to 7 per cent, whatever is the going rate, on the land and on the improvements is used to compute from the income to the capital value.   The age of the improvements and an estimate on how much longer they will be usable is also a factor in estimating value.   In brief, the value to be paid on the open market is the basic consideration.

In buying real estate, all purchases below 60,000 DM can be determined by administrative decision.   Between 60,000 and 100,000 DM, a decision by a committee of the City Council is necessary.   Above 100,000 DM, the whole City Council must approve.

Ninety per cent of the real estate is acquired through negotiation using one of the above three methods of valuation. In 10 per cent of the cases, there is a "depriving;" that is, the owner does not sell voluntarily.   In such cases, an inde-pendent committee of experts enters the proceedings.   A Beamte is chairman, but he must not be a government em-ployee involved in the administration of land.   Normally a

municipal employee from the Vermessungsabteilung who is
experienced in the measuring of land serves on the committee.   In order that the City can establish its case, it must
be proven beyond reasonable doubt that the land is shown in
the Bebaungs Plan for public use.   An administrative appeal
to the Regierungs Präsident, who is the top administrative
official in the Land Administrative District in which the city
is located, is available.   Thereafter, the property owner may
apply to the Court of Justice (second level), with the Presid-
ing Justice thereof, two assistants from the Ordinary Courts,
and two judges from the Administrative Courts, hearing and
deciding the case.

   When the City sells land, the Regierungs Präsident is
not involved.   The sale is not necessarily made to the highest
bidder.   The Real Estate Office takes into account the interests of the city in terms of land-use.   On this basis the
Real Estate Office director determines the best and most
competent firm to whom the property should be sold.   All
sales must be approved by the City Council.

   The City has been purchasing land since the 1920s, at
which time Dr. Konrad Adenauer, then Mayor of Cologne,
initiated the policy of municipal ownership.   The City purchases undeveloped land and leases it for agricultural use
until the appropriate land use has been determined by the Department of Planning.   As of 1966, the City owned 10,000
hectares within the Cologne boundaries, which is 40 per cent
of the city; also 1,000 hectares outside the city. [21]

   By financial necessity, when land is ready for development the City sells in order to purchase more land as a
development reserve.   Control of development is continuously maintained in this manner.   In the opinion of one Baurat
in the Stadtebauamt, there should be greater use of the leasehold device.   Currently, the leasehold policy has been fully
applied in Bocklemund, where the entire community is owned
by the City and leased to private corporations for development.   Usually, the residential development, if leased, is
leased to Housing Associations.   If the City retains ownership, development is speeded by the verified experience that
development can begin even before planning is completed. [22]

   Without adequate drainage, water supply, and sewage
disposal, development is absolutely prohibited.   Normally,
the City, which owns 40 per cent of the land in the City and
most of the undeveloped land, develops the land before sale.

In any event, drainage, streets, and street lights are provided by the City, for which the developer, if a private person or corporation, pays a certain share in accordance with
a complex formula.   Water, electricity, and central heating
are provided by the public utilities, which defray cost through
charges.   These utilities are private shareholding public utilities; however, the City is in each case the largest shareholder, hence holds a policy-determining position.   The City
levies an annual fee for drainage, street cleaning, and sewage and waste disposal, and levies the fee along with the
real estate taxes. [23]   As a result, all development is properly serviced with a minimum of cost to the city.   Furthermore, agricultural land, valued at one or two DM per square
meter, will sell at thirty DM after development. [24]

The 1964 Report shows the purchase of 2,547,176
square meters of land at 46,462,659 DM, and the sale of
1,230,230 square meters at 31,221,197 DM.   The sale proceeded for planned development; the purchase, for various
municipal reasons: the subway, southern extension of the
greenbelt, Neue Stadt (Chorweiler), recreation areas, and
other public uses. [25]

The Konservator Division in the Office for the Arts
and Adult Education (Amt für Kunst und Volksbildung) has
responsibility for the preservation and maintenance of historical monuments and has architectural control in connection with such monuments.   There could be a need for close
cooperation between this division and the Planning Office
and/or the Development Planning Agency.   Recently, however, the major interest of the Konservator Division has involved the preservation of partially war-demolished "Kathe-
drale und Kirche" of ancient origin, therefore the need for
coordination has been less immediate. [26]

One other municipal activity within the functional area
studied in this chapter, which may seem to be administra-
tively separated, is the provision of residential housing.
The securing of emergency housing for people in need is a
function of the Welfare Administration; and the administration of publicly-supported housing, which in West Germany
is considered to be "public housing," is a function of the
Building Administration.   This is less of a separation of related activities than may at first glance appear to be the
case.   The former is clearly a welfare function concerned
with people who need welfare attention requiring casework
techniques of administration.   The latter is concerned with

people who presumably do not need welfare or casework attention. Furthermore, the former provides emergency housing in emergency situations, while the latter provides financial assistance in the securing of better housing for people
in the lower middle-class financial category, and in this connection administers loans and grants for housing construction.

Notes

1. Gliederungsplan der Stadtverwaltung Köln, February 20,
    1964 provided by Mr. Straatmann, Verwaltungsrat.
        In the remainder of the chapter the data on adminis-
    trative organization is based on this official adminis-
    trative chart, unless otherwise specified.

2. Stadt Köln Haushaltsplan, 1965, p. 270.
        In the remainder of the chapter, the data on the
    number of employees in specific agencies is secured
    from the 1965 budget. Included are the number pro-
    vided in the budget for the 1965 fiscal year, former
    credits for personnel, plus supplementary provisions.
        The 1965 Budget is also used for budget specifica-
    tions concerning anticipated receipts and authorized
    current expenditures.

3. Interviews with Mr. Pohl, Baurat, Administration; Mr.
    Riedel, Baurat, Planning Director; and Mr. Klose,
    Baurat, Street Construction Director, Stadthaus,
    Room 369, February 9, 1966.
        Interview with Dr. Gudknecht, Deutscher Städtetag,
    February 9, 1966.

4. Interview with Dr. Lehman-Grube, Specialist in Plan-
    ning, Deutscher Städtetag, February 14, 1966.

5. Von Oberregierungsrat Dr. Ing. Joseph Wolff, "Die
    Bauleitplannung und ihre Sicherung nach dem Bundes-
    baugesetz." Das Bundesbaugesetz und die Gemeinden,
    (Karl Krämer Verlag, Stuttgart, 1964.
        Raumordnungsgesetz of April 8, 1965 (BGB1. IS. 306)
    and Nordrhein-Westfalen Landesplanungsgesetz, May
    7, 1962 (GVB1. S. 229) (Deutscher Gemeindeverlag,
    Köln, 1965)
        Bundesbaugesetz of June 23, 1960 (Bundesgesetz-
    blatt IS. 341) (Ausgegeben zu Bonn am 29 June 1960).
        Landesbauordnung, Nordrhein-Westfalen of June 25,

1962 (mit Begründungen) (Werner-Verlag-Dusseldorf).

6. Gliederungsplan des Stadtverwaltung Köln, February 20, 1964.

7. Verwaltungsbericht der Stadt Köln, 1964, p. 161.

8. Interview with Baurat Riedel, Planungsamt, Stadthaus, Room 181, March 2, 1966.

9. Interview with Baurat Riedel.

10. Verwaltungsbericht der Stadt Köln, 1964, p. 162-163.

11. Interview with Dr. Lehman-Grube, Deutscher Städtetag, February 22, 1966.
Interview with Dr. Rombach, Oberregierungsrat, Köln Regerieungsbezirke, March 4, 1966.
Interviews with Dr. Wiedeman, Ministerialrat and Herr Kitschenberg, Bundesministerium des Innern, Bonn, February 11, 1966.
Interviews with Dr. Tilse and Dr. Ing Winter-Efinger, Bundesministerium für Wohnungswesen und Städtebau, Bad Godesburg, February 11, 1966.

12. The Federal Ministry of Housing, Town and Regional Planning, Bad Godesburg, Report, 1964, p. 25.

13. Verwaltungsbericht der Stadt Köln, 1964, p. 164.

14. Gliederungsplan des Stadtverwaltung Köln, February 20, 1964.

15. Ibid.

16. Verwaltungsbericht der Stadt Köln, 1964, p. 167-173.

17. The Municipal Budget of 1965, however, shows the drainage, cemetery, and park and garden maintenance functions grouped in the Department of Public Enterprises, which would reduce the amount budgeted for the Department of Building Administration to an amount just under 100 million DM. Stadt Köln, Haushaltsplan, 1965, chart, p. 5.

18. Interview with Baurats Pohl, Klose and Riedel, Stadtplanungsamt, February 9, 1966.

19. Gliederungsplan des Stadtverwaltung Köln, February 20, 1964.

20. Interview with Mr. Stemmler, Direktor, Liggenschafts-amt (Real Estate Office), March 4, 1966.

21. Interview with Mr. Stemmler.

22. Interview with Baurat Pohl, Planungsamt, Stadthaus, Room 369, February 9, 1966.

23. Interviews with Mr. Willings, Direktor, Abteilung für Kommunale Entwicklungsplanung, in the Office of the Development Planning Agency, March 17, 1966.

24. Interview with Mr. Stemmler.

25. Verwaltungsbericht der Stadt Köln, 1964, p. 19-27.

26. Ibid, p. 156-158.

Chapter VI

COLOGNE: COORDINATION

The top administration consists of the Oberstadtdirektor, the Stadtdirektor, the Director of Finance (Stadtkämmerer), and nine Directors of operating departments (Beigeordneter), selected by the City Council for 12-year terms of office. Continuing tenure for the City Manager and department heads, as in council-manager cities in the U. S. , may be preferable. The four-year term of office for the Chief Executive and department heads, as is customary in American non-council-manager cities, may be too short. There is much to be said for a 12-year term, giving a sufficiently long term to provide the opportunity to "carry through" with a program without gaining permanent tenure and without escaping popular control. The top management is responsible through the Oberstadtdirektor to the City Council and can be held to account for the administration. City Councilmen are elected every five years and after each election the Council chooses a Mayor. Furthermore, citizens participate in councilmanic committees, thus strengthening popular control. Below the Beigeordneter the staff has permanent tenure. In this way in North Rhineland-Westphalia, a career service is maintained without losing popular control. This is West Germany's answer to the problem of the relationship between the expert and the layman in municipal government.

In order to comprehend the coordination of administration within the city, it is advisable to survey its extent. The administrative plan lists the operating departments in the following order:

Bureau of the City Manager
(Buro des Oberstadtdirektor)

1. General Administration (Allgemeine Verwaltung)

2. Finance Administration (Finanzverwaltung)

3. Law-Security-and Order Administration (Rechts-
   Sicherheits- und Ordnungsverwaltung)

4. School Administration (Schulamt)

5. Administration for Arts and Adult Education (Amt für
   Kunst und Volksbildung)

6. Social Administration (Sozialamt)

7. Health and Hospital Administration (Gesundheitsamt
   und Amt für Krankenanstalten)

8. Building Administration (Bauerverwaltung)

9. Administration for Public Enterprises (Verwaltung für
   öffentliche Einrichtungen)

10. Administration for Industry and Commerce (Verwaltung
    für Wirtschaft und Verkehr)[1]

The major difference in the above listing of agencies
for assignment to the Beigenordneter and the official Structure Plan of the City Administration of Cologne (Gliederungsplan der Stadtverwaltung Köln) is the separation of the School
and Culture Administration into two operating departments:
1) Schools, and 2) Arts and Adult Education; also the separation of Social and Health Administration into two operating
departments: 1) Social, and 2) Health and Hospitals.

The Bureau of the City Manager, the General Administration, and the Finance Administration represent the top
management, or in American terminology, staff and auxiliary.
Through these offices coordination is provided.

The Bureau of the City Manager has one and only one
direct responsibility: the News Office (Nachrichtenamt).
This provides the City Manager direct control of public relations.

The Assistant City Manager (Stadtdirektor) has responsibility for the Statistical Office, the Real Estate Office,
and the Registration Office, which are self-explanatory, and
obviously serve managerial purposes.

The General Administration, which is the central

managerial headquarters, is under the direction of one
Beigeordneter, who is responsible to the City Manager for
three offices:

I. Head Office (Hauptamt)
  1. Supplies and Materials (Beschaffungsstelle)
  2. Mail In and Out (Eingangs-und Versandstelle)
  3. Administration Library (Verwaltungsbücherei)
  4. Data Processing Division (Rechenzentrum)
  5. Administration of Worringen (Verwaltungsstelle
     Worringen)

II. Personnel Office (Personalamt)
  1. Division for General Affairs (Abt für allegemeine
     Angelegenheiten)
     a) Regular and Supplementary Pensions (Zusatsvers-
        orgung, Zusatzversorgungskasse, Ruhegelversorg-
        ung)
     b) Illness Pension (Krankenungterstützungsverein)
     c) Sickness Insurance (Gemeinsame Betriebskranken-
        kasse)
     d) Administration and Savings Bank School (Ver-
        waltungs- und Sparkassenschule)
     e) Institute for Personnel Selection (Institute für
        Personalauslese)
  2. Division for the Personnel Affairs of the Beamten
     and Angestellten (Abt. für Personalangelegenkeiten
     der Beamten und Angestellten)
  3. Division for the Personnel Affairs of the Arbeiter
     (Abt. für Personalangelegeheiten der Arbeiter)
  4. Salaries and Wages Division (Gehalts-u. Lohnabt)
  5. Discipline Division (Disciplinarabt)

III. Office for Examination of the Records of the City
     (Rechnungsprüfungsamt)

     A few observations from the official outline, obvious
though they be, are worthy of note.   The auxiliary functions
grouped in the Hauptamt have both service and supervisory
implications.   Centralized purchasing of supplies and materials is placed in the Head Office, rather in the Department
of Finance.   Open competitive bidding is required for all
purchases above 500 DM.   Likewise, mail distribution is
operating from this control center, rather than from some

obscure point, or worse yet scattered through many places
within the City Hall. Furthermore, the placement of the
Data Processing Division in the Head Office provides the
logical central location for information control. The Administration Library provides more than a service function. It
has policy significance of the highest order.

A newly annexed area of the city (e. g. Worringen at
time of this writing), until it is organized as a Stadtteile or
Stadtbezirke, will be administered directly from the Head Office. This is comparable to the incubating function of the
mayor's office in the U. S. A.

The heavy emphasis on pensions and sickness insurance is highlighted in the Personalamt by being listed as the
first three of five sections in the Division for General Affairs. A School of Administration in the Personnel Office is
in accordance with the best thinking, but is not in practice
in America. What may seem unusual is the inclusion of
"savings bank" in the title of the School, evidencing a marked
municipal interest in this field of activity. Finally in the
fifth and last listed section is the function which in the United
States is too often the one and only function of the Personnel
Office--the Civil Service Commission--which in Cologne is
the Institute for Personnel Selection.

The establishment of a separate division for the personnel affairs of the Beamte and Angestellte and another division for the personnel affairs of the Arbeiter may be considered a "carry over" of class distinction from times past.
On the other hand, there are clearly different personnel
needs among the professional and office personnel on the one
hand and the labor personnel on the other; and it is probably
right that personnel office take full cognizance of these differences.

The placement of a Salaries and Wages Division in
the Personnel Office along with pension and insurance administration, instead of scattering these functions among the departments of finance, pensions, personnel selection and so
on, is worthy of note as a sensible coordination of personnel
functions too often missing in the U. S.

Finally, the very existence of a Discipline Division
may prove shocking to some contemporary psychologists.
Every municipal government must be prepared to face and
deal with disciplinary problems. Normally, this is left en-

tirely to the operating, line official. In Cologne, the Personnel Office has organized a special division to which these matters are referred.

A final obvious observation that needs to be stressed is that the Personnel Office is not an independent board or commission, but is an office, functioning definitely as a staff and auxiliary agency, a part of the "Allgemeine Verwaltung," a part of the management team responsible to the Chief Executive (Oberstadtdirektor).

In addition to the Head Office and the Personnel Office, the Office for the Examination of the Records of the City (Rechnungsprüfungsamt) is placed under the direction of Beigeordneter Dr. Heidecke, who in turn is responsible to the City Manager.

At the top level of the permanent administrative staff is "der Rat," requirement for which is a university law degree. The Oberstadtdirektor, Stadtdirektor, Stadtkämmerer, and the nine Beigeordneter, who are appointed for 12-year terms of office, must also have the qualifications of a senior administrative official (Rat). [2]

The 1964 personnel report classifies the total municipal personnel as follows:

2, 293 Officials and retired Employees (Beamte und ruhegehaltsberechtigte Angestellte)

4, 805 Employees on Active Duty (Tarifangestellte)

6, 078 Laborers (Arbeiter)

508 Apprentices and Assistants on Probation, etc. (Lehrlinge, Praktikanten, usw.)

───────

13, 684   Total

In an interview on February 8, 1966, with Stadtamtmann Stotberger and Verwaltungsrat Stratmann the following classification and totals were given: [3]

7,633 Beamte and Angestellte

5,582 Arbeiter

13,215 Total regular personnel

500 Apprentices, Assistants on Probation (est.)

13,715 Total

The Beamte have life tenure and administrative pensions provided from public funds after 35 years of service
at 75 per cent of the highest salary received. In addition to
life tenure, the Beamte by Land law may be transferred from
one city to another within the Land. The Angestellte have
permanent tenure and are covered by retirement insurance.
The employee contributes 3 to 4 per cent of the annual salary into the retirement fund. The City contributes twice
this amount. Upon retirement at 65, his pension is tax-
free. Widows and children of Beamte and Angestellte receive 60 per cent of husband's pension.

The Beamte and Angestellte are the only two groups
in West Germany that have the equivalent of craft unions.
The Beamte is legally prohibited from participating in a
"strike." All other employed personnel belong to one of 16
trade unions, the Deutsche Gewerkschaft Bund. The City
negotiates with the DGB as regards pay, working conditions
and pension, and hires by contract with the union.

Primary school education in West Germany continues
to age eleven. On the basis of the school record and exam-
inations, selections are made for apprenticeship to the position of Angestellte. After three years of apprenticeship, if
the record is satisfactory, the applicant becomes an Angestellte. Every third year, the employee's work is evaluated
until he reaches 50 years of age. Promotion from one
group of positions to a higher level is possible by additional
schooling and tests. A School of Public Administration (Ver-
waltungsschule) in the Personnel Office is available for those
who wish to become Beamte.

The above arrangements are breaking down the class
character of the bureaucracy at the municipal level, yet simultaneously are maintaining high personnel standards.

The City Manager has weekly meetings with the Assistant City Manager, the Director of Finance, the nine Beigeordneter, the Director of the Head Office, the Director of the Personnel Office, and the Director of the Office for the Examination of the Records of the City. All together, this group is the Verwaltungsrat--cabinet, or management committee. Deputies of the Verwaltungsrat meet with agency, or office, heads as needed, for ordinary day-by-day coordination. Verwaltungsrat Straatmann stressed that supervision and coordination of tasks are performed largely by means of personal contacts, rather than by committee meetings. See 2

Manpower and money are the two essential ingredients in the management of any enterprise. The Finance Administration (Finanzverwaltung) is organized into three offices: 1) Headquarters, which has direct charge of administering federal, state, and municipal funds, and loans for new buildings, 2) Tax Office, and 3) Treasurer's Office.

The Tax Office is organized according to tax source: 1) business tax; 2) real estate tax; 3) entertainment tax; 4) licenses to operate an inn or to serve drinks; 5) fees for waste disposal and sewage disposal; 6) dog tax; and 7) indirect taxes. In addition, there is an Office for the Examination of Books of private firms, utilities, museums, municipal departments, and other agencies (Stelle für Buch-und Betriebsprüfung).

The Treasurer's Office also has a Division for the enforcement of tax collection (Vollstrekkungsabteilung).

The operating budget has steadily grown: 621 million DM in 1964, 642 million in 1965, and 655 million in 1966 (approximately $164 million). For 1966, the capital budget totalled 318 million DM, providing a total for that year of 973 million ($243 million). These totals do not include public transport, gas, electricity, or water, which are provided by shareholding companies, in each of which the City is the largest shareholder.

Deficit financing is prohibited by law. Cologne had had no deficit until 1965, at which time the legal requirement was met by a transfer of funds from the extraordinary, or capital budget (Ausordentilichen Haushaltsplan).

Estimates for each fiscal year are submitted by the head of each municipal agency to the Director of Finance,

who presents the total compilation to the City Manager. After negotiations and adjustments, the City Manager presents
the proposed budget to the Mayor for presentation to the City
Council. The Councilmanic Committee on Finance and Taxes,
which is one of the larger committees, having 17 members,
considers the budget and reports to the Council for action.
Ten members of this committee represent the majority party
and seven the minority party with the chairman a majority
party member. There are two other councilmanic committees concerned with finance: 1) Committee on Investigation
of Expenditures, and 2) Committee on Retrenchment of Expenditures, five members on each. The chairman of the
latter is a member of the opposition party, guaranteeing a
real inspection of expenditures. [4]

        Prior to 1960, the fiscal year extended from April 1
through March 31 of the following calendar year, as in Great
Britain. Since 1960, the fiscal year has been the calendar
year. [5]

        Of the 655,000,000 DM operating budget in 1966,
240 million was allocated to salaries, wages and pensions,
which was 36.63 per cent of the total in comparison with
the usual 67 per cent in American municipal budgets.

        Up to 87.5 per cent of a municipality's financial needs
are provided by the Länder, calculated by means of a formula which takes into account total population, administrative
cost of duties performed for higher levels of government (including the Bunde), and the special needs of the municipality
(equalization) as regards education or other essential services. Cologne is receiving half of its budgetary needs from
North Rhineland-Westphalia.

        Of the municipal revenue, 80 per cent comes from
the business tax, which is a net income tax. Following
World War II, this was the only tax available to municipalities which kept pace with market trends. Except/for government grants, municipalities are still substantially dependent
upon it. [6] The remaining 20 per cent comes from the land
tax, entertainment taxes, innkeeper and liquor licenses, dog
taxes, and fees for sewage and waste disposal, but largely
from the land tax. By virtue of the concern in the U.S.A.
about the reassessment of urban real estate at frequent in-
tervals because of rapidly changing property values, it may
be of interest that there has been no reassessment of property in Cologne for tax purposes since the 1920s. For this

reason, tax rates have to be high. The tax rate varies from
120 per cent on the assessed valuation of forestry land to
250 per cent on the assessed valuation of real estate. The
heavy reliance on business taxes is a current controversy in
Cologne and the obvious need for reassessment of land for
tax purpose could well become one.

The Bunde and the Länder share the personal income
and corporation taxes. On a national basis, over half of this
revenue is assigned by federal law to the Bunde, but by an
equalization system, the financially weaker Länder share a
smaller percentage with the Bunde, and the financially strong-
er Länder share a higher percentage.   The Länder quite obviously administer the tax system for the Bunde.   The question was raised as to the equity of the Bunde receiving on
the average over half of the revenue collected by the Länder,
particularly since a goodly portion of Bunde law is administered by Land and local personnel.   The answer was that the
total financial as well as administrative structure is inter-
twined.   The Bunde, for example, pays for the material and
construction of a major highway or street.   The Land pays
for administration only.   Likewise, in the case of social
services, the Land pays for administrative expenses only. [8]

The usual administrative controls on expenditures are
available to the Stadtkämmerer (Dr. Linpinsel) and the Oberstadtdirektor (Professor Mohnen).   The City Council is responsible for an annual audit.   Every third or fourth year,
the Regierungs Präsident, the chief executive of the administrative district in which the city is located, has an audit
made, for which he is responsible to the Minister of the Interior of the Land.   There are furthermore a Land Court of
Audit (Landesrechnungshof) and a Federal Court of Audit
(Bundesrechnungshof) to which accounting is necessary. Thus
financial accountability is provided.

There are no independent or semi-independent agencies, no boards or commissions outside the network of administrative responsibility to the Oberstadtdirektor.   It is
all within the municipal administrative structure, responsible
through the Oberstadtdirektor to the City Council, where responsibility for all municipal public affairs is finally lodged
and firmly retained.

Outside the municipal structure are enterprises which
are owned and operated by shareholding companies in which
the City owns stock and has representation on the Board of

Directors. In the case of certain public services, the City
is the largest stockholder and has a controlling voice in
policy formation, but these services are not part of the government. In 1966, they were:

1. Gas, Electricity and Waterworks Joint Stock
   Company of Cologne (Gas-Elektrizitäts-und Wass-
   erwerke Köln AG)

2. Cologne Transport Joint Stock Company (Kölner
   Verkehrs-Betriebe AG)

3. The Savings Banks of the City of Cologne (Spar-
   kasse der Stadt Köln)

4. Fair and Exhibition Corporation of Cologne
   (Messe-und Ausstellungs-Gesellschaft mb H Köln)

5. Cologne/Bonner Airport in Wahn Corporation
   (Köln/Bonnar Flughafen Wahn GmbH zu Proz)

6. Cologne-Bonn Railway Joint Stock Company
   (Kölner-Bonnar Eisenbahnen AG)

7. Cologne Cableway Joint Stock Company (Kölner
   Seilbahn-Gesellschaft)

8. Rhine Ferry Cologne-Langel/Hitdorf Corporation
   (Rheinfähre Köln-Langel/Hitdorf GmbH)

9. The Cologne Zoological Garden Joint Stock Company (Atiengesellschaft Zoologischer Garten
   Köln)

10. Cologne Sport Hall Service Corporation (Kölner
    Sporthalle Betriebe-Geseldschaft mbH)

Six of the ten companies are public utilities, providing gas, electricity, water, and public transportation; two
are service companies operating publicly-owned exhibition
and sport halls; one is a publicly regulated savings bank
system, for which the City guarantees investors' savings;
and one is a zoological garden company operating a zoo for
the City on a lease basis. The employees of these firms
are not municipal employees, and the companies are legally

considered to be private companies, or corporations. They are included in the municipal budget only insofar as the City is obliged to maintain physical facilities, such as the publicly-owned exhibition and sport halls, or commitments as regards public transport.

With the possible exception of the Zoological Gardens, all of these enterprises can properly be considered to be business operations, which can be best administered by private companies or corporations; yet these business operations are very definitely affected with a public interest. This legal arrangement is one method of coping with a problem which is everywhere a dilemma.

Within the administrative structure of the municipal administration, there is very little scattering of related functions, and there are no independent entities, special districts, or single purpose governments that escape the attention of the voter and are not accountable to the City Council. Administrative responsibility for everything is concentrated in the City Manager's Office, and he is responsible to the City Council.

Notes

1. Except where otherwise specified, the sources for the remainder of the chapter are the Gliederungsplan der Stadt Köln, February 20, 1964 and the Verwaltungsbericht der Stadt Köln, 1964.

2. Interviews with Verwaltungsrat Straatmann and Stadtamtmann Stohlberger, Rathaus, Room 22, February 8, 1966.

3. Interview with Straatmann and Stohlberger.

4. See Table 9, Appendix.

5. Interview with Verwaltungsrat Feldotto, Deputy City Treasurer, Rathaus, Room 217, February 8, 1966.

6. Haushaltsplan 1965 der Stadt Köln, p. 3.

7. Ibid., p. V.

8.   Interviews with Dr. Schmitz, Finance, Deutscher Städt-
     etag, February 7 and March 14, 1966.

Chapter VII

COLOGNE: INTERGOVERNMENTAL RELATIONS

Every square foot of land, excluding certain forest lands and military reservations, is organized into Gemeinde (communes). As specified in Chapter II, the Gemeinde may be urban, rural, or a combination of both. Their present boundaries were established before the discovery of America. As a result, these boundaries, with exceptions where changes have been made, have little relevance to current needs. There is a phenomenal number of these jurisdictions, and most of them are entirely too small for modern governmental purposes. West Germany has 24,500 Gemeinde, of which more than 11,000 have fewer than 500 inhabitants. Approximately 23,000, or 93.8 per cent, have less than 1,000 population, and 95 per cent have less than 5,000 population. [1] An extreme example of a small Gemeinde is one in Schleswig-Holstein which has a population of 15, all members of one family. [2] The Gemeinde are municipal corporations and have general competence except police and justice, which come under Land jurisdiction. [3]

Due to the large number of small Gemeinde, North Rhineland-Westphalia, Rhineland Palatinate, and Schleswig-Holstein have jurisdictions, known as "Ämter," which perform municipal service and functions that the smallest Gemeinde are incapable of administering. In so doing, the Amt acts as agent for the Gemeinde. Included in the list of services and functions are urban planning and land-use controls. The Ämter are historically old in North Rhineland-Westphalia, but new ones are created by Land law as the need for them become evident. Lower Saxony is attempting to initiate Ämter by voluntary action of the small Gemeinde, called "Samtgemeinde," but this voluntary approach is not proving successful.

North Rhineland-Westphalia has 2,634 Gemeinde, of which 1,875 are grouped into 294 Ämter. The Amt is organized like the Gemeinde with a governing council, elected

for a five-year term, a mayor selected from the council by
the council for a five-year term, and a director, or manager,
selected by the council for a 12-year term.   The only essential differences in the structure of the Amt government from
that of the Gemeinde are the election of the Amt council by
the Gemeinde councils, and the chairman of the Amt council
does not have the status of mayor.

        The existence of a Gemeinde as a Stadt has an his-
torical basis, but normally a population of 10, 000 is necessary.   The Land Minister of the Interior makes the determination. [4]

        With a population of 100, 000, a Stadt becomes a
kreisfreie Stadt, which is in effect a city-county consolida-
tion.

        The Landkreis is frequently translated "county" for
English and American readers; however there are numerous
differences.   The Landkreis has no judicial functions.   Furthermore, it is not organized to perform relatively simple
governmental functions in rural areas, but to help small
Gemeinde perform functions beyond their capacity.   Gemeinde
can contract with the Landkreis to perform specified functions, and the Landkreis are organized and staffed to assume
the urban duties.   Furthermore, the Landkreis is created by
Land law as a municipal corporation. [5]

        The Landkreis is organized like the Gemeinde, with
a governing council popularly elected.   The chairman of this
council is the Landrat, equivalent to a mayor, the political
executive, selected by the council from its own membership,
all of whom have five-year terms.   There is also a professional director, selected by the council for a 12-year term.

        The Landkreis is similar to the county in that through-
out West Germany the Landkreis is the level of government
between the Gemeinde and the Land.   There is also some
similarity in that they are both agents of the Land and simultaneously a self-governing subdivision of the Land. [6]

        There are 425 Landkreis and 140 kreisfrei Städte
(city-county consolidations) in West Germany.   North Rhineland-Westphalia has 57 Landkreis and 38 kreisfrei Städte.
The Landkreis range in population from 30, 000 to 350, 000.
Most of them range from 100, 000 to 200, 000 population,
averaging 150, 000.

Dr. Wagener, who is a department secretary of the
Landkreistag (Association of the Counties) in North Rhineland-
Westphalia, explains the role of the Landkreis in West Ger-
man local government.

> The Landkreis is responsible for those tasks which
> are necessary for the district as a whole and for
> the execution of those activities which exceed the
> capability of the small municipalities. These in-
> clude hospitals, road and waterways maintenance,
> savings banks, social welfare, youth homes, homes
> for the aged, schools--especially for vocational
> and agricultural education as well as secondary
> schools, water supply, public health, veterinary
> supervision, control of air pollution, real estate
> survey, building permits, and licenses for danger-
> ous industrial plants.

> . . . On the average, the income of the Landkreis
> is formed out of 40 per cent given by the local
> communities, 35 per cent given by the state (gov-
> ernment grants) and 25 per cent from its own taxes
> and profits from its own property. [7]

The only tax resources available to the Landkreis are
taxes on hunting, dogs, and licenses for selling liquors.

While the Landkreis is multi-functional, two particularly significant duties which are performed as the agent of
the Land are the administration of Land grants and the control of the police. In North Rhineland-Westphalia, the Regierungsbezirke, administrative district of the Land, has
delegated to the Landkreis the administration of grants to the
local governments. By Land law, the director, chief executive officer of the Landkreis, is in charge of the state police located in the Landkreis.

In the larger Länder, there is an intermediary administrative layer between the central and local governments,
called "regierungsbezirke." The executive of this district,
the Regierungspräsidenten, in North Rhineland-Westphalia is
appointed by and responsible to the Land Minister of the Interior. He is responsible for the supervision of local governments particularly in the following administrative areas:
police, water supply, state forests, planning and housing,
supervision of business and industry, health and schools.
In the performance of all of its supervisory duties, the Re-

gierungsbezirke has interrelationships with all of the Land
ministries, except the Ministry for Bunde Affairs and the
Ministry of Justice.   This means that the Regierungsbezirke
are districts for virtually all state-local government relationships.   In brief, each ministry does not have its own district organization.

North Rhineland-Westphalia is divided into six Regierungsbezirke from southwest to northeast: Aachen, Köln,
Düsseldorf, Arnsberg, Münster and Detmold.   The boundaries patently need redrawing.   Three districts penetrate into
the Ruhr areas, which has made necessary the creation of
the "Siedlungsverband Ruhrkohlenbezirk," and the "Ruhrge-
biet," which is superimposed over the three districts in order to facilitate planning for this strategic area.

The Köln Regierungsbezirke includes seven Landkreis
and two kreisfrei Städte: Cologne and Bonn.   It includes the
entire Cologne metropolitan area, except along the northern
boundary where the Cologne MA overlaps into the Düsseldorf
district.   Leverkusen, a Kreisfrei Stadt of 106,347 population in 1966, borders on the northern boundary of the City of
Cologne, but is in the Düsseldorf district.   The percentage
of persons employed in Leverkusen is 130 to 150 per cent of
the number of employed persons residing there.   The employees not residing in Leverkusen commute from Cologne.
Dormagen, an Amt of 25,285 population in 1966, also borders
on the northern boundary of the City of Cologne, but again is
in the Düsseldorf district.   Here the percentage of employees
to resident employees is above 150, again commuting from
Cologne.   North of Leverkusen are five jurisdictions in one
Landkreis in the Düsseldorf district with employees who commute from Cologne: three Städter and two Gemeinde east of
the Rhine; and west of the Rhine adjacent to Dormagen are
four other Gemeinde in another Landkreis in the Düsseldorf
district.   In all of them are employees who commute from
Cologne.[8]   Of the 1.5 million population in the Cologne metropolitan area, over 225,000 reside in the Düsseldorf district.

The Ministry of the Interior at the Land level with
headquarters in Düsseldorf provides some coordination.

Another governmental level between the Land and local governments in North Rhineland-Westphalia is the Landschaftsverband.   Like the Regierungsbezirke, the Landschaftsverband can be traced back to Prussian days.   Taking cogni-

zance of the local interests of the Rhineland area, the administrative districts in the northern Rhineland area, which was
in Prussia, were organized into a provincial association
(Provincialverband). In 1953, North Rhineland-Westphalia,
recognizing the different interests and traditions of the two
major parts of the Land, created two regional governmental
entities called "Landschaftsverbänder:" 1) Rhineland and 2)
Westphalia. The Landschaftsverband Rhineland includes the
Regierungsbezirke Köln, Düsseldorf and Aachen. The Landschaftsverband Westphalia includes Arnberg, Münster (southwestern portion of the Land) and Detmold (northeastern portion of the Land). Unfortunately, this division also cuts
through the heart of the Ruhr industrial district. All of the
Cologne metropolitan area, however, is within the Rhineland
Landschaftsverband with headquarters in Cologne.

        The Landschaftsverband is a self-governing associa-
tion. In the Rhineland Landschaftsverband are 23 Landkreis
and 17 kreisfrei Städte, elected by the councils of their respective jurisdictions. In the governing Assembly are 133
representatives from the counties and city-counties organized
into party groups in 1966 as follows: 64 CDU, 54 SPD, 14
FDP and one Independent. The Landschaftsverband is also a
legal corporation in public law.

        The responsibilities of the association cover areas be-
yond the financial and geographic competence of the numerous
small jurisdictions within the region: 1) institutional and
highly specialized aspects of public health; 2) institutional
and highly specialized aspects of public welfare, 3) autobahn
and major highways; and 4) culture, such as museums, ar-
chives, and preservation of the countryside.

        In connection with the highways and preservation of the
countryside, the Landschaftsverband enters into land-use regulation. It does not have taxing authority and is financed entirely from contributions from local members (kreis) and by
grants from the Land. The Minister of the Interior has supervisory authority.

        The policy forming body is a council with five-year
terms of office, elected by the councils of the member jurisdictions. One quarter of the representatives of the Kreis
and Kreisfrei Städte in the Assembly of the Landschaftsver-
bund Rhineland are administrative officials of the government
units, which they represent, therefore they are well informed
as regards the administrative as well as the functional prob-

lems of the area concerned.

The council elects a Director General and a Deputy
Director General for 12-year terms.   The staff of 1,450 of-
ficials is organized into ten departments.   In the Director
General's Office are four divisions: 1) Audit Office, 2)
Press and Information,   3) Provident Fund, and 4) Organi-
zation and Methods, including computerized data processing.
The other nine departments include: 1) Administration and
Personnel,   2) Finance and Economic Affairs,   3) Building
Administration,   4) Youth Welfare,   5) Road Construction,   6)
Welfare (ex-servicemen and surviving dependents of ex-servicemen),   7) Public Welfare (blind, physically handicapped,
mentally handicapped, speech defects),   8) Health (hospitals,
asylums, and T. B. prevention and cure), and 9) Cultural Activities.   This last mentioned department has responsibility
for the preservation of the countryside, and the preservation
of the customs and traditions of the Rhineland.

Of the 16.3 million population in North Rhineland-
Westphalia, 8.8 million reside in Landschaftsverband Rhineland with a geographic extent of 33,977 fläche, or 131 square
miles, a sufficiently large area in terms of geography, population, and taxable resources to make feasible the responsibilities assigned to it. [9]

Another type of coordination is made possible by Land
law, which authorizes the formation of "Zweckverbände,"
single purpose districts.   About 256 special purpose districts
have been formed in North Rhineland-Westphalia: water supply, 203; education, 35; and sewage disposal, 18.   Single-
purpose districts have been in existence for 60 years in Germany.   Some of the Zweckverbände are mixed corporations,
based on a public contract; for example, the Rhine-Westphalia Electric Corporation, the largest power production enterprise in Europe, which has a power grid with Austria,
Switzerland and France.   Other Zweckverbände are small
enterprises for local use only; as for example, the Zweckverbände that Cologne is negotiating with Bergisher-Gladbach
and Bensberg, two Städter, immediately east of Cologne within the Cologne metropolitan area for drainage and water pollution control. [10]   A Zweckverband is always only for one
purpose (which can be anything) and is under the legal supervision of the Land government.

Bunde law authorizes the formation of Planungsver-
bände, but this device is generally not used.   There are a

few examples of successful verbände of this nature, but there
are not a sufficient number to consider it a solution to the
problem of planning for larger geographic areas.

One of the major problems, mentioned by everyone
interviewed, is the competition between Gemeinde, cities,
and counties for industries. The Regierungspräsident in the
Cologne district has established a definite policy of regulating land-use in the Cologne district more strictly in order
to curtail the competition for industry. Where subsidies
from the Land for construction purposes are involved, the
Regierungspräsident can coordinate planning as regards
water-supply systems, sewage-disposal systems, hospitals,
streets, and industrial sites.

Another device that would help, according to Dr. Gudknecht of Deutschen Städtetag, is the Arbeitsgemeinschaft, a
joint working association, which is authorized by Land law
in North Rhineland-Wesphalia, but it has been very little
used. This could be used for planning purposes. Planning
must come first. Everything else depends upon it. [11]

Throughout West Germany, but particularly in the
highly urbanized and industrialized Rhine-Ruhr area, there
is a realization that the units of municipal government are
entirely too small. Most of the Gemeinde serve no useful
purpose in contemporary society. Instead of merging them,
they are retained and Ämter are authorized by Land law to
perform the necessary functions, which the small Gemeinde
are unable to perform. In other situations, the county
(Kreis) more and more performs municipal functions.

Herr Blumentrath, Executive Member of the Board of
the Association of German Gemeinde (Deutschen Gemeinde-
tages) estimates that the 24,500 Gemeinde in West Germany
could well be reduced to 7000. [12] Dr. Bockelman, Business
Manager of the Deutschen Städtetag and former Mayor of
Frankfurt, estimates 6000. [13] Both gentlemen are mindful of
the rural areas where smaller jurisdictions may be advisable
and are feasible.

In 1964 a study was made of the technical administrative resources necessary for a minimum size of administrative unit. The minimum population requirement, depending
of course on the number of different municipal functions varies from 6,000 to 50,000. [14] This calculation, however, has
no relevance to the metropolitan setting.

The county in West Germany is well organized to perform municipal functions. At present, there are 425 Landkreis and 140 Kreisfreie Städte in West Germany, providing
a total of 565 units of local government if the county were
used as the smallest unit of local government. Dr. Bockelman, however, considers the county to be too small for current municipal needs in the industrialized, urbanized portions
of West Germany. The entire structure of local government
is too small both in geography and population. Dr. Bockelman sees the need for urban regions that would comprise
several Kreis, but would be smaller than the current Regierungsbezirke,[15] which is comparable to the idea expressed by
John C. Bollens and Henry J. Schmandt in The Metropolis.[16]

In the Cologne MA, there are at least 33 jurisdictions
in toto and parts of five other jurisdictions:[17]

Kreisfrei Städte	2
Städte	8
Gemeinde	19
Ämter	3
Landkreis	1
	33
Landkreis (partial)	5
Total	38

The populations vary from 561 to 859,830. Excluding
the Landkreis, the populations of the jurisdictions range as
follows:

Population	No. of Jurisdictions
1,000- 5,000	9
5,000- 10,000	3
10,000- 20,000	8
20,000- 30,000	4
30,000- 40,000	2
40,000- 50,000	3
50,000-100,000	1
100,000-200,000	1
800,000-1 million	1
	32

Only three of the jurisdictions have 50,000 or more population, which Dr. Wagener established as requisite for overall municipal functions. Actually, the totality should be under one metropolitan government.

Accepting the Landkreis as the smallest local juris-diction in the Cologne Regierungsbezirk, the populations would vary from 107,600 in Landkreis Euskirchen to 859,830 in Kreisfrei Stadt Köln, population entities large enough to cope with contemporary urban problems. The current Landkreis boundaries, however, would quite obviously have to be re-drawn to conform to present urbanization realities.

From the above analysis, it is obvious that there is the same reluctance to change established agencies and to alter well established boundaries as there is in the U.S.A. The supervision from the Land level is better organized in North Rhineland-Westphalia than at the state level in the U.S.A. At the Land level, however, Regierungsbezirke boundaries desperately need redrawing in the light of current economic structure and population distribution.

Of excellent assistance to the cities of West Germany are the studies and services provided by the German Munici-pal Association (Deutschen Städtetag), which was established in 1905, and currently has its headquarters in Cologne. [18] The Association represents approximately 480 municipalities. There are a total of 1000 Städter in West Germany, but many of them exist for historical reasons only, and most of them "still have a prevailing rural character;" therefore the As-sociation represents the major portions of the real cities. [19] The Deutschen Städetag has recently released publications in paperback form on several problem areas under the follow-ing titles:

1. The City Must Live.
2. The City and Its Region.
3. Life in the City.
4. Streets for the City.
5. Space Order - A Manageable Problem?
6. Chaos or Order?
7. Renewing our Cities.
8. Citizen of the City State.

Of equal significance is the Center for Local Govern-ment Studies (Verein für Kommunalwissenschaftung), which was established in 1951 by the German Municipal Association and

the Senate of Berlin.   Seven research departments are at
work:

1. Local Government History
2. Urban Research and Communal Statistics
3. Local Government Law
4. Local Government Politics
5. Local Government Finance
6. Communal Sociology
7. Local Government Economy

> The Center is organized in interdependent depart-
> ments to establish a coordination between the dif-
> ferent disciplines, which did not exist up to now in
> Germany, in their work on the common object:
> The Local Government. [20]

The Academy of Administrative Sciences (Hochschule
für Verwaltungswissenschaften) at Speyer, described below,
has contributed much to the development of municipal administration as an area worthy of serious study.

> The Hochschule is a post-university establishment.
> In addition to a few visiting scholars, some from
> abroad, those attending it are Referendare, young
> men and women who have completed their univer-
> sity studies, mostly within the faculty of jurispru-
> dence at any of the German universities, and who
> next must pass successfully through a probationary
> service, recently reduced to two and one-half
> years.   As civil servants "on revocation," they are
> assigned to various duty stations, mainly different
> courts, but including a period in an attorney's of-
> fice and in an administrative agency.   In keeping
> with their interests, Referendare, in the course of
> this probationary service, may be assigned by the
> participating governments for a semester to the
> Hochschule. [21]

During the last week of March 1966, the author at-
tended an Institute held at the Hochschule for municipal officials from all over West Germany.   Cities in every Land
sent beamte and other municipal officials to Speyer to participate in the Institute.

Dr. Fritz Morstein Marx, who is very active as a
faculty member at the Speyer Academy, escaped from Ger-

many when Hitler came to power, came to the U. S. A. ,
joined the faculty of Yale University as a political scientist,
became Dean, was Deputy Director of the U. S. Bureau of
the Budget, and when he retired from Yale returned to Germany where he is devoting his vigorous energies in direct-
ing German attention to research and study of the practical
aspects of administration with less emphasis on law.

Among serious students of municipal affairs in West
Germany, there is an awareness of the need for action by
the Land governments to reduce the chaos of multiple governments at the local level.   Two major differences between
West Germany and U. S. A. are noticeable.   There is in West
Germany no unincorporated land.   As a result, new municipal entities are not continuously being incorporated, thus
compounding a bad situation.   Furthermore, the German
Kreis (county) is organized to provide municipal services
which the normal American county is not.   As a result, there
is no urban fringe lacking the services and controls of adequate government.   Furthermore, over the substructure of
small, inadequate Gemeinde a superstructure of larger governmental entities has been created to cope with the large-
scale and expensive needs of an industrialized and urbanized
society.   The Amt is nothing more than an expedient device
for escaping the necessity of merging governmental entities
that are too small.   Of greater significance are the Kreis
and the Landschaftsverbände.   Dr. Bockelman's "regional
metropolitan government" is for the future.   This idea among
others will appear in the literature of municipal affairs for
decades, and eventually the practitioners and men of government will become aware of it and make an effort to make
use of it.   This is relevant to all municipal functions, but
particularly to urban planning and land-use controls.

At the Land level, citizen organizations, or pressure
groups, participate in the area of land-use planning.   The
Land Planning Law provides for a Planning Association for
the Rhineland portion of the Land in which representation
from nine Federal agencies, nine Land agencies, and all the
political subdivisions in the Rhineland is mandatory, and representation, or membership, on the part of specified non-
governmental organization is permitted upon application.
The following may be voluntary members:[22]

1.   Chambers of Agriculture.
2.   Chambers of Industry and Commerce.
3.   Chambers of Trades and Handicraft.

4. Labor Unions and Trade Unions.
5. Public Housing Estate Societies and Homestead Societies.
6. Enterprises and Associations of Housing, Agriculture, Forestry, Industry, Mining, Transportation, Power Industry, and Navigation Industry.
7. Organizations of District and Home Care.
8. Scholarly Institutions.

The Planning Association serves as a coordinating agency for the governmental units and as an advisory body insofar as non-governmental organizations are members. The list of non-governmental organizations that may participate is to say the least formidable. Particularly active are the first three listed above. The Chambers of Trades and Handicraft, of which about 20 have joined, are primarily interested in city planning, land use for dwellings, and small business. The Chambers of Industry and Commerce, of which about eight have joined, concentrate interest in regional planning, traffic ways, and utilities. The Chambers of Agriculture have a strong interest in both local and regional planning, and particularly the preservation for farming use of good soil which is claimed for other purposes all too readily. Encouragement to participate seems not to be necessary for these groups.

Dr. B. Rombach, Oberregierungsrat, Köln Regierungsbezirke, writes, "All three [of these Chambers] know what interest they have to protect and report with emphasis on own accord."[23]

The organizational interest and activity in land-use planning at this level is worthy of a separate study by someone who can communicate freely and precisely in German. There are two aspects to the situation. One, the Land government has by law provided an opportunity for citizen organizations to participate. Two, the citizen organizations recognize that the Rhineland region is a more significant area within which to function than the limited area compassed by any one city or Gemeinde. A hypothesis for research may well be: given a real opportunity to participate in public affairs, in which German private organizations have a stake at a governmental level that is commensurate or relevant to the problem, these organizations will participate. If this does not come within the American concept of "pressure politics," it is a preliminary step in that direction. Whether or not the activation of organizational pressure politics is a

desirable goal is another problem and involves a value judge-
ment. The findings of the above proposed research would
provide the base for further encouragement of, or limitation
of, that kind of activity.

Notes

1. Interviews with Dr. Tilse, Ministerialrat, Bundesminis-
    terium für Wohnungswesen und Städtebau, Bad Godes-
    berg, Deichmannsaue, February 11, 1966; and Dr.
    Bockelman, Business Manager, Deutschen Städtetag,
    February 14, 1966.

2. Interview with Mr. Blumentrath, Executive Member of
    the Board of German Gemeinde, Koblenzer Str. 37-
    39, Bad Godesberg, February 23, 1966.

3. Interview with Mr. Könneman, Erster Landesrat, Land-
    schaftsverband Rhineland, Landeshaus, February 10,
    1966.

4. Nordrhein-Westfalen Kleine Verwaltungskunde, Informa-
    tionen über das Innenministerium, herausgegeben vom
    Innenminister des Landes Nordrhein-Westfalen Staats-
    bürgerliche Bildungsstelle, 1965.

5. Interview with Dr. Wagener, Department Secretary of
    the Landkreistag (Association of Counties) in North
    Rhineland-Westphalia, Schäferstrasse 10, Düsseldorf,
    March 10, 1966.

6. Interview with Dr. Rolf Grauhan, Munich, April 5, 1966.

7. Dr. Wagener, Address delivered in Mettmann, England.

8. Statitisches Jahrbuch der Stadt Köln; map between pages
    106 and 107.

9. Nordrhein-Westfalen Kleine Verwaltungskunde, Informa-
    tionen über das Innenministerium, 1965. And, inter-
    view with Mr. Könnemann, Director General, Febru-
    ary 10, 1966, Landschaftwerband Building, Cologne.

10. Interviews with Dr. Rombach, Mr. Decker, and Mr.
    Botschen in the Office of the Regeruings President in
    Cologne, February 10, 1966; and Dr. Gudknecht, Of-

fice in Deutschen-Städtetag, February 14, 1966.

11. Interview with Dr. Gudknecht.

12. Interview with Mr. Blumentrath.

13. Interview with Dr. Bockelman.

14. Wagener, Frido, "Efficiency and Reform of German Local Government," Archiv für Kommunalwissenschaften, 1964, p. 237-258.

15. Interview with Dr. Bockelman.

16. John C. Bollens and Henry J. Schmandt, The Metropolis: Its People, Politics, and Economic Life, (New York: Harper & Row, Publishers, 1965). Chapter 19, "The Shape of the Future."

17. See Tables 2 and 10, Appendix.

18. The Deutschen Städtetag address is Köln-Marienburg, Lindenallee 11.

19. Deutschen Städtetag, Municipal Self Government in Germany, p. 5.

20. Statement by the Verein für Kommanalwissenschaften (Center for Local Government Studies); address: Ernst-Reuter-Haus in Berlin-Charlottenburg, Strasse des 17 Juni 112.

21. Morstein Marx, Fritz, "German Administration and the Speyer Academy," Public Administration Review, December, 1967, Vol. 27, No. 5, p. 407.

22. Nordrhein-Westfalen Landesplanungsgesetz vom 7 Mai 1962 (G. V. Bl. S. 229), sec. 7.

23. Letter from Dr. B. Rombach, Oberregierungsrat, Köln Regierungsbezirke, May 30, 1967.

Chapter VIII

STOCKHOLM: RESULTS OF LAND-USE CONTROL

Thomas Atmer and Bjorn Linn (National Association
of Swedish Architects), analyzing city planning, write,

> The essential task of the moment is to organize the
> city into an efficient tool for living, a city adapted
> to all sections of the community which serves them
> in their work, home life and recreation. [1]

The economic efficiency of a city, including land-use
determination for industry, commerce, and residential purposes, and circulation for men and materials, and adequate
tax base data, which has been the major consideration in
American cities, is not enough. "Cities must be good places
in which to live as well as to make a living."[2]

The Swedish planners moved from major attention to
economic efficiency in the 1920s to emphasis on the residents'
needs for light and air in the 1930s, and thereafter gained
a realization that there were also psychological and spiritual
needs that have to be met in order to make a city a good
place in which to live.

> Town planners will do their share to create a "liv-
> ing environment," not being content simply with ar-
> ranging things so that people breathe and move in
> a healthy environment. [3]

A "living environment" most effectively characterizes
Stockholm.

Four periods of Stockholm's development are discern-
ible: 1) the Old Town (Gamla Stan)--middle of the Thirteenth
Century to the middle of the Seventeenth Century; 2) the city
of Stone--middle of the Seventeenth Century to the end of the
Nineteenth Century; 3) the Garden Suburbs--the beginning of
the Twentieth Century to the 1930s; and 4) the Metropolitan
Plan, which includes outlying communities connected with

140

the metropolitan center by means of the underground or surface railway--1945 to the present.

        Stockholm does not have a history dating back to the
First Century as is true of Cologne, yet preservation of the
significantly historical has not been ignored; and in this respect Stockholm has been very fortunate that the location of
the original city was on an island.   In the middle of the
Thirteenth Century, Birger Jarl, ruler of the Swedish kingdom, built a fortress on an island, at the point where water
rushed from Lake Mälaren into the Baltic Sea.   This site
was selected in order to protect the single, natural inlet
from the Baltic.   This was the birth of Stockholm, said to
have taken place in 1252.   There is evidence that merchants
in nearby Sigtuna, when it burned down in 1255, moved to
Stockholm. [4]   By 1288, a walled town had been established on
the island.   It was a primitive town built almost entirely of
wood.   During the first four centuries of its existence, the
town was repeatedly damaged by great fires.   For example,
during the Seventeenth Century, the southern areas of Stockholm suffered eight conflagrations that burned down whole
parishes within a day or two.

        In 1436, the State Council drew up a charter, which
proclaimed that "Stockholm is the capitol of the kingdom."
The crucial turning-point in Stockholm's history came in the
middle of the Seventeenth Century.   Compelled to rebuild because of the devastating fires, the city in 1640 adopted a
master plan, and the governing officials appointed a city
planner, called a "conductor."[5]   During the Thirty Years
War, when Sweden became a major power and Stockholm became a center of international importance, the population increased fourfold and residential districts developed in the
areas north and south of the central island.   Thereafter, the
residential expanse of the city remained practically unchanged until the last half of the Nineteenth Century.

        Fearful that the atmosphere of the Old City might
change, a special law, part of the Lex Gamla Stan, was
passed on June 30, 1947 to preserve historic buildings and,
in general historic areas.   Under this law (Byggnadslag),
Stockholm is authorized to acquire historically and culturally
significant areas and make necessary repairs and interior
improvements on the buildings.   Thereafter, the City may
lease the properties to private citizens.   Paragraph 44a of
this law, providing loans to private citizens for the repairs
and interior improvements, raised questions which have not

been settled. If arrangements under discussion are adopted,
it would mean that the persons to whom the properties are
leased will be authorized to make the necessary repairs and
interior improvements and receive a loan for this purpose,
paying off the loan by means of the lease payments. [6]

Under another law (Lag om Byggnadsminnen, December 9, 1960), the Riksantiqvarien, a national official, can
designate a house as a "K hus" (culture house) and the owner
thereof is prohibited from demolishing the structure. If the
owner in order to comply with the orders of the Riksantiqvarien is obliged to use the building in a very uneconomical
way, he is to be paid for this limitation on the use of his
property; however, the Riksdag has not provided funds for
the purpose, therefore the national government can do no
more than exercise persuasion. [7]

A third law with the objective of preserving historically or culturally significant structures applies to all of Sweden. The Riksantiqvarien is authorized to propose expropriation of such a structure for purposes of preservation. The
proposal may be made to an "authority," belonging to the
State, or to a municipality, authorizing it to perform the expropriation and to preserve the historically or culturally significant structure. [8]

With the exception of the east and west tips of Stadsholmen (City Island), which are now taken over by automo-
tive traffic, the islands on which the original city was built,
Stadsholmen and Riddarholmen (Isle of Nobility), have been
reasonably well preserved in their medieval layout. The Old
City Island was substantially smaller in the Thirteenth Century. It is a matter of record that the Island raises itself
one meter each century. [9] The boundary of the old town wall
of the Thirteenth Century can be traced in the narrow blocks
along Prästgatan and Baggensgatan. Remains, both of the
thirteenth-century castle and the seventeenth-century palace,
are to be found in the present palace, completed in the
1700s. The foundation of the Riddarholm Church was laid
about 1270 and was completed before the end of the Thirteenth
Century. Since the 1600s it has been used only as a royal
and "famous citizen" burialplace. The Great Church (Stor-
kyrkan), adjacent to the palace, is the cathedral church of
the Stockholm diocese, and is used regularly for Lutheran
Church services. It is situated on the site of the original
church, built between 1260 and 1264. The Parliament Building and the headquarters for many of the national adminis-

trations are also situated in the Old City, the "Gamla Stan."

Most of the structures in the "Gamla Stan" are still
used for the purposes for which they were built: government
office buildings, restaurants, residential quarters, retail
trading, including specialty shops, churches, and semi-public
buildings, such as the House of Nobility. Restaurants in the
Old City have become favorite eating places. For example,
"Den Gyldene Freden" (the Golden Peace) has become famous
without the benefit of special patronage. Anders Zorn, a
Swedish artist, purchased the restaurant and presented it to
the Swedish Academy, which arranged that the restaurant,
which was opened in 1721, would maintain the old traditions.
Residences in the Old City, about half of which have been up-
graded and made comfortable for twentieth-century living,
have attracted attention and may reverse the downward trend
of population in the Old City. [10]

Professor Olof Byström of Stockholm University, and
the Senior Keeper at the City Museum of Stockholm, writes
about the Gösta Berling committee, which was appointed to
plan the preservation of the "Old City" and which submitted
a report in 1965):

> Above all the committee was anxious to preserve
> the Old City as a residential area. Buildings are
> better preserved when used as homes than when
> they are used for other purposes. Offices tend to
> expand and, in due course, require changes in the
> buildings in which they are housed. They also bur-
> den the narrow network of streets with more traf-
> fic than do dwelling units. [11]

Taking into consideration the irregular network of
streets from two to five yards in width and the closely-built
houses, the Gösta Berling committee was well aware that the
limited amount of open space would never make apartments
suitable for families with children, but the central location
and the extraordinary environment would be "stimulating for
childless couples, persons living alone and students." [12]

One exception to the generalization that all of the
structures in the Old City are used for the purpose for which
they were built is the Stockholm City Museum, which is actually situated on a larger island, Södermalm, immediately
south of the Old City, and at the entrance to the Old City Island. This was the historic City Hall. Stockholm's histori-

cal development is here illustrated by both permanent and
temporary exhibitions. [13]

    In addition to pressure being exercised on private
property owners by the government to preserve buildings believed to be historically or culturally significant, private
property owners are likewise opposing the government's taking property in connection with urban renewal projects on the
grounds that certain properties are significant and worth preserving. The Stockholm Chamber of Commerce during the
summer of 1966 was attempting to escape acquisition by the
city of its headquarters on the mainland north of the Old
City Island in connection with a large modernization project,
pointing out that the property in question was built in 1648
and that there are very few old structures left in the Stockholm central business district, and therefore those that are
left should be preserved. At the time, the City was not interested either in the history or the cultural significance of
the property. [14]

    Stockholm's finest contributions in urban design as
well as architecture are creations of the present century.
The City Hall (1923), the Concert Hall (1927), Wenner-Gren
Center (1959), the Folksam Building (1959), Hötorget (1959),
the contemporary church buildings, the park and open-space
areas, and the so-called towns such as Vällingby and Farsta
are merely a few examples; what has been preserved in the
Old City with a few additions in Norrmalm and Södermalm
is sufficient to provide the necessary links with the past and
enable the citizenry to have an historical perspective.

    Overcrowding and a shortage of housing have been
continuous problems for Stockholm. The city population increased during the second half of the Nineteenth Century
from 100,000 to 300,000, and during the next 20 years to
500,000. By 1930 the development of a major portion of the
Inner City was completed, totalling 3,400 hectares, largely
on the mainland north of the Old City and including the islands of Kungsholm and Södermalm and others smaller. The
Inner City was laid out with a gridiron street pattern of
square or rectangular blocks of stone buildings three to six
stories high. Workers with large families lived in one or
two rooms with a kitchen; this size flat constituted 70 per
cent of the entire housing stock in the city. For these reasons, this portion of the city is known as the City of Stone.[15]
Mr. Joakim Garpe, former Commissioner for City Planning,
comments concerning the City of Stone in these words,

> For social housing reasons, the many densely-de-
> veloped and partially substandard residential dis-
> tricts in the inner town erected during the period
> of private capitalism--must undergo radical renew-
> al. [16]

In 1930, the concept of a statistical room was introduced in Sweden as a measuring unit: 22 square meters
(236.7 square feet).   The International Statistical Room is 6
square meters (64-1/2 square feet); a room so small is legally prohibited from being built now in Sweden. [17] In Stockholm, the average size room is 25 square meters, which is
slightly larger than the average size room for all of Sweden. [18] The average occupancy in 1966 was 1.85 persons per
room not including the kitchen.   Mr. Göran Siedenbladh, Director of Stockholm's City Planning Department, estimates
that the average occupancy in 1975 will be one person per
room.   More than two persons per room is now considered
to be "over-crowding." [19]

Of the 4,157 dwelling units built during 1966 in Stock
holm, 32.7 per cent were in the Inner City.   Of the dwelling
units built in the Inner City, 30 per cent were four rooms or
larger; in the Outer City, 45 per cent were four rooms or
larger. [20] The Stockholm Real Estate Office reports that the
average apartment in today's construction is a four-room
unit.   At the other end of the listing were 11 per cent of the
dwelling units having one room without kitchen, and 8 per
cent being without a private bath. [21] This is understandable
in view of the adult proportion of the Stockholm population
that is single, widowed, or separated.

%-age of Total Pop. in Stockholm
as of Dec. 31st of Specified Year

	1950	1960	1966
Adults unmarried	23.77	23.84	26.33
Widowed	5.48	5,89	6.66
Separated	3.83	5.15	5.89
Total Per Cent	33.08	34.88	38.88

Furthermore, 35 per cent of the 105,380 persons who
were searching for housing in August 1966 were interested
in and preferred one-room accommodations.   Another 37 per

cent were searching for two-room accommodations, 18 per
cent desired three rooms, and only 10 per cent preferred
four rooms or more.   The International Urban Studies Project at the Institute of Public Administration, New York City,
reports that Sweden has the lowest average household size
in Europe except Monaco, and the average household for
Stockholm is lower than the average for Sweden: Sweden has
2. 8 persons per household.   Stockholm has 2. 43 persons per
household. [22]

An analysis of the nature of these households in Stockholm is revealing.   The following tabulation presents the
number of private households by number of members:[23]

1	102,079
2	93,086
3	61,488
4	46,697
5	18,039
6+	7,739
Total	329,128

The following tabulation presents the number of private households, with a married head-of-household, by number of children under sixteen years of age[24] residing there:

0	88,584
1	44,168
2	30,926
3	9,152
4	2,498
Total	175,328

The first observation worthy of notice is that only 53
per cent of the households have a married head-of-household.   Of the total number of private households, 59 per
cent are households of one or two, and 77 per cent are households of one, two or three.   Of the households with a married head, 50 per cent have no children and 25 per cent
have one child (leaving 25 per cent with more than one
child).   Considering the relatively small size of the major
portion of the households, it is not surprising that over two-
thirds of the housing construction in 1966 was multi-family
housing; only one quarter was single-family housing, and the
remaining 5 per cent was other types of housing.

The keenest problem of housing has been to build rapidly enough to meet immediate needs. There are long queues waiting for apartments. This housing situation prevails despite: a housing construction record of an average of 5,150 dwelling units each year in the city during the period 1956-1965; the production of 18,000 units per year during the succeeding five year period in the Stockholm metropolitan area; and the continuous loss of population in the city since 1960. Although births have exceeded deaths each year by an average ratio of 2,482 to 1,393, emigration to the suburbs has caused the following annual net population loss:

	Pop. Change	Total Pop. Year's End
1960	+ 1,573	808,022
1961	− 793	807,229
1962	− 3,089	804,140
1963	− 5,697	798,443
1964	− 5,247	793,196
1965	− 6,608	786,588
1966	− 8,177	778,411

It is estimated that by 1975 the population will be 711,900, and that by 1980 the City of Stockholm will be down to 665,200 inhabitants; however while the core city lost 21,301 population during the period from November 1, 1960 to November 1, 1965, the suburban communes gained 103,074.

The population distribution among the Inner and Outer Districts of the City and the immediate suburbs in per cent of total population is shown for 1940 and 1965 and (estimated) for the year 2000:

Distribution of Population [25]		
1940	1965	2000
Inner City 60%	30%	15%
Outer City 20%	40%	25%
Suburbs 20%	30%	60%

Notice the 50 per cent reduction in the proportion of the total population in the Inner City during the 1940-1965 period, and another 50 per cent reduction anticipated by 2000. In the Outer City, a doubling of the percentage of the total metropolitan population between 1940 and 1965 was not sufficient to curtail a continuing loss of population by the

whole city of Stockholm to the suburbs each year from 1960
to 1967. The total population in the Stockholm metropolitan
area is expected to be 1.6 to 1.7 million in 2000.

The overall population density for the Inner City in
1968 was 88 persons per hectare (35.62 per acre); for the
Outer City, 31 per hectare (12.54 per acre); and for the entire city, 42 per hectare (16.99 per acre). [26] The population
density in the immediate suburbs, which belong to the Greater
Stockholm Planning District, ranged from .45 persons per
hectare in Österhaninge, a landskommun on an island in the
Baltic southeast of Stockholm, to 28.04 in Solna, a city bordering on Stockholm to the north, on the highway to Uppsala.
For the suburban jurisdictions, which belong to the Greater
Stockholm Local Traffic Association, the average population
density was 1.73 persons per hectare. [27] Within commuting
distance of Stockholm there is obviously ample space for a
substantial population growth.

Mr. Göran Sidenbladh, Director of Town Planning for
Stockholm, makes the following significant observation,

> Stockholm's ability to plan its physical, economic
> and social development must be attributed mainly
> to one all-important factor: public ownership of
> the land. If destructive fires in the city made
> planning necessary, government control of the land
> made it possible. This tradition of land control
> has a long history. [28]

Private ownership of land was virtually unknown in
Stockholm prior to the Nineteenth Century. The land was
owned either by the national or the municipal government,
and was leased for housing, business or industry. The terms
of the lease might be only nominal, but the lease itself
served to establish the principle that the land did not belong
to the user. During the Nineteenth Century, the lease system was whittled away. The lessors were permitted to acquire full title to the land by the payment of a sum equal to
thirty times the annual lease payment. By 1850, most of
the land area not used for municipal purposes had passed into private ownership. [29]

In 1904, the City Council set out to buy large areas
of farm and forest lands south and west of the city limits
with the intent to build "garden cities" as suburbs for the
metropolis. Concurrently the city extended its boundaries so

that the new suburbs came within the city limits.

By 1910, the City commenced acquiring property in
the CBD.   A 1953 amendment to the 1948 Building Law authorized zonal expropriation, which enabled the City to acquire property on the basis of its current land use without
making public a proposed re-use plan, thus reducing the
cost of land acquisition.

As a result, the City in 1966 owned about half of the
central business district, 36 per cent of the Inner City, and
83 per cent of the so-called Suburban Area inside the administrative borders of the municipality, the Outer Town.   This
totals 74 per cent of all the land inside the City of Stockholm
(see Map #5).   Over twice as much land has been purchased outside the city limits.   The City in 1966 owned land
approximately 40 kilometers (26 miles) outside the city. [30]
By retaining ownership and leasing the property, the City can
control land use for the public interest.

Of the housing construction within the municipal boundaries during 1966, 63.6 per cent was on municipally owned
real estate, leased to the occupant for a period of 60 years
with automatic 40-year extension if notice is not given.   The
rents are fixed for ten-year periods.   Municipal companies
built 43 per cent and cooperatives 20 per cent.   The remaining 37 per cent was built by development companies or
by private persons.   As of 1960, 21 per cent of the total
housing in Stockholm had been constructed by municipal companies, 16 per cent by cooperatives, and 63 per cent by development companies or private persons.   During the past
several years, about one-half of the land owned by the City
and reserved for housing had been made available to municipal companies.   The City also leases to private individuals
and companies for single-family and multiple-family housing.[31]
As a consequence, housing developed particularly since 1960
can be attributed in large part to official policy.

In addition to direct control of construction on municipally-owned property, standards for residential construction throughout Sweden is regulated by the National Housing
Board.   The standards are spelled out in detail in a publication entitled God Bostad (Good Housing).   Editions were prepared and published in 1960 and again in 1964. [32]   In terms
of room arrangements, climate control including sunlight,
shade and ventilation, closet and other storage space, and
physical equipment and facilities, the standards are high.

Map 5. Property Acquired by the City of Stockholm in the City as of 1966.

City Limits
City Property

Source: The Planning Division, Department of Building and Planning, City of Stockholm.

Special attention is given to play space for children, student
housing, housing for the retired and for the handicapped.
Standards for multiple-family construction in Stockholm are
supplemented by Planstandard 1965, prepared and published
by Stockholms Stadsbyggnadskontor (The Office of the Building Board), which includes the City Planning Office. Planstandard 1965 analyzes and establishes standards for different types of multiple-story structures, schools, children's
cottages, nursery schools, day nurseries, vacation centers,
traffic systems, parking facilities, and specifications for
protection zones between traffic and residences. [33] These
specifications, administered by the Building Board insure decent urban living conditions.

The City owns and leases, or directly administers,
recreation and beach areas within and outside the city boundaries, totalling 165 square kilometers, which provide 200
square meters per inhabitant[34] Including commercial harbors
in the category "open to public use," approximately two-
thirds of the waterfront within the city is open to the public. [35]

As of 1960, the urbanized land within the municipal
boundaries of Stockholm was 45. 8 per cent, land reserves
32. 7 per cent, planned open space 16 per cent, and agricultural use, 5. 5 per cent of the total. The above percentages
evidence the distribution of parks and open space, which distributed on three parts of the mainland and 15 or more islands escape verbal description. The park areas are not
large, segregated parks, but rather a system of linked
strips, easily accessible to the pedestrian. Concerning a
mile-long shore of Lake Mälaren, Mr. Peter Shepheard, recognized English architect and landscape designer, commented
in the 1950s,

> . . . here a natural and varied landscape has been
> created in which one can walk or stroll or picnic,
> where mothers can rest and children can play.

> Children's playgrounds are found everywhere in Stock-
> holm's parks, often placed deliberately where
> people can take pleasure in watching children at
> play.

> The scheme for Norr Mälarstrand resulted in the
> clearing out of some wharves and commercial
> buildings from part of the front to restore the

clean, bold sweep of groves and meadows. [36]

Mr. August Heckscher, Commissioner of Parks and
Administer of Recreation and Cultural Affairs for the City of
New York, writing in the autumn of 1967, commented about
the excellent balance between the natural and the man-made
environment in Stockholm. [37] The waters of Lake Mälaren
and the Baltic waters are available to the citizenry, as are
the shores of the Rhine to the citizenry of Cologne, and are
not cut off by expressways, commercial and warehousing facilities, and industry, as all too often occurs in the U.S.A.
This theme of the relation of the world of nature and the
world of the man-made, the ecological approach, is further
evidenced in the "new town" developments.

Since the beginning of the century, more effective
land-use planning and administration, special efforts in residential construction and serious attention to public facilities,
creating a pleasant environment in an urban setting, have
provided higher living standards in Stockholm and have initiated effective   planning for an improved metropolitan Stockholm.

A vital part of the current development of Stockholm
is the building of "new towns," some in the Outer City and
some beyond the administrative boundaries of the City, connected in all instances with the metropolitan center by means
of the rapid mass transit, underground or surface, and the
redevelopment of the central business district (CBD) into a
metropolitan center to which the citizenry will wish to come. [38]
This is the story of modern metropolitan planning in Stockholm.   It should be the subject of a substantial volume.
Here merely a few analytical observations as regards the results of this last stage of planning will be made, paying special attention to the major ingredients thereof: 1) New
towns,   2) Circulation, and 3) the CBD.

Relevant to the new towns is the neighborhood-com-
munity concept, which has played a significant role in recent
Stockholm urban planning.

For administrative purposes, Stockholm is divided into parishes and "town quarters" (stadsdel).   The Outer City
is organized into 11 parishes, each of which in turn is subdivided into two to 13 town quarters, totalling 93.   The Inner City is organized into 16 parishes and 19 town quarters
with little if any apparent relationship between their bounda-

ries. The parish demarcation serves church purposes and
is used for statistical reports by the Stockholm Office of Statistics. The town quarter demarcation is also used for official statistical reports. Neither the parish nor the town
quarter fits closely the socio-economic structure of today.

Göran Siedenbladh, Stockholm Planning Director, recognizes the Swedish indebtedness to the Americans and the
British for the "neighborhood planning concept." Siedenbladh
very properly uses the term "neighborhood" in analyzing
three aspects of the new towns when they were first established: 1) the functional aspect, "meaning that if suburbanites
were to have reasonable access to schools, shops, playgrounds, public transport and, if possible, places of work,
their dwellings must be grouped with respect to walking distances to the facilities;" 2) the social aspect, meaning that
these people would form a social unit; and 3) the architectural aspect, meaning that the neighborhood should be an architectural entity with obvious centers and edge. [39]

The Stockholm planners were thinking in terms of
10,000 population groupings. By 1950 it had been established
that a population of 10,000 was not sufficient to support "good
and complete shopping facilities." To meet that criteria,
some 25,000 people were needed. With this goal in mind,
four units with an average population of 23,000 were built.
With this change in population planning, a shift had been
made from the "neighborhood" concept of a social unit with
"face to face" contacts, to a "community" concept of an in-
stitutionally centered unit with indirect contacts through organizational channels.

In addition to the need for larger population aggregates to make "good and complete shopping centers" economically feasible, the attitudes of the residents of the new
towns, who had been surveyed on several occasions, showed
a desire for larger groupings. Furthermore, the increasing
ownership of automobiles was a motivating factor for the
change. The number of automobiles per 1,000 inhabitants
increased from 37 in 1950 to 175 as of January 1, 1962,
making Sweden the fourth-ranked country as regards num-
bered of registered passenger cars in relation to population,
surpassed only by the U.S., Canada, and Australia. [40]

C. F. Ahlberg, Director of Regional Planning, visual-
izes that with the increase in the use of the motor car the
area of influence of shopping centers will continue to grow.

For that reason the Regional Plan provides for an extension
of "several fairly large shopping and cultural centers with
areas of influence of 50,000 to 150,000 inhabitants."

The overall pattern of Greater Stockholm contemplates
around the nucleus (CBD) a compact formation of fairly dense
residential and business areas of different types (institutions,
wholesale trade, industry) for a distance of three to five kilometers (two to three miles). Surrounding this "inner Metropolitan area," which includes both the so-called Inner City
and certain adjacent areas, "there is a belt containing residential areas with both houses and blocks of flats, and there
is less accent on business and industry," extending from the
CBD approximately 15 kilometers (ten miles) in all directions.

> These strip-like built-up areas follow the main
> lines of communication from the City centre. These
> strips lead to a circle of demarcated communities,
> some 30-40 kilometers (20-25 miles) from the cen-
> tre. For these, industrial areas are assigned on
> a larger scale.
>
> The main structure of the plan is based on the fol-
> lowing argument. The central City area will be
> still the main business area, and the commuting
> traffic will be very extensive. In the period of the
> plan it is impossible--and for several reasons un-
> desirable--to rebuild this central region so that all
> commuting traffic relies on private cars. A public
> transport system is thus indispensable.[41]

The new towns have been situated along the railway
routes of the underground, which extend now from the center
of the city south, west, northeast, and will extend north and
east. Outside the urbanized portions of the city, the underground comes to the surface and the commuters can enjoy the
vistas of fields and forests of the open areas.

Vällingby, the first of the new towns, was offically
opened in 1954 ten kilometers west of the Old City Island by
automobile and about ten miles by rapid transit which swings
around in the Inner City underground. (The Vällingby community is situated in the southern portion of Spånga Parish
in the West End.) The railway enters the shopping center
underground and stops at the station 22 minutes after leaving
Sergels Torg, the central underground station in downtown

Stockholm, adjacent to Hötorget.   The trains arrive and leave every five minutes.   Parking space for 1,100 cars has been increased to accommodate 2,500 (600 in a parking garage and 1,900 open parking).   In connection with the underground station are bus stops and taxi stands.   The Vällingby Center has 193,750 square feet (18,000 square meters) of shopping surface, and 301,392 square feet (37,000 square meters) of space for other community services. [42]

About 80 shops were trading in the Center in 1964. Underground streets are provided for deliveries to the stores, leaving the shopping center surface free of motor traffic. Near the southern edge of the shopping center is a hotel, which includes a police station.   On the southwestern and northeastern corners of the Center are churches.   Other community institutions are a library, cinema, youth center and community center.   Fifty-three civic organizations were listed in 1966 as being members of the Community center, including Lions and Rotary Clubs, cooperative societies, boating and bridge clubs, and other organizations ranging on to political clubs, including the Conservative, Liberal, Social Democratic and Communist Parties.   The Center also has office space for health and welfare institutions, press branches, telephone and telegraph, and for physicians, dentists and other professional services.   There are, furthermore, excellent cafes, cafeterias and restaurants.

Apartment houses penetrate into the edges of the shopping center, having the shops on the ground floor.   Flat blocks, star-houses, low point-blocks and other multi-story residential structures extend 500 meters (approximately 500 yards) from the underground station; and from 500 to 1,000 meters are terraced houses (town houses) and detached single-family housing.   The experience of the Stockholm Passenger Company has established that these are the maximum distances which can be accepted, if demands from the local population for bus service to underground station are to be resisted. [43]   The development that has resulted, provides the overwhelming proportion of the dwelling units in three-story walk-ups (70 per cent), about 20 per cent in elevator high-rise buildings, and only 10 per cent in single-family houses and town houses.

C. F. Ahlberg describes Vällingby as follows,

Vällingby is built like a wheel, the community center--surrounded by a ring road--being the nave,

and the streets and pedestrian paths alternately being the spokes. The streets are surrounding en-
claves or precincts with children's playgrounds, a
nursery school and one or two local food shops of
their own. The interior of such an enclave is free
of motor traffic. [44]

Elementary schools are to be found along with the
children's playgrounds and nursery schools in the green
spaces within the communities. High schools and trade
schools, however, are placed in the community centers within easy access to the rapid mass transit. Furthermore community use of the assembly rooms, gymnasia and swimming
pools is arranged. Mindful of variations in the use of the
term "community," the population of the Vällingby Community
as of 1960 has been given as 63,000.

In 1960, the second new town was opened: Farsta,
ten kilometers south of the Old City Island. (Farsta Community is situated in the Farsta Parish in the South End.)
The architects, Backström and Reinius, who designed Vällingby, also designed Farsta. Interesting variations from the
Vällingby Plan, however, are noticeable. The railway remains at the ground level through the shopping center, thus
providing additional underground street and garage space for
deliveries and storage space for trucks and other motorized
equipment. In Vällingby, a "solid," a large shop building,
around which the central facilities are grouped is the nucleus
of shopping center, while in Farsta, an open space is the
nucleus, the main central square (oblong in shape). The
shopping center has a total of 302,000 square feet (28,000
square meters of shopping space), which was justified even
though the anticipated residential population to be served was
less than in the case of Vällingby--by the nearness of Nynäsvägen, a major highway at the southern edge of the Stockholm MA. There is also a substantial increase in the space
available for other community services: 613,548 square feet
(57,000 square meters), based upon the experience of Vällingby, built six years earlier. Parking space was originally
provided for 23,000 cars, 600 of which were in parking garages. This increase over the original planned for Vällingby
was also based on the nearness of Nynäsvägen, therefore the
expectation of customers coming by automobile, as well as
the general expected increase in the use of the automobile.
Less than one year after the opening of the center the parking facilities were found to be inadequate.

There is a noticeable increase in the average dwelling
standard in terms of the number of rooms and floor space
in comparison with Vällingby, due in part to greater demands
for convenience and in part to the increase in average size
of families. Twice the proportion of Farsta's population is
accommodated in single-family and town houses than in Vällingby. The apartment buildings, however, have been made
larger and higher, so that one third of the residents in Farsta live in multi-story structures eight to 15 stories in height.

Another difference not involving planning that is
worthy of notice is the construction of the Vällingby Shopping
Center by a municipal society, and Farsta by a private company.

The basic pattern of Vällingby and Farsta, however,
are similar. In both there is a basic reliance on the underground for commuting connection with downtown Stockholm.
Both shopping centers provide pedestrian-only streets and
ample space and facilities for customer rest and relaxation.
Farsta has proceeded one step further and provided complete
separation of pedestrian and vehicular traffic. In Vällingby,
11- to 12-story blocks of flats surround and penetrate into
the shopping center. In Farsta, two groups of 14- to 16-
story point-blocks are included in the shopping center, situated at the side of the two parking garages. In both, apartment and multiple-story residential buildings are provided
for a distance of 500 meters around the shopping center, and
terraced houses and single-family houses for a distance of
500 to 1,000 meters. Both communities are organized into
neighborhoods, at least four in the Farsta Community: Gub-
bängen, Hökarängen, Sköndal, and the central Farsta neighborhood. Göran Siedenbladh specifies seven neighborhoods,
which are served by the main center. Open green areas are
provided in both communities with pedestrian-only paths, sep-
arating motor and pedestrian traffic and also providing space
for recreational facilities and schools. Ample provisions
are made in both centers for community organizations, their
headquarters, and cultural programs and activities. Opportunities for employment have been provided in both communities. In Johannelund, about one mile west of the Vällingby
Shopping Center and part of the Vällingby Community, an industrial area was developed. In Raksta, immediately east
of the Vällingby neighborhood, a large office block providing
employment for 3000 has been erected. The Swedish Tele-
communications Service has shown interest in Farsta, has
built facilities, and will expand these facilities. Furthermore

an insurance company has built a branch absorbing 1000 office workers from their central office in Downtown Stockholm.   There has been no attempt in either community, however, to provide employment for all employable persons.
The working population in Vällingby in 1960 was 26,900.   The number of jobs in the community was 9,600.   The working population in Farsta was 20,200, and the number of jobs in the community was 5,800.

Mindful again of the variations in the use of the term "community," the total population of the Farsta Community as of 1960 has been given as 45,900.

The Skärholmen area has the largest community shopping center hitherto developed.   (Skärholmen is situated in the southwestern portion of Hägerstens Parish in the South End.)   It is located on an underground line extending southwest from the Stockholm CBD, approximately the same distance from the city center as Vällingby or Farsta.   This community shopping center is expected to serve a rather large hinterland, larger than the community.   A quarter of a million population is the estimate.   A new feature for the center, which was opened in 1967, is a hotel with 180 apartments and shops for retired people.   Four neighborhoods are planned, one of which, Bredäng, has been built with a neighborhood shopping center which is larger than the normal Stockholm neighborhood shopping centers, and includes a day-nursery, school and church among its cultural facilities.

The three communities and shopping centers described above, Vällingby, Farsta and Skärholmen, were planned and built within the administrative boundaries of Stockholm in the Outer City.   The remaining communities and shopping centers to be mentioned are on the drawing boards at the present writing for development outside of the administrative boundaries of the city.   C. F. Ahlberg states,

> In many suburban municipalities existing built-up
> areas are scattered and unsystematically planned.
> Most residential areas consist of one-family houses
> on large plots.   The task is to reorganize and
> complete the physical community structure of these
> areas as well as to add new neighborhood units
> and communities on the undeveloped suburban
> land. [45]

Plans have been prepared for developments in the fol-

lowing municipalities, all north of Stockholm: Järfälla,
Täby, Märsta, and the Järvafältet area, which involves four
suburban municipalities (Järfälla, Solna, Sollentuna and Sundy-
berg) and Stockholm. This area, a former military training
field, is a large project, for which the Stockholm Regional
Planning Office has prepared a general land-use plan and the
Stockholm City Planning staff has prepared a draft master
plan for the portion within the Stockholm administrative limits. (See Map #3). The five municipalities have organized
a joint committee. A competition among Scandinavian planners was held in September 1966, for which judges were selected by the joint committee, and decisions on the selection
of a planning agency for the entirety of the area were made
by the end of the year. Thereafter, the joint committee
made the necessary decisions as regards the plan and the selection and signing of a contract with a builder. [46]

All of the communities and shopping centers in the
suburban municipalities mentioned above, with the exception
of Märsta, are situated within 25 kilometers of the city core.
Of the employed population, 40 to 60 per cent commute to
the Stockholm CBD, and are therefore not properly designated as "satellite towns" in the British sense. One exception to this generalization is the new town of Märsta, which
is being developed to house the employees of the new international airport of Arlanda. Märsta is 25 miles north of the
Old City Island in Stockholm and is a suburban Kommun within the Stockholm MA. The old kommun of Märsta had a population of 2,000. The new town is being planned for 40,000.

Comparable data is available for five of the community centers. [47] The floor area for shopping purposes in the
five community centers is in total 1,388,592 square feet
(129,000 square meters) and the floor area for other community purposes totals 2,933,190 square feet (281,500 square
meters). Of special significance is the comparative amount
of space devoted to commercial purposes and to other community purposes.

There is ample evidence of a willingness to experi-
ment in planning of new town developments. This, in the
opinion of the author, does not mean a lack of basic principles and policy, but rather a willingness continuously to question both principle and policy in the light of changing circum-
stance. Seven policies have remained firm and unchanged:

    1.   The provision of ample open, green space both

within and between the new towns and the built-up Inner City
and the new town developments. This policy is supported by
the municipal ownership of 83 per cent of the land in the
Outer City. It is also supported by Swedish law. The advantage of this to the general public includes not only the
publicly-owned land, but also the privately-owned land. According to an ancient "all men's right," anyone is permitted
to go on any privately-owned land that is not directly connected with a dwelling, provided no damage is done to trees
or crops. Furthermore, Swedish law specifies that agricultural land shall not without special permission be sold or
purchased for any other purpose, nor be acquired by anyone
who does not prove qualifications in agriculture. For these
reasons, the open green spaces will be preserved as such
and will remain open for general public use.

     2.   The location of new town developments within the
Outer City or the Inner Suburban Section along a rapid mass
transit route or an extension of a rapid mass transit route,
connected with one of the underground systems.

     3.   The routing of motor traffic through the green
belts which surround the communities.

     4.   The placement of recreational facilities, nursery
schools, and elementary schools in the green spaces within
the communities.

     5.   The placement of high schools and trade schools
in the community centers.

     6.   The provision of ample space for non-commercial
community services and social and cultural activities in each
new development in the community center, in the neighborhood centers, or in both.

     7.   The provision in new towns of multi-story housing
within 500 meters of the community center and terraced or
single-family housing beyond the 500 meter distance.

     The nature of the Stockholm economy dictates the ne-
cessity of underground connections with downtown Stockholm.
This city has become more and more the nerve center for
the national economy as well as for the national government.
Administrative headquarters for private and governmental enterprises are being concentrated in the Stockholm CBD. Personnel in these administrative headquarters need speedy per-

son-to-person contacts for effective service and effective decision-making, therefore they cannot be effectively dencentral-
ized.

The pattern of employment location in metropolitan
Stockholm was found to be the same in 1960 as the pattern of
residential location 20 years earlier: 60 per cent   in the Inner City and 20 per cent each in the Outer City and the suburbs. [48]   In brief, while residences have decreased, employment has not.   Certain types of enterprises, which are not
dependent upon a downtown location can and have decentralized, which is to be expected; however because of the changing nature of the Stockholm economy, a reduction of the overall employment in the Inner City is not anticipated.

Ever since World War II, the Swedish government has
attempted to discourage industrial development in and around
Stockholm, permitting it to remain a decision-making center.
As early as 1950, of those employed in Greater Stockholm,
39 per cent were employed in industry and 50 per cent in
trade and public service, while for the entire urban economy
of Sweden the corresponding percentages were 54 and 36.
In 1960, industry and handicrafts employed 28 per cent of
the working force in Stockholm.   By 1965, the percentage
had declined to 24.4.   In 1965, 20.1 per cent were employed
in Public Administration and 31.7 per cent in business, totalling 51.8 per cent.   The next largest category was "communications," wherein 9.6 per cent were employed.   Among
the remaining 14.2 per cent were a wide variety of occupational classifications, including agriculture in the Outer City.
The Stockholm Region (City and County), during the decade of
1955-64 inclusive, decreased in the national proportion of
employed persons in industry from 14.8 to 13.9 per cent.
It is worthy of note that the engineering classification, which
is large throughout Sweden, employed three-fifths of the industrial labor force in the Stockholm Region.   Thereafter,
the printing industry accounted for 14 per cent, the foods industries 7, and chemical technology 7 per cent. [49]   The overwhelming proportion of the labor is demonstrably highly
skilled.

The industry that is in Stockholm is encouraged by
making available sites along railway rights-of-way and along
the major motorways.   Rights-of-way between industrial and
residential property are at least 100 meters in width, which
makes possible a public screen in addition to the screening
by private industry.

The advantages of decentralization within the Stockholm MA, particularly for industry, have been stressed continuously since World War II both from the point of view of
the core city and the suburbs. Traffic-wise it would be advantageous for employees to live near their place of employment. Professor Ahlberg stated the case from another Hy-
resgästernas Sparkasse- och Byggnadsförening (Tenants' Savings and Building Society), point of view in a joint publication of the nationwide building cooperative, and the Swedish
Association of Town and Country Planning in 1956:

> Children who grow up in a purely residential area
> obtain an unreal conception of the community in
> which they are living. It would be valuable both
> for their intellectual and emotional development and
> for the direction of their more mature interests if
> productive work was to enter more directly into
> their field of experience and to influence their im-
> agination and their play. It may prove stimulating
> also for adults to have an element of working life
> in residential districts.
>
> Apart from motives of environmental policy, the
> proposal to introduce "mixed suburbs" appears to
> be the most realistic. [50]

The Inner City has 1. 5 per cent of the land, 30 per
cent of the population and over three-fifths of the employment in metropolitan Stockholm. The portion of the Inner
City, which the Tunnelbaneplan för Stor-Stockholm Report
calls "kärnområdet" (the core of the Inner City) has 100, 000
employed persons, but only 7, 000 residents. For the entire
Inner City, however, the number of residents and employed
persons are approximately the same, slightly over 300, 000. [51]
This situation obviously does not mean a reduction of daily
population movement across boundaries, and more important-
ly on the streets, over the bridges, and on public transport.
In the Appendix, showing Table 15, population and employment in the Stockholm MA in 1960, gives an idea of the
daily commuting traffic. The need for rapid mass transit is
obvious.

The development of an underground system has been
debated since 1930. Planning of the underground commenced
in 1941. Prior to actual construction, preparations were
made for such an eventuality. In the more recently built
"new towns" and suburbs, extensions of tramlines were com-

pletely separated from all other traffic and the rights-of-way made wide enough for the underground and/or metropolitan trains.

Construction on the underground in the Inner City started in 1945. By 1952, Stockholm had two underground lines, one in the south and one in the west. The connecting and most essential link through the CBD and serving the Old Town was missing. The two lines poured people into the CBD while the street network could not absorb the surface traffic which resulted in transferring from one to the other.[52] By 1957 underground service was in operation throughout the Inner City with a total of 41 kilometers of double track and 47 stations. This represented the first of the proposed three "diagnolsystems." A portion of the second "diagnolsystem," which will serve the northeast and southwest, was opened in 1964. The third "diagnolsystem" will serve the northwest and east. The three subway systems when completed will provide 11 branches: six on the mainland south of the CBD and five on the mainland north of the CBD, all within 40 minutes' travel time including transfer time from the T-Centralen in the central business district.[53] The 11 branches will serve seven geographic sectors, three south and four north.

Population requirements outside the Inner City for each underground sector have been estimated at 100,000 minimum and 200,000 maximum. For each system, the estimated population requirement is 400,000. Policy as regards the location of individual stations has been that a station should be so sited that it is surrounded by land of a kind which can be developed to its fullest extent. The minimum distance between the stations should be 1,100 yards and the maximum 2,200 yards. A resident population of 10,000 can be handled by one station outlet. An increase to 15,000 justifies two permanent outlets.[54] Great stress has been given to "traffic standards:" comfort, speed and dependability, also to other amenities for passenger convenience and pleasure. In the CBD, walking distance to the nearest underground station is at most 250 meters. Particularly noteworthy is the attention to design, color and the station environment based on purely aesthetic principles.[55] Stockholm has financed about 20 outstanding artists in the presentation of contemporary compositions and designs on the walls and pillars of the underground stations as well as in the tubes of the underground.

In order to construct the first underground line in the
CBD, because the cut and cover method was used and because
the streets were so narrow, it was necessary to demolish
all the buildings along the route.   The second underground
system is bored deeper than the first, in fact it is bored
through granite, and the third system is planned likewise,
thus causing no disturbance above ground and reducing the
cost of underground construction.   Except for the Brunkel-
bergasen, a high gravel ridge, which extends north-south
through the central business district to a point south of the
present Sergels Torg, there is normally a ten meter depth
to granite.   Private ownership of land extends no more than
two floors below ground level, therefore the City does not have
to purchase property rights for the underground tunneling,
except for the stations.   The current plans provide for five
underground levels, plus a sixth tunnel for utilities.   The
first level is reserved for pedestrian use, the second and
third for rapid mass transit, and the fourth and fifth for
motorized traffic.   The deepest penetration into the granite
is 20 meters (60 feet).   The four-track, two-level line for
rapid mass transit occupy levels corresponding to the third
and fourth basements in the new buildings.   Direct entrances
from the underground have been provided to hotels.   A tunnel leads under a heavily travelled thoroughfare from the
Sergels Torg station to the central station of the main line
railway, thus the local underground is indirectly connected
with the European railway network.

Any greater depth than two floors into the earth would
hit water level.   Private builders must guarantee to the City
that water will be kept out.   Several hundreds of pumps are
now in operation for private construction as well as the public underground construction.   These pumps need to be in-
spected with painstaking regularity. [56]

On December 17, 1964, an agreement between the City
and the County of Stockholm was consumated to form a compact governing local traffic within metropolitan Stockholm.
The compact was approved by the city council and the county
legislative body in 1965.   A new company for all public
transport in Greater Stockholm was formed to take over and
develop the operations of all the different companies operating in Greater Stockholm.   The compact also provided for the
continued extensions of the underground systems and the administration of the three systems.   In the same year, the national parliament authorized national appropriations from the
automobile tax in the form of grants to cover 95 per cent of

the construction costs of the underground systems.   Prior to
1965,   Stockholm had invested in the system 1. 75 billion
kronor ($350 million).   A similar amount, it is estimated,
is needed to complete the present plans.   The Underground
Lines Committee of the Stockholm Executive Board (Stadskollegiet) in 1965 estimated that the proposed extensions
should be completed and ready for operation by 1980. [57]

          Motorized traffic has not been ignored.   A Traffic
Route Plan for Stockholm was submitted by the Master Planning Commission on February 20, 1960.   As far as Lower
Norrmalm is concerned, the major traffic arteries will go
either underground or around.   In addition to the levels for
motorized traffic in the underground tubes, service streets
are underground.   Furthermore, the Traffic Route Plan of
1960 provides a ring road around the CBD, which is partially completed.   To the northeast, it comes as close as one
and one half kilometers to the CBD, but to the south four
and one half kilometers away.   The Traffic Route Plan also
includes inside the Ring two traffic routes of the same standard as the Ring Road, which form a cross over the Inner
City.   Otherwise, motorways, having at least a six-lane traffic capacity and multiple-level crossings, enter the Ring
from all important outer sectors, and do not penetrate into
the Inner City.   The boulevards and streets of the Inner City
are no longer considered to be chief traffic arteries. [58]

          The purpose of both boulevards and streets have been
carefully reconsidered.   What type of street is preferable
as a shopping street: the narrow, pedestrian street or the
wide street with broad sidewalks, big display windows and
lively traffic? Stockholm has excellent examples of both.   The
narrow streets were kept in the historic portion of the city.
The boulevard is now neither a traffic artery nor a shopping
street.   Göran Siedenbladh stated the case for the boulevard
as follows:

          It has returned to what it was meant to be when
          introduced in Paris more than a hundred years
          ago: an open space in the city centre, which
          should enable people to move about more freely. [59]

          With the emphasis on space and freedom for pedestri-
an movement in downtown Stockholm, the implications of this
for the street scene, and the overall interest in the appearance of the city, advertising on buildings came to be regulated strictly by the Local Building Authority (Byggnadsnämn-

den) in the City.   The national Highway Law applies to billboards in the countryside. [60]

Control of parking facilities makes limitation of motorized traffic into the central business district possible. A
1956 traffic study showed a need for 35,000 parking spaces.
Eliminating the long-term parking, the planned parking, capacity in the City Plan of 1962 was limited to 20,000, based
upon the estimated capacity of the street network. All curb
parking is prohibited.   Parking is provided in multi-story
parking structures above ground (12,000 spaces) and below
ground (8,000 spaces).   By 1966, sixteen parking garages
had been built in Lower Norrmalm and approximately 40 in
the Inner City.   Parking garages have been distributed so
that walking distance will not, as a rule, be more than 250
meters.   The restricted parking capacity (20,000 parking
spaces) is defended on the grounds that the standard of public transportation is high. [61]   A projection of commuters'
use of public transport on their way to work from 1962 to
1980 is as follows:

	1961	1980
To downtown area	87%	90%
To other parts, Inner City	71%	50%
To nearby suburbs	52%	15%
To other suburbs	35%	15%

The City Plan of 1962 stresses the vital economic, administrative and cultural importance of the Stockholm CBD to
the entire region.   While this plan covers a wider portion of
the CBD, it gives special attention to Lower Norrmalm and
the immediately surrounding area.   In accordance with the
above-mentioned emphasis, the redevelopment along Sergelsgatan provided two central stations for the underground systems (one at Hötorget and one at the new Sergels Torg); five
18-story office blocks (slab buildings) with two-story terrace
buildings for shops, the roofs of which are used as a high-
level pedestrian circulation system; a pedestrian-only street;
and trees, bushes, patches of green, flowers, playground
space, water, benches and outdoor cafes on both levels.
David Hellden, Architekt, SAR, describes the project as follows,

The five high blocks have not been conceived with
a view to collecting together a mass of offices and
shops, but in order to realize a modern town plan-

ning idea, namely the creation above traffic level
of a kind of metropolitan park from which tall
buildings arise, surrounded by sun, light and air.[62]

Three basement floors provide car-parking in the middle and lower basements and loading bays, storage space and
shops in the upper basement. Service traffic thus has a segregated system of high capacity, permitting pedestrians to
move on its own circulation space unmolested by vehicular
traffic of any sort.

At the north end of the redevelopment, two vital parts
were retained from the pre-redevelopment: one, the historic
Hötorget (Haymarket Square), where flowers, vegetables and
fruits have been sold for centuries and continue to be sold
as in the past. And two, facing the Haymarket Square is the
famous Konserthus (Concert Hall) in front of which stands
Carl Milles' "Orpheus Fountain." In the redevelopment a-
long Sergelsgatan at the south end of the Hötorget on a roof
terrace is a little theater (Sergels Teatern). At the south
end of the redevelopment is Sergels Torg with Stockholm's
version of London's Hyde Park corner, where anyone can
"hold forth" on anything and everything without legal limitation. Mr. Richard Joseph depicts one unique aspect of Sergels Torg as follows:

A long stone wall lines one side of the square, and
this serves as a bulletin board for whatever slogans
or obscenities happen to be currently popular. The
writings last until late each night, when a street
cleaner comes around to wash them off--leaving a
clean blackboard for the kids' scribblings the following day. [63]

At the north end of Hötorget in the evenings, crowds
gather just in case of a "happening." Activity is characteristic of the Hötorget-Sergelsgatan-Sergels Torg redevelopment, which has been described as a "futuristic city of sky-
scrapers and glittering pedestrian malls"; however it is more
than that. It has become a center of human activity.

This redevelopment has become one nerve center for
metropolitan Stockholm; however not the one and only. There
is sufficient geographic scatter of interest in the CBD to keep
people moving and to avoid a too heavy concentration of
people in any one place: numerous "squares," parks, including the island park, Skansen, within walking distance of the

CBD; and along the shores of the mainland and the CBD islands, places where children can play, oldsters sit and watch,
and people of any age rest and relax; also theaters, various
types of museums, restaurants, and in Nybroplan (an open
space on Nybroviken which empties into the Baltic waters),
The Stockholm Pavilion, within which is housed models, maps,
drawings and other presentations of Stockholm's Development
and Redevelopment Plans. There are the usual large city
night clubs and the less usual cellar "boites" like Bobadilla,
once a series of caves belonging to a thirteenth-century mon-
astery, but gone is the monastic mood. Now the vaults of
Bobadilla vibrate with the overpowering din of electronic string
ensembles. The small boutiques and the even newer disco-
tiques, where psychedelic light shows are projected, are likewise popular with the younger set. Along the shores of the
mainland CBD are spots where sight-seeing and pleasure
boats stop for passengers. In addition, residential land and
building use has been protected and retained even in Gamla
Stan, so that people are moving about throughout the CBD
night and day. Furthermore, it is a place to which people
are interested in coming.

The development of "new towns" with open spaces within and around them, the provision of parks, playgrounds and
publicly-used shoreline in the Inner as well as the Outer City,
the improvements in housing, the redevelopment of portions
of the central business district and the protection of other
portions; the provision of rapid mass transit, (which becomes
underground transport in the Inner City); also cooperation with
the other governments in the metropolitan area, have created
a situation which in 1961 won the Abercrombie Award from
the International Union of Architects (for "the organic growth
and internal reconstruction of Stockholm and its region") as
"an example to all other cities because they show foresight
in land policy and intelligent co-ordination of the many problems confronting the modern city. [64] More vital is the development of a metropolis in which people can enjoy living.

Notes

1. Atmer, Thomas and Linn, Bjorn, Contemporary Swedish
    Architecture (Stockholm: The Swedish Institute, 1963),
    p. 1.

2. Wendt, Paul F., "Lessons from the Old World for
    America's City Builders," Appraisal Journal, Vol. 29,

No. 3, July 1961, p. 389.   Requoted in part in Urban
Land, Vol. 26, No. 7, July-August, 1967, p. 10-11.
The House Beautiful in a Special Issue, January 1968,
entitled "Scandinavia: Exploring a Land where Home
Comes First" emphasizes this aspect of life in these
countries.   The material is based on research in Denmark, Finland, Norway and Sweden by a House Beautiful editorial group--Marion Gough, Frances Heard,
Elizabeth Sverbeyeff and Warren Stokes--and photo-
graphed with them by Howard Graff.

3.   Holm, Lennart, "The Master Plan for Stockholm: A
     summary of some important aspects," att bo, Special
     Issue, 1953, p. 1.

4.   During the early Middle Ages, Sigtuna was the capitol
     of Sweden.

5.   Holmgren, Per, "About Town Planning in Sweden with
     particular reference to Stockholm" (unpub. condensed
     version of a series of lectures held in Great Britain
     in April 1967, p. 7-8.)

6.   Interview with Mr. E. G. Westman, Stadjuristen, City
     of Stockholm, Stadshuset, June 1, 1966.   Byggnadslag,
     June 30, 1947, Section 44a.

7.   Interview with Lars Almström, Director, Stockholm
     Chamber of Commerce, June 28, 1966.   Lag om
     Byggnadsminen, December 9, 1960, Sections 1, 2 & 5.

8.   Lag om Expropriation, May 12, 1917, Section 108 (De-
     cember 11, 1964).

9.   Interview with Lars Almström.

10. Interview with Mr. Yngve Larson, former Borgarråd,
     Trafik och Stadsbyggen Roteln.   At the time of the
     interview Dr. Larson was writing a history of Stock-
     holm under a commission from the City's Municipal
     Archives, May 17, 1966.   See Saneringen i Gamla
     Stan (Reconstruction in the Old City) prepared by the
     1960 Committee on the Old City.

11. Byström, Olof, "The Old City," Kontur Swedish Design
     Annual, published by the Swedish Society for Industri-
     al Design, 1965, p. 14.

12. Ibid.

13. In 1966, the City Museum was doubled in size at a cost of four million kronor with an impressive courtyard, surrounded by the wings of the building on three sides and the sea on the north side, thus protected from the noises of the city.

14. Interview with Mr. Almström.

15. Holgren, Per, Op. cit., p. 7-8.

16. Garpe, Joakim, "Stockholm at the Opening of the 1960s," Stockholm regional and city planning (Published by the Planning Commission of the City of Stockholm), 1964, p. 23-24.

17. Interview with Mr. Per Holm, Editor, Plan Tidskrift, June 9, 1966.

18. Planstandard, 1965, prepared and published by the Stockholm City Office of the Building Board, p. 13.

19. Interview with Mr. Göran Siedenbladh, Director, Department of City Planning, Nämndehuset, Room 5101, June 20, 1966.

20. Stockholm Office of Statistics, Monthly Statistical Review, 1967, No. 2, Table V, p. 10*. Unless otherwise specified, the statistical data in the remainder of this chapter are taken from the Stockholm Office of Statistics, Monthly Statistical Reviews.

21. Letter from the Stockholm Real Estate Office, September 6, 1967.

22. International Urban Studies Project, Institute of Public Administration, New York City, Stockholm Report (unpublished), January 1966.

23. Central Bureau of Statistics, Statistical Abstract of Sweden, 1965, Table 32, p. 43.

24. Ibid.

25. Material from Stockholm's Real Estate Office, September 6, 1968.

26. See Table 12, Appendix.

27. See Table 3, Appendix.

28. Siedenbladh, Göran, "Stockholm: A Planned City,"
     Scientific American, Vol. 213, No. 3, September
     1965, p. 107.

29. Ibid.

30. Letter from Mrs. Carin Linden, Public Relations Offi-
     cer, Stockholm City Real Estate Office, September
     6, 1967.

31. Ibid.

32. God Bostad i Dag och i Morgon, prepared and pub-
     lished by Kungliga Bostadsstyrelsen, April 1964.

33. Planstandard 1965, prepared and published by Stock-
     holm's Stadsbyggnadskontor, January 7, 1965.

34. Calmfors, Hans, Town Clerk, Local Self-Government
     in Stockholm, "A Short Presentation" (Stockholm,
     April 1966), p. 21.

35. Letter from Mr. Percy Bargholtz, Assistant to the
     Director, Department of Planning and Building Con-
     trol, October 3, 1968.

36. Shepheard, Peter, Modern Gardens (N.Y.: Frederick
     A. Praeger, 1953); Excerpts from p. 120-128.

37. Heckscher, August, "Scandinavia Observed," House
     Beautiful, Special Issue, January 1968, Vol. 110,
     No. 1, p. 88-89.

38. The so-called "new towns" are not new towns in the
     British sense of self-sufficient urban units, but sub-
     divisions, large enough to be full-scale communities.
     The one exception is the recently planned town of
     Märsta.

39. Siedenbladh, Göran, "Planning Problems in Stockholm,"
     Stockholm regional and city planning (Published by the
     Planning Commission of the City of Stockholm, 1964),
     p. 58.

40.   U. S. National Industrial Conference Board, Road Maps
      of Industry, September 3, 1963.

41.   Ahlberg, C. F. , Director of Regional Planning, "The
      Regional Plan for the Stockholm Area," (1961), Stock-
      holm regional and city planning, 1964, p. 51-52.

42.   The data given in these descriptions of new towns and
      community shopping centers are taken from Professor
      C. F. Ahlberg, Regional Planning Director, Giorgio
      Gentili, Venetian architect, Professor Kell Astrom,
      Architect and City Planner, the Stockholm Chamber
      of Commerce, and personal visits during May and
      June, 1966.

43.   Holmgren, Per, "Integration of Public Transport with
      Urban Development in Stockholm," paper delivered on
      the 16th of September, 1965 to the Town and Country
      Planning Summer School, St. Andrews, Great Britain
      (Mimeographed), p. 4.

44.   Ahlberg, C. F. , "Shopping Centers and Satellite Towns
      in the Stockholm Region." Lecture given at a study
      conference on Regional Planning and Retailing at the
      Gottlieb Duttweiter Institute for Economic and Social
      Studies, Zurich, February 25, 1965. (Duplicated by
      Kungliga Högskolan, Institutionen for Stadsbyggnad),
      p. 2.

45.   Ahlberg, C. F. , Ibid. , p. 5.

46.   Interview with Mr. Kurt Berg, Planner, City of Stock-
      holm Department of City Planning, June 3, 1966.

48.   Stadskollegiets Utlåtanden och Memorial, Bihang nr. 85,
      Tunnelbaneplan for stor-Stockholm. Förslag avgivet
      av Generalplaneberedningens Tunnelbanekommittee,
      1965, p. 7.

49.   See Table 14, Appendix.

50.   Ahlberg, C. F. , "An Outline of a Regional Plan for the
      Stockholm Area," att bo and Plan (joint edition), 1956,
      p. 35-36.

51.   Tunnelbaneplan for Stor-Stockholm, 1965, p. 18-19.

52. Holmgren, Per, Op. cit. , p. 8-9.

53. Tunnelbaneplan for Stor-Stockholm, p. 28-29. Map
      shows the travel time on the various branches on the
      different sectors.

54. Holmgren, Per, Op. cit. , p. 14.

55. Roman, Kristian, "Art Takes the Subway," Kontur
      Swedish Design Annual, 1965, published by the Swed-
      ish Society for Industrial Design, p. 16-25.

56. Interview with Dr. Gunnar Asvärn, Gatukontoret, Stock-
      holm, May 17, 1966.

57. Tunnelbaneplan for Stor-Stockholm, 1965, p. 13-15.

58. A Traffic Route Plan for Stockholm. English summary
      of the Comprehensive Traffic plan submitted by the
      Master Planning Commission of Stockholm (Stockholm:
      Statens Reproductions Anstalt) 1960, p. 10-16.

59. Siedenbladh, Göran, Op. cit. , p. 62.

60. Letter from Mr. E. G. Westman, Stadsjuristen, City
      of Stockholm, October 25, 1968.
         Byggnadslagsstiftningen med anmärkninger och
      sakregister utgivna av A. Bexelius, Justieombudsman,
      A. Nordenstam, Overstathållare, och V. Korlof,
      Regeringsråd (Stockholm: P. A. Norstedt och Söner
      Förlag, 1964.)
         Grunddragen av Byggnadslagstiftningen: 3. Regler-
      ingen av enstaka bebyggelse, p. 28.
         B. S. sec. 53, par. 1, sec. 55 & 66.
         Anmärkningar, p. 455 & 456.

61. 1962 års cityplan, Åke Hedtjärn och Stig Johnson,
      March 27, 1963. Utformning: Axel Vänje, Stads-
      kollegiets Reklamkommittee (Stockholm: Sjösteens,
      1963), p. 26.

62. Hellden, David, "Första Höghuset i Hötorgscity, Stock-
      holm," The Swedish Architectural Review, No. 11,
      1962, p. 298.

63. Joseph, Richard, "Stockholm Swings to the Time of Its
      Youth," Chicago Tribune, June 16, 1968.

64. Journal of the American Institute of Planners, Vol.
     XXVIII, No. 4, Nov. 1962, p. 220. Larson, Yngve,
     "Building a City and a Metropolis," Stockholm Re-
     gional and City Planning, p. 8-9.

Chapter IX

STOCKHOLM: POLICY FORMATION

Although local self-government has deep roots in the
Scandinavian countries, the forms which originated in pagan
times did not last. In the Twelfth Century, the introduction
of Christianity gave rise to a new unit of government, the
parish (socken). Originally a purely ecclesiastical organization, the parish in due course of time assumed a few secular
duties, such as the care of the poor, public health, and public education, which helped to revive public interest in local
government.

The cities developed from centers for pagan worship,
justice and trade. Members of different trades formed
guilds to protect their economic interests, and the cities became strictly regulated societies, governed by one group,
the burghers. Since the burghers needed royal protection,
leadership was exercised in the cities by a royal official.
This official was later replaced by a burgomaster (borgmäs-
tare), elected or nominated locally. The burgomaster and
his counsellors formed the magistrate, a body with partly
judicial and partly administrative duties, while the aldermen
of the city formed its representative body. This organization of municipal government remained in effect until the reforms of 1862, issued as royal decrees. The powers and
priviliges of the burghers and guilds were abolished. Municipal decisions were thereafter made either in a general
city meeting of all eligible citizens or by a representative
body, the city council. An executive committee, elected by
the council, formed the executive, while the magistrate, appointed by the Crown in its administrative capacity, was retained to supervise the activities of the city administration.
The basis of the local system established in 1862 still remains in force. Subsequent local government legislation,
however, has been passed as statute law, eliminating the
magistrate. [1]

The franchise depended on the size of the taxes paid.

A wealthy person had a larger number of votes than a person lacking wealth.   In 1909 the number of votes to be cast by one single man was limited to 40.   Full local democracy, in the sense that practically all adults should have an equal vote, was not established until 1918.

Concerning local self determination (home rule in the U. S.), the Local Government Act of 1930 took a first step by providing that the primary communes (excluding the provinces of counties) had to take care of "common matters of order and economy," provided that the matters had not been entrusted to any other authority. [2]   In 1948 the basic competence rule in the Local Government Act was changed, and this change was repeated in the Local Government Act of 1955, "The local authority should administer its own affairs." [3]

The decisions of a communal council within its autonomous (non-statutory) powers may be subject to inquiry only if an inhabitant of the commune lodges a complaint on the matter.   The complaint is submitted to the county government (länsstyrelsen), and appeal may be made to the Supreme Administrative Court (regeringsrätten).   A vital feature of this procedure is that the council decision may not be altered by the regeringsrätfen and the council may not be ordered to pass another resolution, or make another decision. The council decision may only be voided or left unchanged. Furthermore, only in the instances in which complaints are lodged and the decisions are voided are the decisions in question invalid.   Similar decisions by other councils, which were not subject to complaint, remain in force.   It is also significant that neither municipal auditors nor a state or local authority with the exception specified above have the right to challenge the decisions of a local council. [4]

The Supreme Administrative Court has approved the following types of activities: communes may purchase land as sites for houses and industries.   They may purchase and operate public utilities (tramways, subways, buses, gas and electricity works, markets and harbors).   They may own and operate hotels and restaurants which are considered important for the commune, build official residences for county doctors and veterinarians and contribute to maintenance of a dispensary chemist's shop.   The commune may also contribute to various social and cultural activities from arranging public dances to operating theaters, museums and schools of music. [5]

In accordance with the principle of equality of status, particular members or groups must neither be favored nor discriminated against. For this reason, communal decisions to support private industry through subscription to stocks or shares have been declared illegal. Neither does the commune have the right to relinquish property without compensation to any industrial enterprise for expansion. Furthermore, it may not furnish loans to any enterprise in order to prevent its leaving the commune. [6]

The communal activities elaborated in the paragraphs above and the principles involved have concerned the voluntary, nonstatutory functions. An important part of the communal activities and the largest part of their expenditure are their numerous statutory duties; nevertheless, the communes have a broad sweep of "home rule." This is a far cry from the "few secular duties, such as the care of the poor, public health, and public education, which helped to revive public interest in local government" when the parish spread into secular affairs.

Parliamentary legislation brings specified functions within the category of statutory functions, which makes them obligatory on the part of the communes, and to the administrative regulations based thereon. These regulations normally establish minimum standards, not the optimum. This may be necessary in order to build a national floor underneath the governmental services considered to be essential. The so-called regulated functions include--in addition to the social services, public health, and elementary education-- the following vital functions: town planning and building, housing, fire protection, civil defense and the administration of justice.

The emergence of democracy in local affairs and local self-government are in Sweden contributions of the present century. Prior to the boundary reforms in 1952, direct democracy existed in about 25 per cent of the rural districts, wherein annual citizen meetings, similar to the New England town meeting, made basic policy decisions. In the Local Government Act of 1953, the last remnants of direct democracy were eliminated. The power of decision in all the local units of government is now lodged in the council, the members of which are simultaneously elected every fourth year under a system of proportional representation. The chairman of the council, who is the closest Swedish parallel to a mayor, is elected by the council for a term of one year, but is usually reelected year after year.

According to the Local Government Act of 1955, now
in force, the council in all local jurisdictions elects from its
own membership an executive board of five or more members, known in landskommuner as the "kommunalnämnd," in
the cities as "drätselkammare," and in Stockholm and Gothenburg as "stadskollegium." The Executive Boards are
elected for a four year term starting one year later than the
term of the council. The council simultaneously elects from
the membership of the Executive Board a chairman and vice
chairman. The chairman and vice chairman of the council
may be elected members of the Executive Board, but not as
chairman or vice chairman thereof. The Executive Board
prepares all questions with the exception of nominations and
elections for decision by the council, and is the administrative body which has responsibility for the execution of the
council's decisions. Dr. Nils Andren succinctly states:
"The executive board amounts to the local Government."[7]

In order to expedite the working relationship between
the laymen, who are part-time public representatives, and
the full-time employees, who are the experts, and in order
to reinvigorate the Stadskollegium, the City of Stockholm in
the 1920s created a Cabinet of City Directors, or Commissioners (Borgarrådsberedningen), elected by Council for a
four-year term of office. The City Directors, or Commissioners (Borgarråd), normally are, but are not legally required to be, members of the Council. Prior to 1940, the
Commissioners were members of the Stadskollegium. Since
1940, the Commissioners have not been voting members of
the Stadskollegium, but are required to attend the meetings
without a vote. The Commissioners in Cabinet session pre-
pare proposals for the Stadskollegium consideration. Now
the Commissioners meet at least twice a week, frequently
spending ten to 24 hours per week in meetings, while the Executive Board meets only briefly once a week. It was the
original intent in 1940 to make the Executive Board more in-
fluential, but knowledgeable persons claim that this has not
occurred. Formerly, the Executive Board met for two to
three hours to discuss proposals presented for consideration.
Now, it meets for 15 minutes and signs the necessary papers
for submission to the Council.[8] The Executive Board, however, is still spoken of as the "government." It is still the
politically responsible policy forming body, representing the
political parties and serving in an advisory capacity to the
City Council, and the politically responsible coordinator of

administrative functions.   The Borgarrådsberedningen became
the "real power" when put out of the Stadskollegium in terms
of voting membership. [9]   Mr. Hans Calmfors, City Clerk,
expresses the power situation in these words,

> The political leadership is vested in the politically
> elected commissioners and especially in the leader
> of the majority group who, by virtue of his major-
> ity, is Finance Commissioner and Chairman of the
> Committee of Commissioners. [10]

The executive board may hire a professionally trained
administrative manager, which 130 primary communes (municipalities) have done, and every county council has hired a
county manager.   The manager is appointed for an indeter-
minate period and is responsible to the county council in the
county and to the municipal council through the executive
board in the municipality.   The International City Managers'
Association officially recognizes these cities and counties as
having city- or county-manager governments.

The government of Stockholm is based on a special
law passed by Parliament in 1957, effective January 1,
1958. [11]   The City Council has 100 members, elected by proportional representation on the third Sunday in September
every fourth year: 1962, 1966 and 1970, and holds one session per month, normally every third Monday of the month
at 6 P.M., except in July and August.   Several sessions are
held in December with the adoption of the budget.   The Council at its first meeting elects a chairman and two vice chairmen.   An Executive Board of 12 members plus an equal
number of deputies is elected annually.   Nine commissioners
to head the nine administrative departments are elected by
the Council for the four-year period of the Council.   The political parties are represented proportionately on the Executive Board.   While it is not legally required as regards the
Cabinet of Commissioners, an attempt is made to distribute
commissioner positions in accordance with the party strength
in the Council.   The Chief Clerk serves as secretary for
all three governing bodies: the City Council, the Executive
Board, and the Cabinet of Commissioners, thus ensuring a
"follow through" on the administration of municipal government business.

A unique feature of the Stockholm administration is
the 50 boards, which are grouped within the appropriate departments by the Executive Board.   Each board has seven to

nine members plus an equal number of deputies, appointed
by the City Council. The Commissioner heading a particular department, who is responsible for the work of his department to the Cabinet of Commissioners, of which he is a
member, to the Executive Board and to the City Council, is
chairman of the important (administrative policy-making)
boards in his department, thus providing an administrative
co-ordination of the multi-sectored administrative arrangement.   Council members and non-council members serve on
the boards.   One distinctive advantage is the membership on
the boards of citizens who have no official connection with
the municipality, except for membership on the board in question.   This is the Swedish way of getting non-political party
and non-administrative hierarchy citizen participation in municipal government.   This arrangement provides opportunity
for a mixture of expert, political party and non-political
party lay opinion in the operational policy.   Expert opinion
weighs heavily.   Political opinion has the final voice.

        The modern political party system emerged in Sweden
after the Four Estates were replaced by a bicameral representative Riksdag in 1866.   As is normally the case, the
party structure parallels the governmental structure.   In
Stockholm, the party structure starts with the neighborhood
political clubs.   At the election district level are representative assemblies and executive committees, selected by the
district assemblies.   Each party has a city-wide assembly
of district representatives, which selects an executive committee for the party in the municipality: Social Democratic
Party, nine members; Conservative Party, 13 members; and
the Liberal Party, 20.   The executive committee, which is
actually a subcommittee of a larger governing board of 50
or more, has a full-time staff directed by a party secretary.

        Normally, a citizen joins a political party by enroll-
ing in one of the party's neighborhood clubs or special units.
As of 1960, the Social Democratic Party had 58 neighborhood clubs, 93 workingmen's trade clubs, 75 union locals,
46 women's clubs, 13 white collar worker clubs, seven re-
ligion-oriented clubs, and one youth organization.   The Conservative Party had 30 neighborhood clubs, 27 women's
clubs, one businessmen's club, one white collar worker club,
and one youth organization.   The Communist Party had 24
neighborhood clubs, 24 workingmen's clubs, one woman's
organization and one youth organization.   The Liberal Party
was split into two organizations: 1) the Liberal Party,

Stockholm Division, and 2) the Progressive Citizen's Association.   Each had neighborhood clubs and special units. [12]

It is commonly understood that no one becomes a civic leader in Stockholm without party affiliation, yet about 75
per cent of the eligible voters remain outside party affiliation.

There is no law concerning the procedure for nominating candidates to office.   Nominating procedure is left entirely to the party itself.   The Social Democratic, Center
and Communist Parties have established rules of nomination
that apply uniformly throughout the country.   The Liberal
and Conservative Parties, on the other hand, have developed
several different systems.   The party organization in each
constituency nominates its own candidates for national as
well as local elections, with the exception of the Communist,
which requires central approval of candidates.

Every citizen 21 years of age with the exception of
those legally declared insane or placed under guardianship
are entitled to vote.   The voting register is compiled annually by the local authorities.   The individual citizen need not
take any steps to be included in it.   He is allowed to inspect
the register when it has been compiled and to lodge complaints against it with the County Governor's Office.   If a
citizen moves from one constituency to another, he may vote
in the old constituency until his name has been included in
the register of the new constituency in which he actually
lives. [13]   Swedish electoral law aims at providing practically
all who are entitled to vote with an opportunity to do so.   A
voting card, which can be used as proof of eligibility to vote,
is issued prior to every election by the local election committee to every person on the election register.   A person
may submit at the polling booth a sealed envelope containing
the ballot of the spouse providing proof is presented that the
spouse personally sealed the envelope and is eligible to vote.
Voting takes place in hospitals.   A person who is absent
from his electoral district, but is in the country, may mail
in his vote.   Anyone eligible to vote who is absent from the
country, may vote at a Swedish embassy, legation, or consulate. [14]   The above described arrangements for voting partially explain the high voting participation in Sweden.

General and local elections are held alternately in
every even year: 1) elections for the Second Chamber of the
Riksdag in 1960, 1964, 1968 and 1972;   2) local elections in

1962, 1966 and 1970.   The election day for all popular elections is the third Sunday in September.   The term of office
begins on January 1st of the following year, except in Stockholm where the new term begins October of the same year.
With the exception of the six city-counties, the voters in the
local elections receive two ballots, one for the city council
and one for the county council.   The county councilors and
the city-county councilors elect the members of the First
Chamber of the Riksdag at the October session for eight-
year periods of service, one-eighth of the representation
each year.   This in effect throws national politics into the
local campaigns and elections, and partially explains the high
participation in local elections.

     In Stockholm since World War II, close to 80 per cent
of the eligible voters participated in every municipal election
except in 1946, and over 80 per cent in every election to the
Second Chamber of the Riksdag except in 1958.   In the 1966
municipal elections 80. 4 per cent voted, and in the 1968
Riksdag elections, 87. 4 per cent. [15]   In the elections to the
councils of the six city-counties, the voting participation percentages for 1954 was 81. 3, 1958, 79. 6; and 1962, 80. 3 per
cent. [16]   For all of Sweden, the voting participation percentages in the county council elections were for 1954, 71. 91;
1958, 79. 2; and 1962, 81. 0 per cent. [17]   Elections to the
Riksdag in 1964 showed that the age group 40 - 60 participated over 89 per cent. [18]

     Ever since the adoption of universal male suffrage in
1909, the Social Democratic Party has been the largest party
in the Second Chamber of the Riksdag.   From 1917 to 1920,
the Social Democrats participated in the government in coalition with the Liberal Party, and in 1918 with the Liberals
effectuated universal suffrage.   Since 1932, the Social Democratic Party has been the largest party in both houses of the
Riksdag, and the largest party throughout Sweden.   The party
membership as of 1964 in Stockholm was as follows:[19]

Social Democratic Party	106, 875
Conservative Party	15, 971
Liberal Party	7, 730
Communist Party	3, 478
Center Party	115
Total	134, 169

     The number of eligible voters for the municipal elec-
tions in Stockholm ranged from 532,836 in 1950 to 569,515

in 1966.[20] In brief, the 106,875 registered party members in
the Social Democratic Party represent a small minority, therefore the observation that the Social Democratic Party has almost
four times the membership of the other parties combined is not
too significant.

Sweden has had a list system of proportional representation since 1909 for all elections, a variation of the d'Hondt system whereby each party's total vote in a given election district
is divided by a predetermined set of divisors.   A candidate e-
lected in more than one district can choose the district which he
shall represent.   The voter casts a ballot for a political party
and the candidates are elected from the top of the list down, depending on the number of seats won in the election, the party
having decided the listing of the candidates on the ballot.[21] With
the proportional voting system, smaller parties have the opportunity in multi-member districts of pulling together scattered
votes to gain seats that would not be gained in single-member
districts of a majority system election. As a result, in Sweden
having proportional representation in all elections with multi-
member districts, there is a tendency for no party to gain a majority.   Coalition governments are therefore necessary, particularly at the local level as in Stockholm where the political representation since World War II has been as follows:[22]

Party	1948	1950	1954	1958	1962	1966
Social Democratic	38	43	41	45	49	38
Liberal	23	35	31	19	23	28
Conservative	22	17	20	30	23	24
Communist	17	5	8	6	5	10
Total	100	100	100	100	100	100

The elections for the Second Chamber of the Riksdag
produced the following results in Stockholm during the 1960s:[23]

Party	1960	1964	1968
Social Democratic	11	10	11
Liberal	6	6	5
Conservative	6	5	4
Communist	2	2	1
Center	0	1	1
Total	25	24	22

In the elections to the Riksdag, the Social Democrats had only a strong plurality, maintaining an even balance through the Sixties; and in the municipal elections of 1966, the Social Democrats definitely lost strength.

The coalitions in Stockholm have been the Social Democrats and a small number of Communists versus the Liberal and Conservatives. The balance of power is always very narrow, which "means that on most issues they somehow or other arrive at a compromise even when there has been very strong disagreement initially."[24] One example of an issue on which a compromise was reached is the division of building land between private builders and the municipally-owned building societies. There were strong party disagreements when the "Zonplan" was adopted in 1962. Party issues have also emerged on the ever-present question as to whether the city should exercise expropriation powers and thus place the City in charge of redevelopment or leave the redevelopment to the private owners.

The result of the 1966 election was a new majority: a precarious Liberal-Conservative majority replacing a precarious Social Democratic majority with Communist help. By virtue of these alignments, numerous knowledgeable persons speak of the "bourgeois parties" versus the Social Democrats, which with fair accuracy describes the political power structure.

Following the 1966 election, the party representation on the Executive Board was five Social Democrats, one Communist, three Liberals and three Conservatives with a Conservative as chairman. On the Board of Commissioners, there were four Social Democrats, three Liberals and two Conservatives.[25]

The 1966 election was actually a vote against the Social Democrats who sustained a loss of 11 seats in the City Council. The other three parties gained seats: the Liberals and Communists, five each, and the Conservatives, one seat. While there was a coalition swing to the right, this did not represent a conservative reaction. Voter dissatisfaction has been expressed. One analysis was a loss of voter confidence in the ability of the Social Democratic Party to maintain full employment.[26] Other issues revolved around inflation, taxes and housing shortages.[27] All of these issues were as much national as local. The 1968 Riksdag election, however, showed the Social Democratic Party in its

former position of plurality strength, winning one-half of the
Stockholm seats in the Second Chamber with the Liberals,
Conservatives and Communists losing one seat each and the
Center Party keeping its one seat.   The 1970 municipal elec-
tion will show whether the 1966 election results were only a
temporary flurry in the Stockholm political scene.

          Constituency boundary lines were redrawn prior to the
1966 elections.   The city had for the 1962 municipal election
six districts.   For the 1966 election, the city was divided
into seven districts, or constituencies.   An apparent effort
was made to equalize the population, to provide greater mixture of economic levels and to reduce the Inner City and
Outer City concentrations in the election districts.   Districts
I and II were extended from the Inner City into the Outer
City.   District III in the Inner City, including a scattered
population in the east and north, gained two parishes.   Districts IV and V lost one parish each.   A new district (VII)
was established in the west end of the Outer City.   The extent of the changes is evidenced by the following tabulation:

District	Number of Parishes 1962	Parishes Transferred Out	Parishes Transferred In	Number of Parishes 1966
I	5	2	1	4
II	4	1	2	5
III	7	0	2	9
IV	3	1	0	2
V	3	1	0	2
VI	5	5	2	2
VII	0	0	(Old VI minus 2)	3

          Since the Social Democratic Party is strongly organ-
ized on the election district basis, the boundary changes may
have produced an unanticipated handicap to that party in its
campaign for the 1966 municipal election.

          Sharp contrasts between wealth and poverty are virtu-
ally absent from Stockholm.   Economic analysis of elections
is therefore handicapped not only by the absence of economic
extremes in wealth, but also by the relatively even scatter of
income levels through the city.

The highest average income and the largest number of persons with capital of 80,000 kronor and over are found in Oscars Parish in the eastern portion of the Inner City, which is part of District III. The five lowest average income parishes are also in the Inner City, but four of these parishes form Södermalm Island, immediately south of the Old City Island, which together in 1962 formed District I, and the fifth parish is located immediately north of the Old City Island. Three of these parishes still form District I. This brief income and capital analysis is partially reflected in the elections. The highest percentage of votes for the Conservative Party in each election appeared in Oscars, Hedvig Eleanora and Engelbrekts Parishes in the order named, the high income East End in the Inner City, District III. [28] Districts I, IV, V and VI (formerly, only a part of VI) have provided the power base for the Social Democratic Party. The highest percentage of Communist vote in the municipal elections was also noticeable in this area.

With the exception of District III, which provides a relatively high Conservative vote and a relatively low Social Democratic and Communist vote, the election returns show that each party has a surprisingly even voting strength throughout the city from election to election. Of interest, however, is the Social Democratic strength in the Outer City (Districts IV, V, VI and VII), particularly in the higher income parishes of Hässelby and Spånga in the West End, and Farsta, Skarpnack and Vantor in the South End. In summary, there is real competition in Stockholm between the Social Democrats and the Liberals for the vote from the moderate center. [29]

It is estimated that there are at least 2,000 formal interest groups in Stockholm. They obviously vary in significance. Sweden is highly unionized. Out of a total of 3,244,084 in the labor force in 1965, 1,563,273 were members of the Swedish Federation of Trade Unions, 489,359 of the Central Organization of Salaried Employees, and 73,636 of the Swedish Confederation of Professional Associations. [30]

Throughout Sweden, about two-thirds of the 700,000 plus members of the Social Democratic Party are collectively affiliated through unions. Affiliation is exclusively on the local level; and within the party, union members do not retain, as in the British Labor Party, a separate identity. The Social Democratic Party's local organizations are based on both individual membership and block affiliation through union membership. [31]

The Liberal Party has been supported by about 15 per cent of the "labor" vote, which approximates one-third of the Liberal Party support.

National law distinguishes between "economic" and "idealistic" organizations. The former are obliged to register with the government, keep records on their activities, and in other ways conform to commercial regulations. The latter are largely free of state supervision. In Stockholm, the Federation of Trade Unions, the Confederation of Professional Associations, the Employers' Confederation, Consumers Cooperatives, Tenants' Associations, Real Estate Owners' Association, Chamber of Commerce, and the motor vehicle associations (economic organizations) are all vital in relation to municipal government. The Chamber of Commerce, for example, has the opportunity to present its views before the planning authorities commit themselves on new town plans.

The Swedish Federation of Trade Unions is particularly concerned about the predicament of the workers who sell a home in a rural or small town area at a low price because there is no demand for housing and move to Stockholm and must compete in a high priced market for limited housing. To cope with this situation, the unions HSB (Tenants' Savings and Building Society) and the Svenska Riksbyggen, are building housing for workers; they also advocate goverment construction of housing and rent control. [32]

The Stockholm Chamber of Commerce and the Real Estate Association advocate the lifting of rent control. Their contention is: lift rent control and housing investment will increase and residential construction will increase, meeting a serious housing need. [33] The Chamber also believes that there has been too much redevelopment moving too rapidly, but only the Conservative Party has openly opposed the City acquiring and owning property in the Inner City. [34]

Among the nonpartisan issues are water pollution and the ever-present problem: who gets the housing? There are several ad hoc pressure organizations. For example, the Södermalm Society (Föreningen Södermalm) has been very active in promoting its views on how the proposed redevelopment of their part of the city should be planned. The so-called "Stadsmiljögruppen," loosely translated "City Environ-

ment Group," composed of writers, artists, architects and
others professionally interested in protecting historic scenic
and other interesting environments, has been active in connection with the redevelopment plans both public and private.
There was also, as of October 1968 and no doubt continuing
indefinitely, relatively spontaneous and unorganized pressure
for more service facilities (nurseries, restaurants, cleaning
services) in the small residential units. The Tenants' Association has joined in this campaign. [35] Another nonpartisan
issue is the question of high versus low density development.[36]

Pressure activity takes place indirectly through the
numerous boards and administrative agencies with the members of the city council, but also directly with the commissioners and council members. The commissioners are frequently contacted by organizations, receive letters and calls
by the leaders and spokesmen of organizations, and visits
from delegations of members of the organizations.

The range of citizen interests represented on the 100-
member council is exceptionally wide. The occupational
groupings given below are listed according to the number per
group.

Vocations of Members of the Stockholm City Council[37]

1. Directors and Managers   20
2. Secretaries   11
3. Education (Principal, School Masters, Teachers)   9
4. Editors and Journalists   9
5. Borgaråd (City Directors or Commissioners)   8
6. Ombudsmän   7
7. Miscellaneous Professional (Archivist, Curator,
       Criminologist, Church Adjunkt, Economist,
       Physician)   6
8. Housewives   5
9. Bureau Directors and Division Chiefs   4
10. Lawyers   4
11. Engineers   3
12. Office Employees   3
13. Cashiers   2
14. Inspectors   2
15. Miscellaneous (Consultant, Fil. Stud., Pol. Mag.,
       Pol. Stud., Police, Printer, Surveyor)   7
                                                      Total   100

The directors, managers and secretaries include, in addition to persons employed by ordinary business firms, employees of consumer cooperatives, unions and professional associations. Almost one-third of the membership belongs to this category. Educators, editors and journalists are the second largest category. It is difficult to determine from the job titles in the official listing of the council members how many are civil servants. There are no legal restrictions similar to the Hatch Acts in the United States. In addition to the City Directors, there are other government employees, and they constitute a significant group in the Council. Noticeable is the small number who could be classified as "workers." Even the Communist Party members are in managerial or professional positions. Noticeable also, in contrast to U.S. experience, is the small number of lawyers.

Requirements for city council membership are age (23 years) and eligibility as a voter in the city. Thirty-four of the 100 members of the council, elected in 1966, were new members, 24 men and ten women. The total number of women after the 1966 election was 25, two fewer than in the 1962-66 term.

In sharp contrast to the Cologne councilmanic committee structure, the Stockholm City Council has very few actual committees in the normal sense of the term. They are as follows:[38]

1. The Executive Board, described above in this chapter, with twelve council members and twelve deputies, serves as the major councilmanic committee on administration. Stadskansliet, which was organized in 1920, has approximately 188 personnel, who serve as staff for the City Council, the Executive Board and the Board of Commissioners. The Statistical Office is also responsible to the Executive Board, functioning as a resource agency.

2. The Election Committee of nine council members and nine deputies prepares nominations for councilmanic election to positions in the administrative boards and agencies. This committee is provided a secretary.

3. The Committee on Administrative and Accounting Review has seven members and seven deputies, one of whom is a member of the Council. This so-called committee is actually a board, which performs the administrative and accounting review.

4. The Committee on the Retail Sale of Intoxicants
has seven council members, also a secretary and an inspector. The Council, in addition, appoints the membership of
a Temperance Board, elaboration on which is not necessary
in this connection.

Stockholms Kommunalkalender lists as "More Important Communal Committees and Delegations" 27 additional
committees and entities, to which responsibilities have been
delegated of a non-administrative nature for purposes of investigation, counsel and the performance of functions supplementary to the normal municipal functions. Members of the
City Council, in addition to non-official citizens, are serving
on each of the 27 committees.

In addition, the 50 administrative boards and agencies
serve partially in the capacity of councilmanic committees.
A motion by a member of the Council may be referred to
that board or agency which has the requisite experience and
competence, which then reports back to the Council through
the Board of Commissioners and the Executive Board, where
the political decisions frequently are made. Council members are appointed by the Council to serve on the 50 boards
and agencies in addition to non-official citizens for six-year
terms of office. Judges, lawyers and policemen are not
eligible to serve.

The meetings of these various boards, committees
and agencies are closed to the public. The minutes of the
meetings, however, are available for public scrutiny with the
exception of references to someone's private life. Meetings
to the City Council are open to the public.

Each member of the Council usually serves on two
city boards and is a deputy on two other boards. They attend the board meetings with regularity and inform the board
chairman of any anticipated absence so that arrangements can
be made for a deputy to attend. Board meetings are scheduled on week day afternoons every other week. Subcommittee meetings of the Social Welfare Board, which occur every
week, is the most demanding on the councilman's time. In
addition, members of the Council serve on the boards of 20
joint-stock companies, in which the City owns some or all
of the stock and city representation on the board of directors
is considered to be essential. Attending meetings--of boards,
council and/or communal committees, and political parties,
participating in informal conferences, and drafting reports

obviously consume a substantial portion of a council member's time.

The City Hall provides admirable facilities. Party meetings can take place in separate conference rooms. After an election, they meet simultaneously and the party leaders rush back and forth in the corridors to consult and persuade in the selection of commissioners for the following four-year period.

A week before a Council meeting the agenda, with supporting material, is received by council members through the mail. Also during the week a supplementary list of minor questions is mailed out. On Friday afternoons preceding council meetings, a council member meets with his party group at the City Hall to form party positions on the questions and issues. He must notify the party chairman if he has to be absent from the Council meeting, so that his vote can be "paired off" with an absentee from the opposition.

At the Council meeting, the chairman presides from a table on a dais. Three chairs are placed on each side of the table. On the one side two seats are reserved for the two vice-chairmen and on the other side one is reserved for the chief clerk, who serves as secretary to the Council. A table for stenographers is placed immediately in front of the dais. To the left of the chairman's dais are desks for the nine commissioners. The 88 other members of the Council are seated at desks arranged in three rows around the dais. As of the 1966 elections, to the right of the dais were seated the ten Communist members and the 38 social Democratic members of the Council, and to the left of the dais were seated the 28 Liberal members and the 24 conservative members, overflowing into the right section of the Chamber. To the left of the dais is a rostrum from which addresses may be delivered to the Council. To the right and above is the public gallery nine rows deep with a sufficiently steep incline to provide everyone with an excellent view of the proceedings. Upon entry into the public gallery, each person receives a printed copy of the agenda, showing the old business and the new business scheduled for that session, also reporting the current status of the operating and capitol budgets. The proceedings are clearly audible.

The chairman presents the business before the Council. Interpellations, written questions to a commissioner concerning matters under his jurisdiction, which were submitted for answer at the previous session, are answered. Occasionally, discussion follows. On each proposition, the clerk reads the roll and each member casts his vote of "yes" or "no." He can abstain, request to have the proposition tabled, or recommitted, but he cannot introduce his own amendment from the floor. A few addresses may be delivered to the Council. Most of the motions are approved unanimously and it is not surprising that citizens of Stockholm find little to attract them; public attendance is slight at council meetings.

Supporting this unanimity in the Council is unanimity in the preparation of business for the Council. Bertil Hanson writes concerning the Board of Commissioners:

> The commissioners present technically correct policy decisions to the Collegium and the City Council, leaving little for these bodies to decide. During six years of service in the Collegium, he (a veteran politician) had seen the commissioners' joint recommendations fail in only 5 of 5000 cases.[39]

The hypothesis that the permanent expert staff control the determination of public policy is not established. The commissioner, working through the boards under his chairmanship, controls all major appointments, which is a factor that the ambitious civil servant cannot ignore. The practice of stressing technical qualifications makes it advisable for the civil servant to be technically well qualified for high administrative appointment, yet since the commissioners want men with whom they can work amicably and effectively, technical competence alone provides no guarantee for promotion to directorships. If there is any question of priorities among governmental enterprises, the political leaders make the decisions in their bargaining with one another, and they want immediately responsible to them administrative personnel who will cooperate.

Furthermore, the commissioners seek and gain professional reputations by attending professional conferences both at home and abroad, lecturing at the universities and professional schools and abroad, and writing for publication in professional journals. The leading politicians also show a willingness to adopt the jargon and outlook of professional specialists, cite professional scholars and award generous grants of public funds for new research projects. It is not a situation wherein the technical experts control the adminis-

tration, but a situation wherein the technical experts and the
politicians are working in the same technically-oriented atmosphere.

The institutional pattern has some relevance to this
situation. The proportional representation system of elections provides a survival of party combinations in a multi-
party setting. Party regulated nominations and multi-member districts make possible "safe seats" for the party leaders.
The customs of sharing seats in the Executive Board, the
Board of Commissioners and the other administrative boards,
and the reappointment of incumbents, further increase the
security of the political leaders.

Since the proportional system of elections gives the
citizen an opportunity to vote for a party rather than for a
person, the fortunes of individual politicians are decided by
the personal relationships developed within the party. Ac-
quaintanceships, personal attributes and the favors of existing leaders become the principal factors affecting advancement to high political office and power. Once in office--in
a position to make policy--the successful politicians tend to
formulate unanimous "technically justifiable" decisions, usually acting with the assistance of professionally trained, per-
manently employed civil servants. The parties have regularly retained most of their shares of high places. Mr. Hanson
specified that in 56 instances from 1920 to 1960 when places
might theoretically have been lost by the parties, only six
losses were actually suffered. [40] After any given election, no
more than one party is likely to have to give up any commis-
sionerships, and that party will probably lose only one or
two, at most three. All former commissioners receive a
pension, irrespective of age or other employment--therefore
commissioners do leave voluntarily; however two-thirds of
the commissioners have succeeded themselves, and some have
served for more than 20 years.

The necessary support within the party is the only
matter of prime importance. They need not worry about public reaction to their decisions as long as the party is not
worried. They can avoid making all questions political questions. They can instead regard most questions as "technical" and heed recommendations of specialists. The wise and
politically astute policy is, "play it safe." There is no need
for "rocking the boat" either within the party or as regards
party group agreements. There is, therefore, the co-pres-
ence of a restrained competition for power and a conciliatory

"technically" oriented pattern of policy-making.

The commissioners are obviously neither obliged nor inclined to apply partisan considerations to problems of policy-making. As a matter of fact, they succeed in confining open party differences to a small minority of the questions. These are questions that have strong human interest angles, that can attract attention and enliven the party followers, particularly the questions that involve basic party principles. These are the questions that become the subjects of City Council debates.

These basic party principles may be nothing more definite than "helping the needy" for the Social Democrats, "self reliance" for the Conservatives, or "freedom" for the Liberals, yet they have significant meaning for the party followers and can stir them to action.

There is outside of the institutional pattern or governmental structure a vital factor that has a bearing on the restrained competition for power and the conciliatory, "technically"-oriented pattern of policy-making. This factor is the coincidence in the views about values and proprieties that are held by several types of community leaders, not only politicians, but also journalists, clergymen, civil servants, educators, businessmen, labor leaders and others who are vocal. There is no complete agreement on values; nevertheless, the widespread acceptance of like value postulates is clear enough to permit reference to a "community consensus." That which gives value and meaning to life, it is generally agreed, is a home, a family, a regular job with proper income, friendly contacts and an opportunity to engage in leisure activities.

A small country, a small, homogeneous population, sharing the same cultural norms and undergoing similar formal instruction in the schools are in the background and provide a partial explanation for this consensus. Furthermore, in Stockholm is a large middle class without extremes of wealth or poverty, concerned with comfort, contentment and happiness. In Stockholm is also an informed electorate that has been educated in the union-sponsored workers' institutes and folk high schools, if not in the universities. These citizens have acquired the speech and the ideas of the formally educated, and form part of the consensus on matters which otherwise would not come within range of their thinking. The consensus of all major citizen types in Stockholm is

therefore due to factors not controllable by the politicians.
The politicians are, in fact, part of the consensus themselves.

Freedom of speech, press, communication and propaganda are accepted by the community, and no political party
can remain unattentive toward conspicuous dissatisfactions.

The hypothesis that the heavy emphasis on expert
technical solutions to problems and the use of technical criteria in policy-formation constitute a shield to protect the
politicians and responsible governmental officials from public
criticism remains unproven.   Politicians and policy-forming
public officials have a seemingly valid premise for handling
non-party, technical questions as they do.   The objectives,
which they have in mind, are relatively non-controversial,
being shared by public officials and the general public alike.
In brief, the objectives come within the area of "community
consensus" and therefore are not usable as party issues.
The realization of these objectives poses problems so complex that only technically trained, expertly competent personnel, unemcumbered by extraneous political considerations,
can effectively provide answers to them.   This is increasingly true of metropolitan problems, not only in Stockholm but
throughout the world.   Furthermore, within the technically-
oriented atmosphere of Stockholm the solutions are by and
large acceptable.   Freedom of the press, speech, communication and propaganda remains available to those who may
be dissatisfied.   For these reasons, a substantial doubt can
be raised about the contention that public officials deliberately take refuge behind a technical curtain as a protection
against public criticism.

The one significant problem is the slowness of the
decision-making process through the labyrinth of boards and
committees and the inevitable delay involved in getting bi-
partisan agreement prior to city council consideration and
action.

There has been concern among students of public affairs in the apparent apathy of the citizenry in municipal affairs and discussions have been held on "how the communes
might create a more alive public interest in their activities."[41]   Proposals include:

1.   Public meetings where interested citizens would have
the opportunity to debate comprehensive municipal projects.

2.   Group meetings to which citizens representing
particular interests would be invited for discussions.

3.   Distribution free of cost of a periodical containing information about municipal affairs to all households.

4.   Municipal referenda.   A Royal Commission studied this proposal with a majority of the commission recom-
mending voluntary consultative referenda and a minority rec-
ommending decisive referenda in municipal affairs.

5.   Change of the electoral system from proportional
representation to a single-member district majority election
representation.

Proposals one through three have merit and are without question worthwhile on the premise that interest cannot
be stimulated unless the citizens have information and some
knowledge about the problems that face the municipality and
the contemplated proposals for dealing with the problems.
The individual citizen, however, may have to be shown that
the problems and proposals do concern him personally and
with sufficient impact to get him involved.

Local government in the United States has had a mixed
experience with local referenda.   One generalization is possible.   There has been no firm evidence to prove increased
citizen interest and participation in local affairs in the states
that authorize local referenda.

Changing the electoral system is a serious proposition.   Contrary to the usual opinion in the U.S.A. concerning the proportional representation system of elections, this
system has provided Stockholm with a political stability which
may not be possible under a single-member district majority system.   With a complete change in top management
whenever there is a change in administration, would there
continue to be the carry-over of policy from one administration to another?   There certainly would not be the carry-
over of top personnel.   There are obviously advantages and
disadvantages to each electoral system.   The single-member
district majority system does enable the individual voter to
get closer to his member of the council.   In terms of city-
wide policy-formation, does this advantage overcome the disadvantages of "ward politics," as we know it in the U.S.A.?

Furthermore, a change from the proportional repre-

sentation system to a single-member district majority election system would certainly have repercussions on party politics in Stockholm that the political parties would not relish
considering seriously. There does seem little likelihood, for
better or for worse, that the voters of Stockholm will have
to vote on any such change.

The general public in Stockholm apparently accepts as
adequate the information received from the press concerning
council meetings and sees little advantage to be gained from
personal attendance at council meetings. The recourse for
the private citizen with a grievance is to submit his case in
writing to the appropriate city board. The outcomes, it is
said, do not depend on the citizen's resourcefulness or influence. As a result, the dissatisfied citizen gets a hearing
and the commissioner does not have to be bothered by individual, detailed and sometimes petty cases. The City Council is normally beyond the reach of the individual citizen who
does not represent a citizen's organization. Individual citizens have the opportunity to participate in municipal affairs
through political party activity, commitment to one of the
"economic" citizen organizations or pressure groups, service
on one of the 27 supplementary councilmanic committees on
which non-council members have seats, and service on one
of the 50 boards. Political party and pressure group activity
is open to all citizens. Other opportunities are limited.

In Stockholm, the political party seems to be the all-
important channel for public policy determination. It is,
therefore, amazing that such a small number of the eligible
electorate have seen fit to avail themselves of the opportunity to join a political party and become active in it. However, an over 80 per cent participation in municipal elections
may raise reasonable doubts concerning a real citizen apathy
in Stockholm affairs. An apparent apathy may exist only as
regards specific procedural aspects of municipal government.

Notes

1. Andren, Nils, Local Government in Sweden (Stockholm:
    International Graduate School for English-Speaking Stu-
    dents, University of Stockholm, 1957 - Mimeographed),
    p. 4.

2. Andren, Nils, Modern Swedish Government (Stockholm:
    Almquist and Wiksell, 1961), p. 188.

3. Lagenfeld, Per, Local Government in Sweden (Stock-
    holm: The Swedish Institute, 1964), p. 5.

4. Wåhlstrand, Arne, Local Government in Sweden, A Re-
    port by Director at the School of Social Work and Mu-
    nicipal Administration, Gothenburg (Mimeographed
    Manuscript undated), p. 25.

5. Andren, Nils, Modern Swedish Government, p. 189.
    Langenfelt, Per, Op. cit., p. 7-8.

6. Wåhlstrand, Arne, Op. cit., p. 7.

7. Andren, Nils, Local Government in Sweden, p. 16.

8. Interviews with Mr. Hans Calmfors, Chief Clerk, City
    of Stockholm, May 16, 1966; Mr. Folke Lundin, Com-
    missioner, Department of Greater Stockholm, May 24,
    1966; and Mr. Joakim Garpe, Former Commissioner
    in the 1950s, June 2, 1966.

9. Calmfors, Hans, Local Self-Government in Stockholm,
    A Short Presentation, April 1966 (pamphlet), p. 15.

10. Calmfors, Hans; Rabinovitz, Francine F. ; and Alesch,
    Daniel J. , Urban Government for Greater Stockholm
    (New York: Frederick A. Praeger, Publishers, in
    cooperation with the Institute of Public Administration,
    New York, 1968), p. 36.

11. Kommunlag för Stockholm, 1957.

12. Hanson, Bertil, Stockholm Municipal Politics (mimeo-
    graphed) Joint Center for Urban Studies of the M. I. T.
    and Harvard University, 1960, p. 76-78.

13. Andren, Nils, Modern Swedish Government, p. 45.

14. Ibid. , p. 54.

15. See Table 16, Appendix.

16. Central Bureau of Statistics, Statistisk Årsbok, 1965,
    Table 439, p. 394.

17. Ibid. Table 437, p. 392.

18. Ibid. Table 434, p. 389.

19. Ibid. Table 430, p. 385.

20. Stockholm Office of Statistics, Monthly Statistical Review, 1966, Numbers 9-12, p. 4*.

21. In casting a ballot, a voter may delete one or more names from a list, but this occurs very infrequently.

22. Calmfors, Hans; Rabinovitz F. and Alesch, D. J., Op. cit., p. 22.

23. Stockholm Office of Statistics by correspondence through Mr. Svante Fornö, Secretary, March 10, 1969.

24. Letter from Mr. Percy Bargholtz, Assistant to the Director, Department of Planning and Building Control, October 3, 1968.

25. Calmfors, Rabinovitz and Alesch, Op. cit., p. 42.

26. Letter from Mr. Enar Lindquist, Svenska Kommunförbundet, August 10, 1968.

27. A Conservative Party Handbook in the 1966 campaign was highly critical of the housing shortage and the growing queues waiting for housing accommodations.

28. Stockholm Office of Statistics, Monthly Statistical Review, 1967, No. 1, Table XI, p. 42*-47*. Stockholm Office of Statistics, Ibid, 1966, No. 4, Table VI, p. 11*.

29. Ibid. No. 9-12, Table III, p. 21*.

30. Statistisk Centralbyrån, Statistisk Årsbok, 1965, p. 221.

31. Andren, Nils, Modern Swedish Government, p. 25.

32. Interview with Mr. Ramsten, Ombudsman for the Swedish Federation of Trade Unions, Hagagatan 2, Stockholm, June 9, 1966.

33. Interview with Mr. Lars Almström, member of the
     Board of Directors, Stockholm Chamber of Commerce,
     June 16, 1966.

34. Interview with Mr. Arne Östrom, member of the Board
     of Directors, Stockholm Chamber of Commerce, May
     25, 1966.
          Interview with Mr. Thomas Michelsen, editorial
     writer, Stockholms Dagens Nyheter, June 27, 1966.

35. Letter from Mr. Percy Bargholtz, Assistant to the Di-
     rector, Department of Planning and Building Control,
     October 3, 1968.

36. Interview with Mr. Thomas Michelsen, editorial writer,
     Stockholms Dagens Nyheter, June 27, 1966.

37. Stockholm Office of Statistics, Monthly Statistical Re-
     view, 1966, Nos. 9-12, p. 28*-29*.

38. Stockholms stadskansli, Stockholms kommunalkalender,
     1966 (Stockholm: Kungl. Boktrykeriet P. A. Norstedt
     och Söner, 1966), p. 102-103, 106-109 and 111-125.

39. Hansen, Bertil, Op. cit., p. 137.

40. Ibid, p. 124.

41. Wåhlstrand, Arne, Op. cit., p. 58-59.

Chapter X

STOCKHOLM: ADMINISTRATION

Urban development in Stockholm is the responsibility
of the Building Board, shared with the Real Estate and Street
Boards.   The Industry Board performs a supporting role with
the provision of utilities as needed.   The Board of Finance
has a significant role, which looms larger in policy formation as finance and credit problems become more vital in the
entire process.

The Building Board has been placed in the Department of Greater Stockholm (Stor-Stockholmroteln), in which
have been placed two other agencies that have influence on
urban development and land use: the Greater Stockholm Delegation, which coordinates policy with the other communes in
the Stockholm metropolitan area, and the Council for the
Preservation of the City's Beauty (Skönhetsrådet), which has
no formal powers, but is consulted on matters to be placed
before the Building Board and thus can influence policy indirectly.   Whenever specialized boards within the Stockholm
Administration are involved in intercommunal problems their
respective commissioners are temporarily added to the Greater Stockholm Delegation; thus it serves as a coordinating
agent for the entire Stockholm administration.   The Municipal Housing Agency, which has responsibility for the distribution of new dwelling units built with municipal and/or other
governmental subventions, was recently transferred from the
Real Estate Department to the Department of Greater Stockholm in order to provide continuous coordination in housing
throughout the metropolitan area. [1]

The Building Office in the Department of Greater Stockholm has responsibility for city planning, surveying, building
permits and building inspection.   The Real Estate Office in
the Department of Real Estate has responsibility for housing,
acquisition of land, relocation for urban renewal purposes,
demolition, reconstruction and/or new building by the City,
contracting with private firms for these operations and su-

201

pervision of them and the management of land and buildings owned by the City.

The actual purchase and sale of municipally owned land and buildings is administered through Aktiebolaget Strada, which is a municipally owned corporation serving as an agent for the City. The Director of the Department of Finance is chairman and the Director of the Real Estate Department is vice-chairman of the Board of Directors of Strada. Furthermore, four municipally owned building corporations actually construct the buildings, residential or commercial, which the City Council decides should be built by the municipality. These corporations are responsible to the Real Estate Office.

The Traffic and City Building Department (literally translated from the Swedish) seems to be misnamed. It is that one of the nine departments which lacks a definite focus. Its responsibilities range from streets, parks, sports and recreation, to cemeteries, refuse and sewage disposal, as well as civil defense. It shares responsibility with the Department of Greater Stockholm for traffic planning. Within the Traffic and City Building Department are four boards, each having jurisdiction over its portion of the overall administration: 1. Street Board; 2. Cemetery Board; 3. Sports and Recreation Board; and 4. Civil Defense Board. Since the Street Board is the relevant agency for the purposes of this chapter, the department will hereafter be referred to as the "Street Department."

Likewise involved in urban development are the utilities under the Industry Board in the Public Works Department (Industriroteln): the Gas and Water Works and the Electric Works. Discussions have been held concerning a reorganization in order to bring water--in the Public Works Department under the Industry Board--and sewage disposal--in the Street Department under the Street Board--into one department under one board.

Since urban development planning is largely under the policy direction of the Building Board in the Department of Greater Stockholm, which includes the Greater Stockholm Delegation and the Council for the Preservation of the City's Beauty, these boards and/or agencies will be analyzed below.

The Building Board has nine members: three Liberals, two Conservatives, three Social Democrats and one Communist.[2] The Commissioner of the Department, who is also

Chairman of the Building Board and the Greater Stockholm
Delegation, is a Liberal. The eight deputies include two
Liberals, two Conservatives and four Social Democrats. The
occupations represented are: one former commissioner,
"who now holds several part-time posts, the most important
being one of chairman of a kind of a planning board for the
arts subjects in our universities (facultetsberedning)," one
lawyer, one school teacher, one journalist, one director from
Kooperativa Förbundet, one senior official from a drug firm
(Astra), one director of the "Children's Day" organization,
and one director from the National Farmers' Union. Among
the deputies are one president of a trade union, one ombudsman from another union, four with the title of "director,"
one civil servant and one employee in the city's Street Cleaning Division of the Street Department.

The other policy-forming body in the Department of
Greater Stockholm is the Greater Stockholm Delegation,
which has two Liberals, two Conservatives and three Social
Democrats, who are, variously: two journalists, one employee of an economic research bureau, one director from
Svenska Bostäder--a building society which the city owns,
one employee from the Social Democratic Party organization,
and one director from an unspecified firm. Among the deputy members (two Conservatives, one Liberal, and three Social Democrats) are one journalist, one lawyer, one civil
servant, one general secretary of a political youth organization, and two women who are members of the City Council,
occupations not specified.

The narrow balance of political power is here illustrated, as well as the wide distribution of occupational and
economic interests represented.

The advisory Council for the Protection of the City's
Beauty has been in existence since 1919. In 1931, it became advisory as regards the restoration of historic buildings. By ordinance on November 17, 1941, the City Council
established that the "Skönhetsrådet" shall have 12 members
for two-year terms. At least eight shall be knowledgeable,
or expert, in the fields concerned, and the ordinance pro-
ceeds to spell out in detail the qualifications of the members.
Two shall represent the Royal Academy for the Fine Arts
and the remaining six shall represent one each from six specified institutions including the Nature Preservation Committee of the Royal Academy of Sciences and the Swedish Architects Association.

204   Stockholm

    The decision-making significance of the Building
Board and the Greater Stockholm Delegation emerges in
the observation that seven of the nine members of the
Building Board and six of the seven members of the
Greater Stockholm Delegation were members of the City
Council. By legislative specification as to membership,
the overwhelming proportion of the members of the Council for the Preservation of the City's Beauty are not members of the City Council. Due to both the specialized and
the advisory nature of the Council, this is understandable.

    The Director of the Building Office, Mr. Göran Siden-
bladh, has been and is considered the Town Planning Director; and insofar as the technical work is concerned, he functions in that capacity with numerous interrelationships with
top personnel in other agencies.

    The department of Building and Planning has a total
staff of 412 employees. Mr. Sidenbladh has a staff of 40
persons in a Management Bureau and six in an Administration Bureau. The former is a unit for administrative intelli-
gence.

    The Planning Division is staffed with 79 employees,
36 of whom are planners (arkitekts) and seven, engineers; it
is organized into four bureaus. A Traffic Division is staffed
with 35 employees, most of whom are engineers, and is organized into five bureaus, four devoted to traffic planning.
An additional bureau, staffed with four engineers, is assigned
the duty of planning the eastern link of the circumferential
motorway around the central business district.

    The City Surveyors Division is staffed with 205 em-
ployees, mostly engineers and draftsmen, and is organized
into four bureaus and a field section. Prior to a 1954 reorganization, this division was the City Engineers Office,
directly responsible to the Building Board.

    Two other units in the Department of Building and
Planning are the Building Permit Bureau, which is staffed
with ten planners (arkitekts), four engineers and three miscellaneous, totalling 17 employees, and the Building Inspection Bureau, which is staffed with six engineers, 13 inspectors, and four miscellaneous, totalling 23 employees. Thus
a significant portion, though not all, of all the city agencies
involved in urban planning and the implementation of plans

are in the one department.

The nine bureaus in the Department of Building and
Planning, four bureaus in the Planning Division and five
bureaus with traffic and transport planning duties, are organized geographically and functionally, but each bureau provides
all the necessary planning within its assignment and within
the framework of previous planning. In brief, there is no
separate advance planning staff in the Stockholm planning organization. The previous planning has been performed by
personnel from the various departments and agencies as
needed under the direction of the Master Planning Commission, responsible to the Executive Board.

In 1951, the Executive Board created a special committee (delegation) to deal with the controversial planning
problems in Lower Norrmalm. On February 17, 1955, the
Executive Board instructed this special committee to assume
responsibility for preparing recommendations concerning the
controversial planning involved in the connecting link for the
underground railway system in the CBD and other difficult,
long-range general planning problems. The delegation was
named "generalplaneberedningen" (long-range planning delegation) and is now known as the "Master Planning Commission." This commission has in its membership the top de-
cision-makers as regards long-range planning from the City
Council, the Executive Board, the Board of Commissioners,
the heads of relevant agencies and a committee of experts
from relevant agencies. Included among the agency heads
are the Directors of the Departments of Finance, Building
and Planning, Streets, Real Estate, and the Director of the
City Tramway and Transport Agency. This group in committee session can make necessary decisions for submission
to the Executive Board and thereafter to the City Council for
councilmanic action. [3]

In accordance with the National Building Act of
1947, as amended in 1959, a master plan, which is a long-
range general plan specifying land uses, must be prepared
by cities and boroughs "to the extent required as guidance
for normal planning;" and a town plan (stadsplan) or building
plan (byggnadsplan) must be prepared, but "must not embrace an area larger than can be realized within a reasonable period of time." [4] The master plan, serving as a guide
for more detailed planning, has no legal effect; however the
county and national administrations in reviewing town plans
or building plans will analyze them on the basis of the mas-

ter plan and will raise questions about deviations therefrom and may refuse approval if the deviations are too serious and the explanations for them are considered to be inadequate. The town plan or the building plan, on the other hand, is a legal instrument and is legally enforcible.

Since 1960, what supervision is provided in urban planning is provided by the architect's office (planning) in the county government and that consists largely in checking the town plan with the master plan and both with national standards. Ratification by the national government, if necessary or requested, is normally quite pro forma. This national review is performed by the Ministry of Communications, which as regards urban planning operates under the jurisdiction of the National Board of Building and Planning. [5]

Since 1964, the National Building Law has superseded local building ordinances and is therefore the sole building law in effect in Stockholm. [6] National law also regulates the composition, organization and procedure of the communal Building Boards, but the essentials of the planning process are at the local level. National legislation, however, authorizes the County Governor to issue a ban on all building within a prescribed area of the commune while a plan is in preparation. This ban is effective only for one year, but can be extended annually, provided the commune evidences a real effort in the preparation of a plan. [7]

Mr. Erik Wannfors, Arkitekt SAR and Division Director in the National Planning Board, gives the following elaboration on national planning policy,

> As the community is responsible for all physical planning these legal rules may be considered as an expression for another basic principle of the Building Act: Society has to decide where and when dense development should be allowed.

This means that in Sweden no land owner has a prior right to exploit his land for high-density building. His basic right is restricted to low-density building of a rural character. It may not necessitate public water supply, roads or other common facilities. The right to use the land for urban development comes into existence first when the municipal council has adopted a town plan or a building plan for the area in question and this plan has been sanctioned by the state authorities.

The aim of this legislation is to encourage the creating and growth of well integrated villages or
cities and to prevent the establishment of settlements which are poorly planned and socially unde-
sirable. [8]

The Nature Conservation Act of 1965 also prohibits
rural development in areas which are considered valuable for
their scenic beauty or for outdoor recreation. The owner
may claim compensation if he is thereby prevented from realizing a building value.

Local government initiates and performs planning with
the one exception of regional plans, which the national government can order be performed and specify the region for
which the planning shall be provided. A regional plan is a
long-range, general plan, dealing largely with inter-communal problems requiring coordinated action. It may broadly
indicate land use, traffic routes, water supply, sewage disposal, recreation areas, and protection of shores and other
undeveloped areas. After the national government has ordered the preparing of a regional plan for a specific area,
the communes inside the specified region must form an organization, a regional planning association for the performance of the joint planning. Orders have been issued for nine
regions in different parts of Sweden. For two of these, the
Stockholm and Borås regions, the regional plans have been
ratified. In the Stockholm situation, the national government also appointed the governing board and nominated the
chairman. Since 1966, however, the board has been and is
elected by association members. When the national government orders the formation of a regional plan, it defrays 50
per cent of the cost of formulating the plan, subject to review and approval. The effectuation of a regional plan, however, devolves upon the communal governments through the
preparation and administration of master plans and town, or
building plans. [9]

The Stockholm Regional Plan was prepared during the
years 1952-1958, and was unanimously accepted in December
1958 by the Regional Planning Association Executive Board. [10]
The Regional Plan is projected to the year 1990, and is being revised to the year 2000 projection. The Stockholm Master
Plan was prepared during 1945-1952. The Master Plan covers a 25 year period, but is being updated by the Master

Planning Commission. [11]   The Zonplan of 1962, which was
adopted by the City Council to protect residential areas and
limit the extension of commercial land uses in the Inner City,
is treated as though it were a Master Plan. [12]   The most recent Town Plan was adopted by the City of Stockholm in
1945; however, so many "delstadsplaner" (plans for portions
of the city) have been approved which modify the Town Plan
of 1945, that it no longer has legal effect. [13]

The Town Plan, or Building Plan, which is only for
the urbanized areas, must be specific: the street layout, location of parks, harbors, railway rights-of-way, building
sites (public, residential, commercial and industrial), including coverage of the site, building position, height, access to
traffic routes and utility easements.   It is worthy of notice
that the Building and Planning, Real Estate, and Street Departments are located together in Nämndhuset, facilitating
the intercommunication that is obviously necessary in the planning process and the interchange of papers and approvals in
the implementation of the plan.   This intercommunication involves: 1) exchange of information concerning subsurface
conditions, drainage and capacity of sewer mains from the
Street Department to the planners in the Building Department;
2) exchanges between the engineers and surveyors in the
Building Department and the personnel in the Land Division,
Building Division and the Urban Renewal Division in the Real
Estate Office and the engineers in the Street Office; and coordination 3) between the traffic planners in the Building Department and the engineers in the Street Office; 4) between
the planners in the Building Department and the engineers
and other technical personnel in the Urban Renewal Division
of the Real Estate Office; 5) among the planners in the Building Department and the Land, Housing, and Architect Divisions in the Real Estate Department and the Park Division in
the Street Department in planning residential developments in
the Outer City; 6) among the Fire Corps in the Street Department and the other agencies in Nämndhuset concerning
safety measures in the interest of fire prevention and access
for fire-fighting purposes; and 7) among the Building Department and the housing agencies in the Real Estate Department.
This list only partially covers the necessary interrelationships.   Technical missing links of great importance are the
Gas and Water Works and the Electricity Works personnel
from Nämndhuset.

A few additional specific contacts, which are essential but need not be as numerous as the contacts previously

listed between agencies located in Nämndhuset, are: 1) the City Antiquarian as regards the presence of stationary archaeological remains that require special attention and care; 2) the Health Board as regards noise and sanitary problems; 3) the Boards of Education as regards school sites; and 4) the Social Welfare Boards as regards sites for kindergartens and day nurseries. In Stockholm the starting point of the entire planning process may be Stadskollegiet on the basis of a recommendation from the Master Planning Commission, the Department of Finance, the Real Estate Office, or the Building Department. Thereafter, the planners in the Department of Building enter the planning picture, and the intercommunication process continues.

Having completed the intercommunication among the relevant agencies concerning the town plan, or parts of it, the Building Board on the basis of comments and criticisms gives conditional approval. The completion of the plan is announced in the press and is made public for a three-week period. A special letter is sent to the property owners in the area covered by the plan and adjacent to the area in question. Citizen objections may be submitted by mail. After the three weeks, the Building Board considers the objections, and forwards the plan to the Executive Board for submission to the City Council. [14] When and if approved by the City Council, it is forwarded to the County Governor's Office, where the County City Planner (Län Arkitekt), who is an employee of the National Building Board, may recommend that it be revised. In the case of highly significant plans, final approval is given by the National Department of Communications. [15]

With the plan officially approved, the implementation of the plan comes under national supervision which, however, is now very general. Before construction may start, a building permit must be secured from the Building Permit Bureau of the City Building Office. The application form requires: specifications concerning outer-wall material, treatment of the facade, roofing material, building plan and "situations-plan," which includes a little more than a site plan, in addition to identifying information such as location of the proposed building site, and name and address of the applicant. The form includes spaces for the comments and signatures of the following officials or offices, also the date the form was received and the date on which the reply was submitted: 1) the Fire Chief, 2) the Chief of Housing Inspection, 3) the Master of Chimney Sweepers, 6) the City Antiquarian (if relevant), 7) the Health Department, 8) the Factory Inspector (if industrial), 9) the Building Inspection Bureau, 10) the Division of City Planning, 11) the Division of Traffic, and 12) the City Engineer. [16] When approved, the Building Permit Bureau forwards the form to the Building Board.

The Building Permit Bureau also has jurisdiction over billboards and signs, which are regulated by the municipality through the Town Plan. Billboards and signs that do not comply with the requirements of the Town Plan are prohibited by the Building Permit Bureau.

The city is divided into four districts for building inspection purposes with one or two inspectors assigned to each district. Prior to the beginning of construction, one architect and one engineer meet with the builder to settle moot questions. Thereafter, inspections are made by building inspectors at the following stages: 1) foundation, 2) building framework, 3) building under roof, 4) the completed building. The first inspection, which is the meeting with the builder, and the last inspection are made by the Building Permit Bureau. The other inspections are made by the Building Inspection Bureau. Inspections are also made by the personnel of the Health Board, and Fire Corps and in the case of industrial construction by the factory inspector. The Building Inspection Bureau is authorized to inspect at any time. The Inspection Bureau also has the responsibility for testing any technical building innovations. [17] Finally, building and health boards, contrary to the usual agency powers, may levy penalties and fines to bring about compliance with local ordinances and laws. [18]

To summarize the development of raw land into residentially occupied property, six chains of activities are involved:

1. City planning through the City Council with County Government approval.

2. City surveying and subdividing.

3. City street and utility planning and construction.

4. Contractors' planning for residential, commercial, and public construction.

5. Contractors' securing building permission and

state loans for construction.

6.   Individual families securing state aid for the pur-
      chase or rental of individual dwelling units.

Mr. Per Holm, Arkitekt SAR, editor of Plan Tidskrift, estimates that the normal time span between the beginning of city planning to actual occupancy of a residentially
developed area is approximately five years. [19]   In an interview at the headquarters of the HSB (Tenants' Savings and
Building Society), the statement was made that it takes from
three to four years to plan and construct a large layout
(block of flats). [20]   Mr. Nils Oelrich, Stadsarkitekt in charge
of the Building Permit Bureau, Department of Building, City
of Stockholm, estimates that in the case of multi-dwelling
apartments, construction begins approximately two and a half
months after the application for a building permit.   In the
case of a single-family house, only one month elapses between the application and the beginning of construction.   If
the builder is in a hurry, the digging of the foundation can
start in two weeks. [21]   There are obviously numerous variables in these estimates.

No private construction, however, can take place in
the city without a "stadplan" or "delstadsplan," showing specifically what is to go where, a full elaboration of required
land use.   Furthermore, in the Outer City, where the overwhelming proportion of the private development now takes
place, the city owns 83 per cent of the land.   This provides
added assurance of adequate control.   The City, therefore,
is in a position to specify where residential, commercial and
industrial buildings shall be placed, and what kinds of residential, commerical and industrial uses land should be put
to, considering the public interest.

Public construction must also comply with the official
plans with out qualification.   Compulsory acquisition of land
by the City, which is now normally necessary only in the Inner City, is possible by several methods of expropriation,
which in the U.S.A. is termed "condemnation by eminent do-
main."   The national Building Act and a special Acquisition
of Land Act provide for this.   Prior to 1953, only "site expropriation" was available to the City.   Under this law, which
is still in force, the City is authorized with the approval of
the national government to acquire any site, for which a plan
has been approved and is officially in effect, providing the
owner is unable, or unwilling, to execute the project which

the plan specifies without undue delay. If the City intends
to redevelop several city blocks, involving realignment of
streets, changing parcel boundaries and planning for the area
as a unit, the willingness of a property owner to build a new
building on his parcel in accordance with the existing town
plan may not meet the requirements of the situation.

To cope with this problem, the City of Stockholm requested and secured the passage of the so-called "Zonal Expropriation Law," which became effective July 1, 1953, just
prior to the planned redevelopment of Lower Norrmalm. Under this law, the City can acquire compulsorily an entire
built-up area, or zone, if redevelopment is considered to be
necessary in the interest of changes in public transport, land
use and/or development, and that the redevelopment cannot
be performed piecemeal, but must be coordinated for the
area, or zone, as a whole. A provisional draft of the new
plan must be attached to an application to the national Minister of Communications for expropriation rights. The new
plan is not made public; only the planning officials and the
Minister of Communications are informed about the specifics
of the plan. This means that the compensation award will be
assessed in accordance with the earlier official plan. The
property owner is not given the advantage of increased values
brought about by public action of improvement in the area.
The City profits from its own improvement action, and speculation is prevented. Another advantage of zonal expropriation is the right of "prior admittance" before the legal proceedings are completed; also the City is legally able to make
revisions in the development plan while demolition and the
expropriation proceedings are being completed. [22]

The judicial proceedings begin with a summons to the
property owner to appear before the Court of Expropriation,
a special court within Stockholm's law courts. The purpose
of the proceedings is to determine the compensation that
should be paid the owner. The court consists of one judge,
two elected assessors (one chosen by the property owner),
neither of whom is a specialist and two specialists (one a
building specialist and one an architect). Appeals are possible, first to the Court of Appeals and thereafter to the Supreme Court. About three years can be involved in the legal hearing and appeals. The City is liable for the legal
costs, regardless of whether the City or the property owner
wins the case. For this reason, appeals are almost invari-
ably taken. Consideration was being given during the summer of 1966 to a change in this portion of the legal require-

ments, making the property owner, if he loses the appeal,
liable for the costs of appeals. Expropriation is considered
to be final only after a final judgment has been rendered and
ratified by the national government.

At the time of "prior admittance" to the property in
question, the City provides a formal guarantee of payment
through the appropriate commissioner and the department director. When the compensation is finally determined, the
property owner is awarded 6 per cent interest on this sum,
effective from the date of "prior admittance."

A preliminary report to The Acquisition of Land Act
specifically states that the offical Town Plan in force at the
time of court action should be the basis for the property valuation, but this can fluctuate during the expropriation proceedings due to inflation or other changes in the real estate
market. Normally, the courts assess the value of the property as the market price when the final decision is pro-
nounced, but in the case of "prior admittance," the value as
of the day the City gains possession governs.

The court delays are not too serious for the City.
The Court of Expropriation has given the City a period of
five years in which to complete a transaction, which upon pe-
tition of the City was extended three years, and then has
been extended once again.

Agreements with property owners have been negotiated, making court action unnecessary. In such negotiations,
the City and property owner voluntarily agree on valuation.
The City may agree to permit the property owner to clear the
site and to erect a new building on the cleared site. The
land becomes municipal property, but is leased to the previous property owner for the purpose of erecting the building
and occupancy of the same, if he so wishes. The term of
the lease is at 60 years, renewable, if the City does not
need the site for another purpose. The rent is fixed for
periods of ten to 20 years.

The principles for valuation of the land are based on:
1) comparables in land valuation, or 2) the hypothetical, or
potential, value on the basis of land use permitted by the
Town Plan. If a building is involved, the income from it is
capitalized. The same principles for valuation are used in
all cases. In the event of an expropriation, both the property
owner's experts and the City's experts appear before the

court to testify.

Under the Expropriation Law of 1953, the City is authorized to expropriate more property than is needed for the redevelopment in order to be able to capitalize on the contemplated improvement by gaining the increase in values of immediately surrounding territory.

The Master Planning Commission has presented a 1967 CBD Plan, which includes converting parts of several major thoroughfares into new pedestrian malls. When the idea of converting narrow streets into pedestrian malls was first suggested in the 1950s, bitter protests were voiced by merchants in the CBD; however as automobile traffic clogged the downtown streets, these same merchants changed their minds, and many of them are now active supporters of the new traffic patterns, including the pedestrian malls. [23]

Urban renewal is now taking place in Lower Norrmalm, the planning of urban renewal is extending into adjoining areas, and has been proposed for 30 blocks in Södermalm (south of the Old City Island). Certain streets will be closed to vehicles and converted into play space and protected walkways. A system of collector streets will be provided, from which cul-de-sacs emanate. Footbridges and underground access roads will separate pedestrian and vehicular traffic. All parking will be underground. Spot redevelopment is planned. [24]

The planning attention given to the central business district redevelopment and renewal and the actual redevelopment and renewal taking place in the Stockholm CBD may well be instrumental in reducing the natural magnetic attraction of activities from the CBD to the outskirts of the city. The City now owns half of the CBD, which greatly facilitates the processing of actual redevelopment. [25]

Mr. Lars Almström, one of the directors of the Stockholm Chamber of Commerce, well illustrated the attitude of the business community: "The CBD is now being renewed. During the next ten to 20 years, the gray area will be renewed." [26]

Mr. Göran Siedenbladh emphasized the need for renewal of the Inner City by the statement that four-fifths of the housing in the Inner City needs to be renewed. [27]

"Save the best and scrap the rest" has become a key slogan in Stockholm's drive for renewal of the Inner City.

The major problem in Stockholm has been to provide sufficient good housing for the increasing population in the Outer City and in the metropolitan area and also for those who wish to live in the Inner City. There has been controversy between those who advocated large-scale construction of housing regardless of quality and those who insist on high standards. "Hög Kvalitet" (High Quality) has consistently gained the upper hand. The problem, therefore, has been "overcrowding."

During the 1930s, the Swedish Government adopted a "social approach" housing policy. Low-income families with at least three children, pensioners (over 67 years of age) and farm workers were granted priority in regard to rehousing. Rents were partially subsidized for these groups, also national loans were made available to the builders to stimulate housing construction for the specified groups.

During World War II, Sweden experienced a reduction in housing construction, skyrocketing rents and inflation. As a result, the national government during 1941-42 changed its housing policy from the "social approach" to one of general applicability for all inhabitants, the "general approach." In order to keep rents in new houses at levels equal to the 1939 rents of comparable standard houses, a rent freeze was applied, a modified form of which is still in effect. This rent control was supplemented by measures which provided mortgage-loan funds to encourage production and to allay builders' fears of future carrying charges, which might be a bar to their willingness to invest in rental housing. There was also a legal requirement of selecting tenants from the municipal registry of applicants.[28]

This change in housing policy highlights two important characteristics of Swedish thinking on social policy: first, the belief that concentrating low-income families with large numbers of children in specific housing developments causes an unfortunate degree of social segregation, and, second, the belief that state aid should be used to produce a high volume of housing at reasonable levels of rent or cost, depending on other devices to supplement the rent paying capacity of low-income families. The needs of low-income families are met by family allowances for children paid to all mothers, irrespective of income, and housing allowances paid on the basis

of a means test applied to the taxable income of the bread-
winner related to the number of children in the family. These
allowances are tax exempt and are never paid in cash.   A
tenant deducts them from his rent or a homeowner applies
them to his amortization and interest payments.   The concentration of low-income families caused by the previous housing
policy has been reduced by permitting families to remain in
these developments irrespective of income and by making va-
cancies available to families irrespective of income.   Subsidies are granted to municipalities for the construction of a-
partments for the aged, and subsidies are paid to the aged
homeowners who secure improvement loans to improve their
housing.   The construction of special housing for the aged is
based on the need for making special care available to them.
Every effort, however, is made not to institutionalize these
apartment buildings but to mix them with the surrounding
neighborhood. 29

        The governmental relationships in regard to housing
boil down to the following formula: the national government
assumes responsibility for providing loans and subsidies, research in building technology, and statistical analyses of the
housing market.   The local government assumes responsibility
for planning and organizing the housing program, inspection
to assure conformity with housing and sanitation standards,
acquiring land to provide building sites, and passing on applications for state loans and rent allowances to large families.
In Stockholm, the Housing Division (Bostadsavdelningen) in
the Real Estate Department administers the housing loans and
allowances.

        At the occasion of the author's first interview in Swe-
den with a Secretary of the Swedish Municipal Association,
the statement was made, "Water pollution is a serious problem throughout Sweden.   Air pollution is not at present." 30

        Increasing concern has been expressed in Stockholm as
regards pollution of the waters and streams in the Stockholm
area.   Sewerage systems, including pipe lines and treatment
plants, cover Stockholm and a portion of the suburbs.   Eleven
communes north of Stockholm formed the Käppla Association
for the planning and construction of pipe lines and a joint
sewage treatment plant.   Stockholm and the communes southwest of the City with Södertälj formed a joint corporation for
water supply and sewage treatment, which will be in operation in the early 1970s, so that the major portion of the
Stockholm area will be serviced.   Two water purification

plants provide 80 per cent of the water supply in Metropolitan Stockholm, largely in the southwest. [31]

The Limnological Institute at Uppsala University reported in 1966 that 800 tons of phosphorus and 7000 tons of
nitrogen are dumped each year into Lake Mälaren, not including the amounts from Stockholm. Most of the phosphorus
comes from the suburban communes, a substantial half from
synthetic laundry sources, slightly less than a half from
toilets. A few industrial sources were also mentioned. [32]

There is a national water law and national water
courts, providing some supervision of the waterways. Stockholm has control over the waterways within her territorial
jurisdiction; however, to construct a bridge it is necessary
for the City to gain permission from a national water court.
The main problem is one of cooperation among the communes. [33] Plans have been sketched to tunnel the outflow
from the sanitary sewers in the Stockholm-Uppsala region to
the Baltic, which would partially protect Lake Mälaren. [34]
To provide complete protection would require the close cooperation and coordination of six counties and, possibly, action by the national government.

Concerning air pollution, a conference on national air
protection personnel (Statens Luftvårdsnämnder) met in Stockholm in 1965. Following this conference, the Stockholm City
Council passed an ordinance prohibiting the running of automobile motors when parked. [35] On December 7th and 8th,
1967, the International Meteorological Institute in Stockholm
called a Joint Organization of Economic Cooperation and Development conference on air pollution. (A surprise at this
conference was the paper delivered by Dr. E. Erikson of the
International Meteorological Institute, presenting evidence that
the Institute has discovered that rain in Stockholm contained
acid attributed to air pollution originating in the Ruhr.)[36]
Concern about air pollution is increasing among city officials in Stockholm.

Several planning problems emerged in interviews and
in Swedish planning literature. The most vital seemed to be
the following:

Mr. Göran Sidenbladh, Director of the Building and
Planning Office, in an interview June 20, 1966, stated:

The functional aspect of neighborhood and commu-

nity planning is still valid and is still followed.
The landscape-architectural aspect is also still
valid and is followed.   The social aspect is something else.   It is changing.   Even the commercial
aspect is different today. [37]

Dr. C. F. Ahlberg, Director of Regional Planning,
dealt with this problem area of planning in a statement in
which he recognized that neighborhood planning is important
to town planning.   He developed the thesis that an attempt
has been made to give the population of a metropolitan center deeper roots--a greater sense of fellowship.   Dr. Ahlberg continued:

> A neighborhood unit, however, is not a world in it-
> self.   It functions only as a section of a large
> town, and life in such a section can be understood
> only when regarded in its relation to the whole.
> Therefore it is just as important that the inhabit-
> ants of the various districts of Greater Stockholm
> should have the feeling that they are Greater Stock-
> holmers as it is that they should feel at home in
> and at one with their particular neighborhood unit.
> From an architectural point of view it is as im-
> portant to give Greater Stockholm a physical struc-
> ture which makes the city as a whole more tangible
> as a unit, as to form the individual districts into
> visually comprehensible units. [38]

Mr. Thomas Atmer, Arkitekt SAR, Stadsbyggnadsekreterare, Building Office, in a critique of planning stated
that the major weakness of planning neighborhoods and communities is the danger of planners trying to force development unnaturally. [39]   Many Swedish planners are concerned
about a "confused individualism."   A thoughtful compromise
needs to be reached between "forcing development unnaturally" and the "confused individualism."

The problem of design, the architectural aspect, to
which Mr. Sidenbladh and Dr. Ahlberg referred, has gained
substantial attention.   The purpose is to prevent, or fore-
stall, the architectural chaos of the Wilshire Boulevard type
in Los Angeles, where each structure is an entity unto itself without any relevance to the architecture of surrounding
structures and without reference to the total effect.   This
presents an unresolved problem, which challenges the design
professions in particular, as Laurence B. Holland specifies

in his Introduction to Who Designs America?   He asks:

> . . . how to accommodate the distinctive building,
> product, or plan, to the full context of competing
> design projects and large-scale design undertakings,
> and to the physical and social forms already exist-
> ing in the community. [And he asks] . . . how
> to harmonize the exercise of individual creative
> talent, the pressures of powerful economic interests
> and impulses, and the full range of human need and
> aspiration within a democratic community. "[40]

This analysis should commence with the individual a-
partment, the home, which must be well maintained in order
to have a satisfactory apartment building, which must be well
designed and maintained in order to have the good neighborhood, which must be well designed and maintained in order
to have the good community; and we continue through the city
to the metropolitan area, each being dependent upon the con-
stituent parts, which together shape and affect the total.

Citizen participation in the planning process, which
concerns Mr. Atmer, seems to be limited in Stockholm to
suggestions and/or objections, mailed to the Department of
Buildings during the three-week period prior to submission
of a plan to the City Council.   In addition, however, surveys
are made of citizen opinion in specific areas, for example in
Vällingby prior to the planning of Farsta, the results of
which are seriously studied, considered and used.   These
surveys cover the "livability" aspect of the results of planning.   Another source of guidance on the "livability" of different types of buildings, room arrangements, and environments and the practicality of differing types of facilities and
equipment are continuously investigated by the National Swedish Institute for Building Research, which conducts intensive
research into these and other relevant problems for use by
government, local and national, and the building industry.
The broad scope of research activity by the Institute is evidenced by its organization into the following six departments:
1) Land Planning, 2) Building Design, 3) Heating Installations, 4) Building Production Techniques, 5) Climitology,
and 6) Economic Analysis.   Dr. Lennart Holm graciously
provided the author with a set of file cards showing 74 research assignments to the staff, involving a fascinatingly interesting and practical research program. [41]

The Stockholm planning agency is fortunate in having

access in the metropolitan area and its environs to several
specialized research institutes as well as access to two well
established and recognized universities for relevant research
assistance, which resolves one significant administrative
problem. Thus the Stockholm planning agency is able to secure well researched data concerning the actual human needs
of the Stockholm society.

The procedure, if not the organization, provides an
integration of research, planning and implementation.

Notes

1. Stockholms stadskansli, Stockholms Kommunalkalender
    1966 (Stockholm: Kungl. Boktryckeriet, P. A. Nor-
    stedt och Söner, 1966) is the source for the data in
    this chapter unless otherwise specified.

2. Information concerning the party affiliation and occupa-
    tions of members of the specified boards and agencies
    after the 1966 election were received by letter from
    Mr. Percy Bargholtz, Assistant to the Director, De-
    partment of Planning and Building Control, October 3,
    1968.

3. Holmgren, Per, About town planning in Sweden with
    particular reference to Stockholm (mimeographed,
    undated). A condensed version of a series of lec-
    tures given in Great Britain in April 1967), p. 10.

4. Aström, Kell, City Planning in Sweden (Stockholm:
    Victor Pettersons Bokindustri AB, 1967), p. 60.

5. Planning Office of the National Board of Building and
    Planning, Town and Country Planning in Sweden
    (Stockholm, July 1961, mimeographed), p. 4.

6. Interview with Mr. E. G. Westman, Stadsjuristen, City
    of Stockholm, June 1, 1966.

7. Calmfors, Hans; Rabinovitz, Francis F. ; and Alesch,
    David J. , Urban Government for Greater Stockholm
    (N. Y. : Frederick A. Praeger Publishers, 1968), p.
    90.

8. Wannfors, Erik, Planning in Sweden (mimographed).

Lecture held at the Reed College Conference on Urban Development in Portland, Oregon, May 3, 1963, p. 12.

9. Ibid.

10. Ahlberg, C. F., "The Regional Plan for the Stockholm Area" (1961), Stockholm Regional and City Planning (Published by the Planning Commission of the City of Stockholm, 1964), p. 37.

11. The first sentence in the Introduction to A Traffic Route Plan for Stockholm 1960, submitted by the Master Planning Commission of Stockholm, reads, "The Traffic Route Plan for Stockholm is a step in a master plan under continuous revision."

12. Interview with Mr. Göran Sidenbladh, Director, Department of Building and Planning, June 20, 1966.

13. Interview with Mr. E. G. Westman.
The first sentence in the Introduction to 1962 Års City Plan reads,
The rebuilding of Stockholm's Central Business District has hitherto followed the Town Plan, which on the basis of the decision of the City Council in 1945 concerning the development of Lower Norrmalm was in 1946 modified by the city planning office of that date. The Master Planning Commission's Committee of Experts now submits on instructions from the Master Planning Commission a new CBD plan.

14. Interview with Mr. Sidenbladh.

15. Interview with Mr. Erik Wannfors, Division Director, National Board of Building and Planning, June 28, 1966.

16. Till Stockholms Stads Byggnadsnämnd (bk IV. 081. 1966. 1. 10. 000).

17. Interview with Mr. Nils Oelrich, Architect in charge of the Permit Bureau, Department of Building and Planning, June 2, 1966.

18. Interview with Mr. E. G. Westman, June 15, 1966.

19.   Interview with Mr. Per Holm, Arkitekt SAR, Editor of Plan Tidskrift, June 9, 1966.

20.   Interview with Mr. Uno Petersson, Bostadshyresgater-nassparkasse och Byggnadsförening, Flemingsgatan 41, Stockholm, June 2, 1966.

21.   Interview with Mr. Nils Oelrich.

22.   The law and proceedings concerning expropriation are taken from the following sources:
      a) A. Bexelius, A. Nordenstam & V. Korlof, Byggnadslagstiftningen, Byggnaldslagen och Byggnads-stadgan med anmärkningar och sakregister (Stock-holm: P. A. Norstedt & Söners Förlag, 4th edition, 1961).
      b) Scarlat, Alexander, Laws and Procedure of Ex-propriation in Sweden (Information Centre Sweden, un-dated).
      c) Westman, E. G. , "Zone Expropriation on Lower Norrmalm in Stockholm (1961)," Stockholm regional and city planning, 1964, p. 65-75.

23.   Aström, Kell, Op. cit. , p. 129-130.

24.   Ibid, p. 149-152.

25.   Interview with Mr. Åke Hedtjärn, Deputy Managing Di-rector of Strada, City Corporation, which buys and sells real estate for the City of Stockholm, June 3, 1966.

26.   Interview with Mr. Lars Almström, Director, Stock-holm Chamber of Commerce, June 16, 1966.

27.   Interview with Mr. Sidenbladh.

28.   Silverman, Abner D. , Assistant Commissioner for Man-agement, Public Housing Administration, U. S. A. , Se-lected Aspects of Administration of Publicly Owned Housing, Great Britain, Netherlands and Sweden (Washington, D. C. : U. S. Government Printing Office, 1961), p. 199-201.

29.   Ibid, p. 202-210.   Dr. Silverman presents an excellent analysis of "Housing for the Elderly. "

Administration 223

30. Interview with Mr. Enar Lindquist, Secretary, Svenska Stadsförbundet, April 26, 1966.

31. Interview with Commissioner Folke Lundin, Greater Stockholm Department, May 24, 1966.

32. Editorial titled "Mälaren hotad" in Stockholms Dagens Nyheter, June 5, 1966, p. 2.

33. Interviews with Mr. E. G. Westman, June 15, 1966; and Mr. Romson, Secretary, Law Department, Swedish Association of Municipalities, June 13, 1966.

34. Stockholms Dagens Nyheter, June 5, 1966.

35. Interview with Mr. Thomas Michelsen, Editorial Writer, Stockholms Dagens Nyheter, June 27, 1966. A report of Statens Luftvårdsnämndkonferens in Stockholm was published, Luften, Bilen, Människan (Stockholm: P. A. Norstedt & Söner Förlag, 1966).

36. Dr. E. Eriksson, International Meteorological Institute, Tulegatan 41, Stockholm, through Mr. William J. Napeir, Urban Affairs Advisor, Office of Education and Information, U. S. Department of Health, Education and Welfare, March 20, 1969.

37. Interview with Mr. Sidenbladh.

38. Ahlberg, C. F., "An Outline of a regional plan for the Stockholm area," Att Bo (Stockholm: Tryckeriaktiebolaget Tiden, 1956), p. 42.

39. Interview with Mr. Thomas Atmer, Stadsbyggnadssekreterare, Stadsbyggnadskontoret, May 10, 1966.

40. Holland, Laurence B. (editor), Who Designs America? Princeton Studies in American Civilization (Garden City, N. Y.: Doubleday & Co., Inc., Anchor Books, 1966), p. 30.

41. Holm, Lennart, The National Swedish Institute for Building Research, 1966 (duplicated by the Institute). In this brochure, which is available in English, Dr. Holm presents the legal basis, the organization and the work program of the Institute.

Chapter XI

STOCKHOLM: COORDINATION

The Stockholm municipal administration has no one
Chief Executive.   Gradual evolution of an administrative system has produced a collective top management, which has
been described and analyzed in part in the previous two chapters.   Legally, the Executive Board in a collective capacity
has full responsibility for the administration.   Responsible
to the Executive Board is the "Stadskansli," which in English
is "The City Management Office," the Chief of which is Director of the Department of Finance.   The Office is organized into the following divisions:[1]

1.   Secretarial Division, the Chief of which is the
City Secretary, or Town Clerk.   The division has a staff of
23.

2.   Judicial Division, the Chief of which is the City
Solicitor.   Staff of 13.

3.   Finance Division, the Chief of which is the City
Finance Secretary.   Staff of 15.

4.   Organization Division, the Chief of which is the
Organization Director.   Staff of 27.

5.   Administrative Operations, the Chief of which is
the City Secretary.   Another secretary is operating superin-
tendent of the division, which has a staff of 37.

6.   Handbook Division, the Chief of which is a Secretary.   The staff of seven prepares for publication Stockholm
kommunalkalender.

The Statistical Office is also directly responsible to
the Executive Board.

The municipal administration is organized into nine

224

departments: 1) Finance,   2) Personnel,   3) Real Estate,
4) Traffic and City Building,   5) Industry,   6) Welfare,   7)
Culture and Education,   8) Health, and 9) Greater Stockholm.
The nine Commissioners manage their respective departments and, with a few exceptions, chair the boards within
their respective departments.   Overall coordination is provided in part by the bi-weekly meetings of the Board of Commissioners, of which the Director of the Department of Finance is chairman, and in part by the City Management Office, of which the Director of the Department of Finance is
the Chief.   The Director of the Department of Finance comes
closest, therefore, to the position of an acting administrative
chief in the operations of the municipal government in Stockholm.

    The administration is a career service below the Ex-
ecutive Board, the Board of Commissioners, and the other
boards and policy-forming agencies appointed by the City
Council.

    Attention will be directed first to finance agencies
and financial policies.   Two boards are involved in the Department of Finance, both of which are chaired by the Director of the Department of Finance: the Finance Board (Drät-
selnämnden), and the Tax Board (Direktionen för uppbörds-
väsen).

    The Finance Board has responsibility for the prepara-
tion and administration of the budget, the accounting function,
and a central data processing operation involving a staff of
300.

    There is a legal requirement that the budget for the
succeeding fiscal year beginning January 1st be passed not
later than December 8th.   During the first half of the year,
each board presents a draft budget for the coming year, specifying personnel and all other costs and also the direct revenue that can be anticipated.   From these submissions, an
itemized budget is prepared by the Budget Division.   The Finance Commissioner negotiates with the chairmen of the various boards and agencies concerning changes.   The resulting
document is presented to the Executive Board where changes
may be made.   The draft budget is then available for public
scrutiny for a short time.   Usually no one takes advantage
of this opportunity. [2]

    Debate may be continued by minor parties in the City

Council.   Once passed by the Council, the budget is binding
on all the boards and agencies.   Since 1958, the Department
of Finance has annually prepared a four-year operating budget, which in 1966 was extended to a five-year operating budget.   This facilitates financial planning.   Likewise since 1959,
a five-year capital budget has also been prepared annually
for Executive Board scrutiny and approval. [3] Approval that
is given applies to the capital investment plan in general and
not to the specifics.   Neither the operating budget five-year
projection nor the five-year capital budget is legally binding,
except those portions that are included in the annual budget
for the coming fiscal year.   A legal limitation specifies that
no portion of the capital resources may be used to meet current expenditures.   The operating budget may not be balanced
in this manner.   In the first five years of the Sixties, the
City of Stockholm had an operating budget surplus (shown in
millions of kronor):

1960 - 49. 4 SKr
1961 - 37. 2 SKr
1962 - 12. 9 SKr
1963 - 17. 7 SKr
1964 - 12. 6 SKr

Instead of using the surpluses to diminish the tax requirements for the following year, the surpluses have been
placed in a special fund, which has eased the borrowing requirements for the City. [4]

There has been discussion of the advisability of changing from the itemized budget to lump-sum authorizations in
order to grant more leeway for administrative discretion;
however, no change has been initiated in the form of the budget.

Accompanying the budget document is a budget message, which presents the accomplishments of the past year,
the objectives for the coming year, and the proposed programs for subsequent years, including anticipated revenues
and expenditures.   Prospects for the future are based on several possible alternatives as regards the economy of the city,
the region and the nation.   This budget message is printed
in full with the budget document and summarized verbally to
the Council.

To ensure autonomy of action by local governments in
Sweden, they have been given an independent power of taxa-

tion and may levy taxes without limitation from above.   An
unusual feature of local taxation in Sweden is believed to be
the absence of the real estate tax.   The Statistical Abstract
of Sweden specifies for the counties and the City of Stockholm
the value of real estate "liable to real estate duty."[5]   Actually, 20 per cent of the "taxation value" of real estate is
counted as income and added to other income.   Real estate is
valued on the basis of land potential in accordance with the
existing city plan for the area in question.

General assessment of real estate for tax purposes is
made every five years: 1965, 1970, 1975.   Special assess-
ments are made each year on property that has increased or
decreased in value that year by at least one-fifth through rebuilding, fire, or other change in the condition of the property.   The market value generally exceeds the assessed value.
All property is assessed.   National income tax is not paid on
state-owned property, whereas local income tax is paid in
full.[6]

The tax rate is determined by dividing the sum that is
needed by the total of assessed incomes of individuals and
corporations in the City.   "The sum that is needed" is determined by totalling the amount of revenue available from
other sources and deducting this from the planned expenditures.   The remainder must be covered by the income tax.[7]
The tax rate in Stockholm was 15 per cent for 1965, and was
increased to 17 per cent for 1966, which means 17 kronor
per 100 kronor of taxable income.   The five-year financial
plan anticipates a tax rate of 17.73 per cent by 1970.   This
has been called by municipal and national officials "a very
low tax" and "a modest tax."[8]   It is below the national average for municipal income taxes.   The Stockholm income tax,
however, is proportionate, while the national income tax is
progressive, which creates a political problem.   If the national government finances a program, the higher income
groups must pay a higher share of the program.

The current revenue sources are as follows:

20% municipally owned and administered enterprises
16% grants from the national government
14% miscellaneous other taxes, such as the entertain-
      ment tax, also licenses, fees, and charges
50% the ungraduated municipal income tax

100% total

Municipalities are not authorized to engage in business activities for a profit; however, the accounting procedure in dealing with depreciation and amortization for utilities and housing provides income beyond costs of operation.

The largest grants are specified for the building of schools, mental hospitals and other public facilities.

Unique other sources of revenue, large enough to be included in the national Statistical Abstract of Sweden, are a duty paid by foreign artists (Artistskatt), dog licenses (Hundskatt), and a portion (determined by the national government) of a seamen's tax (Sjömansskatt). [9]

The ungraduated municipal income tax rate is not limited or regulated by the national government, but as a matter of administrative convenience is collected by the national government and thereafter the municipal shares are distributed to the individual communes.   For this reason, the City must inform the national tax collection agency of the rate of taxation established by the City Council.   Since the national government collects the municipal income tax, the Stockholm Tax Board receives the amounts forwarded from the national tax collection agency through the County government and functions under county supervision.   The Stockholm Tax Board maintains the necessary tax records.   A staff of approximately 400 performs the function.

Municipal budgets have surged upwards sharply since World War II.   Municipal income taxes, collected by the national government for local governments, on a per capita basis increased from 45.39 SKr (Swedish Kronor) in 1954 to 73.50 SKr in 1964, which is more than a 50 per cent rise in income taxes within a decade. [10]   The City of Stockholm Operating Budget has totalled:[11]

> 2,025,832,000 SKr in 1962.
> 2,899,624,000 SKr in 1965.
> 3,273,496,000 SKr in 1966.

This shows more than a 50 per cent expansion in a four-year period from 1962 to 1966, and a 12+ per cent jump in one year, which means the same rate of budgetary growth, if continued.

The Stockholm Capital Budget for the five-year period totals 4,095,000,000 SKr.   The administration had recom-

mended 4, 301, 600, 000. [12]   For 1966, the Capital Budget totalled 1, 874, 842, 128 of which 995, 322, 248 came from special
funds and represented in part the payment of fiscal advances
and deficits, listed in the allotment of the Capital Budget
totals as "Increase of available regular capital resources,"
leaving 879, 519, 700 Skr expenditures for specified, substan-
tive purposes from Capital Budget. [13]   Of the 879,519, 700
SKr, real estate purchases were alloted 105,010,000 and
595, 153, 000 were alloted to construction and reconstruction.
This represents a tripling of the 1965 expenditures for real
estate and almost a one-third increase in the expenditures
for construction and reconstruction. [14]   The overwhelming
proportion of this part of the Capital Budget was thus alloted
to urban development.

     Between 1946-1963, local government investments in
terms of capital improvements have recorded by far the
greatest advance in comparison with private and national government investments.   The local government investments experienced a fourfold increase while total investments had only
slightly more than doubled.   Private investments remained
at the same level until the early years of the Fifties when an
upward trend started that has so far continued.   There has
been an obvious interaction between the public and private investments during the past decade.   When private investment
declined, public investment expanded rapidly and vice versa.[15]
This public policy led to a necessary regulation of public investments, both local and national, during a period of heavy
private investments.   Largely for this reason, sanction by
the national government has been necessary to raise loans
beyond specified limits.   The sale of bonds with maturity
dates longer than five years and/or exceeding 5 per cent of
the taxable income of the commune is severely restricted.
The Ministry of Finance and the Bank of Sweden have particularly held back on authorizing loans for communes like
Stockholm where the tax rate has been less than the national
average.   There were complaints about the national government's reluctance to permit the negotiation of loans from a-
broad.   "We could borrow from the United States and France,"
said one official, "but the Bank of Sweden said, 'No.   The
Balance of payments will not permit it'." [16]

     The reason may partially have been that also relevant
to the need for limiting foreign loans was the deliberate policy of limiting public investments during periods of rising private investments.

Since 1957, it has been necessary for Stockholm to
finance a growing proportion of its capital investments from
current revenues. In 1966 only 22 per cent of the long-term
investments could be financed by bond issues of greater than
five years maturity. [17] This is a particularly serious financial problem for a city like Stockholm, which faces rapidly
growing urban development needs.

Concerning local government financial control, all
boards throughout Sweden, including the Executive Board,
have to submit to audit, exercised by auditors appointed by
and working on behalf of the City Council. [18] In Stockholm,
this audit is performed by the staff of the Council Committee
on Administrative and Accounting Review (Revisionsutskottet).
Thus the elected representatives retain final financial control.

The second department listed in the official Stockholms Kommunalkalender 1966, is the Personnel Department
(Personalroteln). Two boards are also involved in this department, the Wage and Salary Board (Lönenämnder), and the
Personnel Training Board (Personalutbildningsnämnden). Both
of these boards are chaired by the Director of the Department of Personnel.

The responsibilities of the Wage and Salary Board
have gradually extended beyond the purpose specified in the
title, which was the purpose in 1911 when first established.
They now include, as well as wages, the policies and prac-
tices of appointment, bargaining with municipal employee unions, pensions, personnel counseling, and personnel health.
The Personnel Consultant and Personnel Health Divisions
grew out of consultations between the Swedish Municipal Association and the municipal employee unions in 1947. Thereafter, both the Association and the unions pressured the City
of Stockholm on this matter. After World War II, the two
new divisions were formally made part of the Stockholm Personnel Department.

Employes are classified in three categories; officials
(ambetsmän), employes (tjänstemän), and workers (arbetare).
Ambetsmän constitute the highest level of the career service, including top-level career supervision, ombudsmän and
professional groups such as architects, physicians and lawyers. All other municipal employes, not classified as
"workers," are tjänstemän. [19] Charts #1 and 2 in the Appendix,
prepared by the Personnel Director of the City of Stockholm,

show the growth of municipal salaried employes and wage
workers in the City from 13,000+ to approximately 16,000 in
each category, totalling close to 32,000 at the end of 1964.[20]
An additional 8,000 were employed by the companies owned
by the City. According to the Calmfors, Rabinovitz and
Alesch study, by 1967 a substantial increase had taken place
in both categories.[21]

Any vacancy in the municipal service is advertised
with specifications as to the necessary qualifications, which
are determined locally by the Board involved with the approval of the Personnel Department (Wage and Salary Board)
and specified in part in municipal ordinances. Only the general qualifications of certain professional positions are specified in national legislation, particularly in fields such as
city planning, land surveying, public health, medicine and
education. Applicants apply to the operating Board involved
and those with the best records are interviewed. Inter-
viewees who are accepted are employed for a probationary
period, varying from six months to one year, during which
time he can be summarily dismissed if he does not measure
up to expectations. Each board hires and fires its personnel
under the overall personnel regulations of the City, which
are determined in part by collective bargaining.[22] If an applicant feels that he has not been given a fair opportunity,
or a former employee feels he has been dismissed unfairly,
an appeal can be made to the Appeals Board (Besvärsnämnd),
appointed by the City Council to hear and decide complaints
over employment, working conditions or discipline.

The City of Stockholm has four Social Högskolor (Social High Schools), which provide courses in administration.
Most of the graduates enter the public service. Courses on
municipal problems and courses relevant to municipal problems are given at the University of Stockholm. Academic
records of such courses, if favorable, and research papers
submitted at the University of Stockholm, are helpful in making application for a municipal position.

Some of the boards provide courses which introduce
the new employee to the Stockholm government, also instruct
him as regards the salary system, personnel organization and
his rights as a municipal employee. The Personnel Training
Board, established a decade ago, is in the process of developing in-service training, which consists largely of circulat-
ing employees from agency to agency under close supervision.
In 1961, Örby Castle was made available to the Board for

course instruction. Over a dozen rooms are usable as class-
rooms, in addition to the kitchen and banquet hall on the first
floor and sleeping quarters on the top floor. The above described arrangements represent a beginning and speak well for
the future of an effective in-service education program for
municipal employees.

A Local Government School in Sigtuna (north of Stockholm), which is closely associated with the Swedish Municipal Association, the Swedish Association of Communes, and
the Swedish Association of Country Councils, conducts three-
day seminars and one-week and two-week courses for elected
and council-selected as well as appointed officials, which
serve very effectively as in-service education for municipal
government officials. [23]

A 1965 law gives all municipal employes and workers
the legal right to engage in collective bargaining. The national Swedish Trade Union of Communal Workers has a membership of 140,000; the Swedish Central Organization of Communal Salaried Employees, 40,000 members; and the Swedish
Communal Professional Association, 20,000 members. In
total, 200,000 local government employees, including
workers, tjänstemän and professional personnel are organized. The overwhelming proportion of local government employees are thus unionized. [24]

The Swedish Municipal Association on behalf of the
cities, the Association of Swedish Communes on behalf of the
other communes, and the Association of Swedish County Councils on behalf of the County Councils represent their respective members in negotiations with the national unions of local
government employees. The national government approved
this centralization for purposes of negotiations by Act of 1954.
Mr. Lars Gräslund, Personnel Director, City of Stockholm,
elaborates on the process involved insofar as the Swedish
Municipal Association is concerned as follows:

> The central bargaining delegation of this associa-
> tion, at present 20 members, is elected for a per-
> iod of three years by the congress of the associa-
> tion. The agreements negotiated by the central
> delegation are not legally binding on the municipali-
> ties but are forwarded to the members as recom-
> mendations by the central parties. These recom-
> mendations are supposed to be applied in unchanged

form by the municipalities and since 1951 there has
been a clause in the rules of the association which
requires members, on the pain of expulsion, to follow recommendations which are formulated by the
central bargaining delegation. The municipalities
have on the whole been loyal to their organization
even if the discipline has sometimes wavered,
chiefly owing to the shortage of manpower. [25]

Most of the collective contracts for workers in private
industry expire during the first quarter of the year. Negotiations, which were started during the previous year, are
usually concluded in February or March. When the central
agreement between the Swedish Employers' Confederation and
the Confederation of Swedish Trade Unions has been signed,
the Swedish Municipal Association enters into negotiations
with the Kommunal Arbetsförbund (the Association of Communal Workers) on behalf of the cities. The negotiations
concern chiefly the adaptation of the SAK - LO agreement
(between the national Employers' Confederation and the national
Trade Union) to the municipal field. If the negotiations
move smoothly, agreement may be reached in April. On the
other hand, negotiations may continue until June or July. The
assistance of a mediator has occasionally been necessary.

Negotiations with salaried employees follow a different
pattern. The national government and the associations of local governments have agreed that it would be to mutual advantage to coordinate salary policy. The Municipal Association
therefore waits for the national government negotiations.
Normally negotiations comprise a packet, including salary
scales, classification of jobs, overtime pay, shift pay and
other economic problems and benefits. After the national
government agreement has been reached usually in the middle
of April, this agreement is applied to the municipal area.

As regards negotiations with the Communal Workers Association, the Central Organization of Salaried Employees and
the Swedish Confederation of Professional Associations, the
agreements reached have to be applied at the local level by negotiations with the local unions and thereafter application must be
made to each worker and each employee. In the municipal field,
after 1966, each contract, which previously was reviewed every
two years, shall be reviewed every three years.

Neither party (employer or employee) can go to court
without negotiating first. The Labor Court has jurisdiction

over any problem regulated by a union contract.   Otherwise,
the administrative court or the regular courts are available.
Mr. Lars Gräslund specifies,

> There is no compulsory arbitration in Sweden, and
> no legislation which enables the government to
> solve labor disputes over the heads of the parties.[26]

Legal limitations on offensive actions are very few.
Since January 1, 1966, national and local government civil
servants have practically the same right to go on strike as
employes in private enterprise.   Likewise since 1966, the
salaried employes and the workers have basicly the same
rules, hence the same rights.   The negotiating parties may
resort to strike, blockade, lock-out and other coercive
measures if they do not agree about questions covered by a
collective agreement, just as may employees in private enterprise, but first they must negotiate.

Stockholm has two salary scales.   Scale A covers the
bulk of the municipal service, has 27 salary grades with adjustments for three cost-of-living zones in the city and has
four salary classes in each grade.   The employee, after
three years' employment, automatically moves into the salary
class above until after nine years he reaches his final salary,
except for age-allowances, placement of his position in a
higher grade, adjustment of the scale, advancement, or promotion.   Scale B includes the higher officials at a higher
salary level with eight salary grades.   There are no cost-
of-living adjustments and no age-allowances.   The grading of
jobs and the general level of the salary scale is decided by
collective agreements.   An employee can get a pay raise
either by the placement of his position in a higher grade or
by an adjustment of the scale.   In 1964, the amounts of the
salary scale in Stockholm were increased by 3 per cent and
at the same time about a third of the Stockholm officials
were placed in a higher salary grade.

The collective agreement with the workers contains a
clause that "payment by results," which is in effect piece-
rate setting, shall be the normal form of remuneration; however, the agreement also provides for "time wages."   The
1960-1961 Central Wage Agreement between the Swedish Employers' Confederation and the Confederation of Swedish Trade
Unions is significant because it prohibited sexual pay dis-
crimination, which was accepted by the Swedish Municipal
Association for adoption by the municipalities. [27]

The salary of the municipal employee in Stockholm
compares favorably with the salaries in the national government.   The top rank of the Stockholm administration is actually better paid than the chief national administrative officials.   The municipal worker earns on an average more than
his counterpart in private industry; he also is in a favored
position in other respects: sick pay, pension and security
of employment.   Since the entire municipal career service is
unionized, the salaried employees compare favorably with the
workers as regards pay and working conditions.   Chart # 3
in the Appendix shows the trend in salaries and wages from
1955 to 1964.   While during this time the consumer price index had moved from 100 to 135, salaries moved from 100
to 173 and wages, to 184.   In annual leave, the advantage
favors the salaried employees at salary grade 14 or above,
while salaried employees below salary grade 14 has the same
holiday leave as the workers:[28]

Employee's Age	Working Days of Annual Leave
under 29	24
30 - 39	27
40	30

Mr. Lars Gräslund admits that there is the danger
that municipal employees may get a more favored treatment
than the employees in the private sector.   Local government
cannot be closed down like a factory.   Furthermore, it is
difficult to apply cost accounting to many municipal services.
Along this line of reasoning, Mr. Gräslund states,

> The trade unions have not always been able to re-
> sist this temptation.   The incitement for the em-
> ployees to demand more than their fair share is
> not lessened by their realizing that the municipali-
> ties find it hard to endure conflicts.   Even the
> threat of a conflict exerts a powerful pressure on
> the municipal representative when it comes from
> nurses, doctors and firemen to pick a few examples
> at random. [29]

Retirement normally takes place at age 65.   Employees are seldom retained after age 67.   Three years of
employment is necessary to qualify for a pension, which a-
mounts to 62 per cent of final pay.   After four years of retirement, the pension is 75 per cent of final pay, and after
12 years of retirement, the full amount.   The surviving

spouse receives 31 per cent of the pension. The pension is
non-contributory, the government paying the full amount. [30]

Concerning the possibility of dismissals, with the eventuality of loss of pension rights, a person employed for ten
years or more, or a person who has reached the age of 40
with five years' or more employment, can be dismissed if
the service he performs becomes superfluous, but he must
be given a one year's notice. In practice, however, such
employes are normally transferred to a new task.

Two characteristics of the municipal employee in
Stockholm are worthy of notice. Foreign workers total 10
per cent of all the workers, largely in the hospital services,
and communists are not excluded. [31]

The entire wage and salary structure for business, industry and government may be responsible for inflation in
Sweden. Due to a shortage of manpower there is intense
competition for personnel. Furthermore, the municipal wage
and salary policy is based on the premise that the problems
of the municipalities demand the best skills and abilities a-
vailable in order to cope with the increasingly complex urban
problems. Stockholm has provided a wage and salary policy
to attract the best available in all three categories: ämbets-
män, tjänstemän and arbetare. The Stockholm leaders hold
to the view that the highest caliber is equally necessary
from bottom to top in the municipal service. If wages and
salaries are high in the overall economy, they need to be
higher in the public service, particularly at the municipal
level.

Swedish literature on the Stockholm Government has
stressed the important role of finance in top management
policy-making. Personnel selection has played an equally important role on a more decentralized basis; however top management has provided the necessary financial support for effective personnel selection.

The individual citizen has his opportunity to hold the
individual municipal employee, or administrator, answerable.
The public ombudsmän, officers of the Riksdag, are available to citizens who have complaints about municipal officials in regard to malfeasance or nonfeasance of obligatory
functions. The ombudsman is authorized to hear and investigate such complaints on behalf of the citizen, bring the attention of higher officials to the administrative error or dere-

liction, follow through on a correction and negotiate if necessary, and initiate court action if a legally punishable derelic-
tion of duty is involved, or explain to the citizen his misunderstanding if the complaint is based on a misunderstanding.[32]
The citizens also have access to the board in charge of a
particular function by mail to make complaints as regards
any aspect of the administration of that function. Furthermore, complaints from citizens that come to the attention of
a member, or members, of the City Council may result in
an interpellation, which must be answered at the next session
of the City Council. In these ways, the municipal administration of specific functions can be made responsive directly to
the citizenry.

Administrative policy coordination takes place through
the Board of Commissioners, which is responsible to the
Executive Board, and the Executive Board, which is responsible to the City Council.

Administrative management coordination is provided
through 1) the Departments of Finance and Personnel, 2)
the City Management Office, and 3) the Board of Commissioners.

Thus, the multiple parts of the complex municipal
structure of Stockholm seem to be pulled together adequately.
With one exception, they are all under the final control of
the City Council. The one exception are the 20 relatively
independent quasi-public corporations under partial municipal
control. In the case of corporations, in which the City owns
all the stock, the board of directors are all selected by the
City, in most instances by the City Commissioners. In the
case of corporations, in which the City owns a portion of
the stock, only the board members who are selected by the
City (Commissioners) are responsible to the City. Studies
and investigations have been and are being conducted to discover some means of making all the quasi-public corporations in which the City has an interest reasonably more responsible to the Stockholm Government. [33]

Notes

1. Specific information concerning the administrative struc-
    ture and the functions of agencies are taken from
    Stockholms Kummunalkalender 1966 unless otherwise

specified.

Stadskollegiets utlåtanden| och memorial, Bihang
1966, Nr 1B, Stockholms stads utgifts och inkomstat
för år 1966, Lönebilaga (Stockholm: K. L. Beckmans
Tryckerier Ab, 1966). This salary ordinance is used
for the personnel number per division and agency, unless otherwise specified.

2. Hjelmquist, Ingvar, Director of the Local Government
School, Sigtuna, Local Government Finance in Sweden,
Summary of a Lecture given at the IULA-course at
Sigtuna, October 8, 1965 (mimeographed copy), p. 9.
Information concerning budget procedure in Stockholm
was secured from conversations and lectures at the
Sigtuna School, June 17, 1966.

3. Stadskollegiets utlåtanden och memorial, Bihang 1966,
Nr 1C, Stockholms stads utgifts och inkomst för år
1966, övriga bilagor; p. 626: "Driftbudetberäkningar
för femårsperioden 1966-1970," and p. 609: "Inves-
teringsplan för femårsperioden 1966-1970." All financial projections in this chapter will be taken from
this document.

4. A statement regarding the Budget Situation, September
8, 1965. "The Operating Budget" (mimeographed),
signed by H. J. Mehr, Finance Commissioner.

5. Central Bureau of Statistics, Statistical Abstract of
Sweden (Stockholm: P. A. Norstedt & Söner, 1965),
p. 355, Table 411.

6. Letter from Mr. Hjalmar Mehr, former Commissioner
of Finance, currently Commissioner, Department of
Housing and Real Estate, November 19, 1968.

7. Interviews with Mr. E. Wannfors, Division Director,
National Building and Planning Board, June 28, 1966;
and Dr. Gunnar Åsvärn (Sociologist), Secretary,
Gatukontoret, May 17, 1966.

8. Ibid.

9. Central Bureau of Statistics, Op. cit., p. 358 & 359,
Table 413.

10. Ibid., p. 363, Table 418.

11. Stadskollegiets utlåtanden och memorial, Bihang 1966, Nr 1A, Stockholms stads utgifts och inkomstat för år 1966, p. XLII & XLIII, "Totalsammandrag." Source for the Operating Budget total for 1965 and 1966.
    Calmfors, Hans, Rabinovitz, Francis F. and Alesch, David J., Urban Government for Greater Stockholm (N. Y.: Frederick A. Praeger Publishers, 1968), p. 109, Table 19. Source for the Operating Budget total for 1962.

12. Stadskollegiets utlåtanden och memorial, Bihang 1966, Nr 1C, p. 610 & 611, "Totalsammanstallning for investeringsplanen 1966-1970.

13. Ibid., p. 548, "Fördelning av bruttoutgifterna på de i staten upptagna utgiftsrubrikerna (forts.) Kapitalbudgeten."

14. Ibid.

15. Hjelmquist, Ingvar, Op. cit., p. 3-5.

16. Interview with Dr. Gunnar Åsvärn, May 17, 1966.

17. Stadskollegiet utlåtanden och memorial, Bihang 1966, Nr 1C, p. 548.

18. Hjelmquist, Ingvar, Op. cit., p. 10.

19. Interview with Mr. Enar Lindquist, Secretary, Swedish Municipal Association, April 26, 1966.

20. Gräslund, Lars, Personnel Director, City of Stockholm, Conditions of Employment for Employees of the Swedish Local Government (mimeographed brochure, undated), Appendix 6.

21. Calmfors, Rabinovitz and Alesch, Op. cit., p. 45.

22. Interview with Mr. Wilhelm Forsberg, Personnel Commissioner, June 14, 1966.

23. Interview with Dr. Ingvar Hjelmquist, Director, Local Government School, Sigtuna, June 17, 1966.

24. Interview with Mr. Gräslund, Secretary, Swedish Mu-

nicipal Association, April 27, 1966.

25. Gräslund, Lars, Op. cit., p. 8. The bargaining pro-
     cedure with the unions is secured from this source.

26. Ibid., p. 1.

27. Ibid., p. 4-6. Also, text of Central Agreement between
     SAF and LO for 1960-61, p. 2.

28. Gräslund, Lars, Op. cit., Appendices 7 & 15.

29. Ibid., p. 5.

30. Interview with Mr. Wilhelm Forsberg, Personnel Com-
     missioner, June 14, 1966.

31. Ibid.

32. See the following titles: Anderson, Stanley V. (editor),
     Ombudsman for American Government (Englewood
     Cliffs, N.J.: Prentice-Hall, Inc., 1968).
          Rowat, Donald C. (editor), The Ombudsman, Citi-
     zen's Defender (Toronto: University of Toronto Press,
     1968).
          The American Assembly, Columbia University,
     The Ombudsman, Report of the Thirty-second Ameri-
     can Assembly, October 26-29, 1967.
          Thierfelder, Hans, Zurn Problem eines Ombuds-
     mans in Deutschland (Köln und Berlin: G. Grotesche
     Verlagsbuchhandlung K. G., 1967).
          Gellhorn, Walter, Ombudsmen and Others, Citi-
     zen's Protectors in Nine Countries (Cambridge, Mass.:
     Harvard University Press, 1966).
          Rosenthal, Albert H., "The Ombudsman--Swedish
     Grievance Man," Public Administration Review, XXIV
     (December 1964), p. 226-230.

33. Interview with Mr. Romson, Secretary, Law Division,
     Swedish Association of Municipalities, June 13, 1966.

Chapter XII

STOCKHOLM: INTERGOVERNMENTAL RELATIONS

During the 1930s and 1940s, it became self-evident in
Sweden that there were too many communes, that numerous
of the smaller communes were financially unable to perform
their functions satisfactorily, and that something had to be
done about it. The division into communes introduced in
1863, when local self-government was reactivated, was still
in effect and the boundaries relatively unchanged. Many of
the smaller communes had shrunk to less than 100 inhabitants. The smallest had 69 inhabitants. A parliamentary
committee was established in 1943 to investigate the situation and to report a recommendation. On the basis of the
recommendation reported, Parliament approved in 1946 a
proposal to merge the small rural communes into larger
units, and entrusted to the County Governors' offices the task
of solving the many problems that emerged during this effort to get the smaller communes to agree to merge. Pressure was used. The objective of the proposal was to make
2000 to 3000 the minimum size of a commune. Six years
were involved in the effort. By 1952, the number of rural
communes had been reduced from 2,281 to 816. [1]

During the following decade, only a few minor mergers took place. By the end of 1963, the number of rural
communes had been reduced to 777. The number of cities
remained unchanged, 133. Boroughs had increased to 96,
eight more than in 1952, making the total number of communes 1,006. [2]

In the Fifties, the population movement from the rural
areas to the urban concentrations had come more swiftly than
had been anticipated, and it was obvious that this exodus
from the rural to the urban areas was far from ended. Furthermore, the local governmental responsibilities had grown
substantially both in the number of duties to be performed
and the financial burdens involved. It was estimated that a
population of 5,000 to 6,000 was necessary to finance and

241

administer an old people's home, a population of 6,500 to
7,500 to finance and administer a compulsory nine-year comprehensive school, and a population of 8,000 to 10,000 to
finance and administer a public health service.

The number of communal associations (kommunalförbund) had been reduced from 935, in 1951, to 181 in 1953
during the period of mergers of small communes; however,
the number of such communal associations had risen to 247,
involving 671 communes, and the number of communal com-
pacts had also risen, to 753, by 1960. There was an obvious need for larger communal entities, particularly in the
fields of school administration, health and hospital care,
provision of water, city planning, housing, industrial development, and fire and police administration. [3] In order adequately to maintain local responsibility for these functions,
action was necessary to enlarge and make financially responsible the communal entities. In February 1961, a Parliamentary committee, appointed by the State to consider again
the problem of communal governments, reported a new proposal which Parliament adopted in 1962. It provided for
"municipal blocks" within which the communes should form a
collaboration council to which participating communes should
elect representatives. The function of the council was to develop plans for municipal cooperation. The municipal blocks
were thought of as inducements to future mergers of the
communes within a block. Knowledgeable experts in the
field recommended that it should be mandatory that collaboration council members be selected in every block in order
to make the transition to mergers smooth and effective. The
national government, however, opposed any mandatory provisions. Since the communes were not to be forced into
mergers, neither should the collaboration be based on anything but "free choice." Yet it was emphasized that it would
be in the interests of all the communes to participate, and
that the collaboration councils would be used by the state authorities as introductory agencies to future mergers.

Again the national government delegated to the County
Governors' offices responsibility for implementing the proposal, specifically the responsibility for preparing guidelines
for the municipal blocks. The total number of municipal
blocks was fixed at 282. Of this total, almost a half com-
prised two to four communes and 37 were single communes
that did not need to be brought into combinations. The
largest number of communes in one block was in Gotland
(island) where 14 communes were formed into one block,

which included the entire county. The block formations were
based not on the population as of January 1, 1964, but as of
the estimated population in 1975, at which time it is anticipated that 8,000 shall be the minimum. This can not be a
legally mandatory minimum, but is a reasonably safe statistical approximation.

The 1952 Parliamentary proposal for reducing the
number of communes in Sweden was concerned only with the
small rural communes, bringing the smallest communes into
community-related entities of larger than 2,000 to 3,000 population in order that they would be financially able to perform the most essential local functions. The 1964 Parliamentary proposal, however, included all of Sweden and attempted to make the communal blocks coincide with commercial and industrial areas, so that they would comprise areas
in which commerce, finances, and communications systems
were complementary. Among the variables used were population movements, commercial traffic, telephone communication, newspaper circulation and economic transactions.

The communal blocks were formed one county at a
time. Each county administration made investigations and
recommended block formations. In many cases, the county
administration revised its recommendations on the basis of
critical comments by the communes. In other cases mutual-
ly agreed upon adjustments were made, while in several
cases, there was agreement from the very beginning. The
final result was that 770 communes supported the county administrations' recommendations, while 220 worked for other
solutions. The national government made significant changes
in the county administrations' recommendations, Of the final
282 communal blocks, 183 were identical with the county
recommendations. The decisions by the national government
were made in conference with the county administrations, at
which meetings the dissatisfied communes were represented.
Finally, hearings were held under the Department of Interior's
auspices, at which 150 dissatisfied communes were heard.
The major opposition came from the smallest communes. A-
mong the communes with less than 2,000 population only 29
per cent were in agreement with the county administrations'
recommendations, while among the communes with more than
10,000 population, 60 per cent accepted the county recommendations without complaint. During the investigations,
statements by the political party representatives and the press
debate seemed to indicate that the communal reorganization
would take place without political party opposition. The quiet

on the political front, however, did not last. The Social
Democrats, Liberals, and Communists supported the communal reorganization, while the Conservatives and Centrists
were in opposition. Deviations from party policy were numerous. By the beginning of 1965, nearly all the communal
blocks had either been formed or were in the process of being formed.

The parliamentary committee plan of 1961 for the formation of communal blocks excluded the Stockholm, Gothenburg and Malmö metropolitan areas with the thought that
larger administrative entities would be needed in the metropolitan areas for reasons other than the small population in
individual communes. [4] Most of the communes in Stockholm
County have more than the 8,000 population, which is the
basis for the block formation program; nevertheless the Department of Interior recommended to Stockholm County that
communal blocks be formed. In 1963, the Stockholm County
administration submitted a 31 communal block delineation,
18 of which were single commune blocks. [5] In 1965, the national government required the formation of communal blocks
in Stockholm County, grouping the 53 communes into 24
blocks. Thirteen of these blocks were within the Stockholm
metropolitan area, as defined in Table 3 in the Appendix,
which is equivalent to the Greater Stockholm Local Traffic
Association. [6]

The Swedish Commune Association and the Swedish
Municipal Association have avoided interfering in the communal controversies and differences of opinion. Instead the
associations have attempted to convince the communes with
advice and information on the advantages of block formation
and have assisted in the preparation of guidelines for communal blocks. On the initiative of the national Building
Board in the spring of 1964, a work group was established
to develop guidelines for planning within the communal
blocks. The work group consisted of representatives of the
Building Board, the Housing Board, the Swedish Communal
Association and the Swedish Municipal Association under the
chairmanship of the General Director of the Building Board.
The work group decided to carry through a problem inven-
tory within a communal block of "normal size and make-up,"
and selected Hudviksvallsblocket, involving five communes,
for the case study. The report was published and distributed in 1965 by the Swedish Commune Association. [7] In this
manner by providing sample studies, guidance was given the
communal blocks by the National Building Board and the com-

munal and municipal associations.

The criticism has been made that the 1962 law is vague on the responsibilities, duties and powers of the "collaboration councils," or "cooperation committees," which have been formed in each communal block containing more than one commune. [8] The intent and hope are that once collaboration and cooperation have been initiated, the communes within a block will develop sufficient common interests to wish to continue working together and to be ready within a reasonable period of time to merge. The overall responsibility of the collaboration council obviously is to get the communes within a block to collaborate in any way possible. Specifics in the law concerning responsibilities, particularly as regards duties and more specifically as regards powers, might well have proven to be self-defeating.

Even before the 1862 establishment of municipal government apart from the parish, organized cooperation between parishes by means of contracts, the creation associations and the establishment of companies was practiced. [9] Ever since, an extensive and growing use has been made of these cooperative devices until the 1950s, at which time the first effort at reducing the number of communes was initiated. In the metropolitan areas, except for the formation of communal blocks in the 1960s, which involves potential reduction, the use of cooperative devices has continued unabated.

As regards associations, Swedish law distinguishes sharply between "kommunalförbund" and "kommunförbund." A kommunalförbund comes into existence by virtue of state action and is regulated under public law, the Law on Communal Associations of May 31, 1957. [10] This kommunalförbund steps into the competence of a commune and legally represents the commune and it therefore can be given any number of functions. A kommunförbund, on the other hand, is an agreement between communes under civil law, which is not covered by the communal law. The kommunförbund can be given one or more related functions only, and does not before the law take the place of the commune. Furthermore, a communal association (kommunalförbund) is regionally limited, involving neighboring communes. A commune association (kommunförbund), on the contrary, is not so limited and may involve communes scattered anywhere in Sweden. [11] For this reason, the municipal associations within a metropolitan area are normally in the form of kommunalförbunder.

Prior to an examination of the particulars in the
Stockholm MA, a glance at the background of the relations
between Stockholm and the suburban cities, boroughs and
communes is presented. Director Lennart Lyström, Greater
Stockholm County Committee (Storlandstingskommitten), very
briefly describes this background as follows:

Stage 1 (before 1900).   The suburbs wanted to join
with Stockholm.

Stage 2 (1900-1950).   Stockholm wanted to annex the
suburbs.

Stage 3 (after 1950).   Cooperation. [12]

The contract device has been used extensively. Mr.
E. G. Westman, Stadjuristen, Stockholm, stated that every
year new contracts were negotiated by the City of Stockholm
with neighboring municipalities. He was not sure, but there
may be 100 such contracts involving, in general: education,
welfare, health, hospital services, housing, public transportation, fire protection, and the utilities such as water, gas,
electricity, drainage and sewage disposal. The one criticism
that Mr. Westman specified was that these contracts were
perpetual. He preferred to make them ten- or 20-year contracts, which would make them periodically reviewable and
subject to revision, hence providing more effective technical
and policy control. [13]   These contracts are of different types.
For example, one commune contracts to perform a municipal service for another commune which does not have the
specified municipal service. Or, two communes, each of
which performs a specified municipal service, contract with
each other that under certain circumstances each commune
shall be prepared and willing to service the other commune.
Or, again, two or more communes contract for joint administration of one or more municipal services.

In 1946, a Cooperation Council of Stockholm Suburbs
(Stockholms Förorters Samarbetsnämnd) was created by voluntary action in order to secure cooperation in matters of
common interest. Twenty-six communes in the inner and
outer rings surrounding the City joined. The matters of common interest that particularly concerned them were town
planning, community development, housing, water, and sewage treatment. The council has no technical staff; however,
the existence of the council, in addition to providing cooperation among the suburbs, facilitates negotiations with the City

of Stockholm in the development of cooperative agreements.[14]

The cities, boroughs and communes within the Stockholm MA, including the City of Stockholm, petitioned the national government in 1950 to create a Regional Planning Association and by order of the national government Stor-Stockholmstraktens Regionplansförbund was created in 1951, joining the City of Stockholm and 44 communes in Stockholm County and one commune (Upplands-Bro) in Uppsala County in one planning unit. The membership, structure and planning jurisdiction are prescribed in the legislation creating the Association. Stockholm has 33 representatives and the suburban communes, 52 representatives on the Association Assembly. An Executive Board of nine delegates, four selected by Stockholm and five selected by the suburban communes with the chairman and the vice-chairman appointed by the Crown, serves as the executive. The Greater Stockholm Regional Planning Office has a professional planning staff which in addition to providing long-range planning for the Association, assists the communes with long-range planning. The staff is currently updating a 1990 plan to a year 2000 plan.[15] Normally a planning agency is advisory only, therefore it is quite appropriate that the decisions of the Greater Stockholm Regional Association are not binding on the communes; however the county and the national administrations in passing on town plans (communal plans) will compare them with the regional plans, raising questions concerning failure to comply, and will refuse to approve serious deviations.

Stockholm assumed the initiative in 1954 with a reorganization on its administrative structure, creating a Greater Stockholm Department, establishing within the department the Greater Stockholm Delegation under the chairmanship of the Commissioner of the Department. The function of this delegation is to represent the City in dealings with the suburban communes, regional agencies and regional problems. The Building Board and the planning staff were also placed in the Greater Stockholm Department, thus emphasizing the planning aspect of this regional relationship. The reorganization became effective in 1955.

Three years later, the Greater Stockholm Planning Board (Stor-Stockholms Planeringsnämnd), a voluntary association of Stockholm with 18 communes forming the inner ring of suburbs, was formed. This association included in addition to Stockholm five cities, five boroughs and eight communes (landskommuner). The board has ten members

and ten deputies, half selected by the Stockholm government
and half by the Cooperation Council of Stockholm Suburbs.
The chairmanship is rotated between a Stockholm member
and a suburban member. From the very beginning, the major responsibility has been the housing problem. The other
problems of special interest and concern to this Association
are also of an "action program" nature, including the regional provision of water purification, sewage disposal, industrial location, traffic, certain educational problems and capital
investment programing. The Association is voluntary in
every sense of the word. Its decisions are not binding on
member communes, yet the Association has become one of
the most significant of the agencies for cooperation in the
Stockholm metropolitan area.

The City of Stockholm contacted the County of Stockholm in 1952 concerning joint planning of hospital services.
Delegates met in 1957 and agreed on the proposition of joint
planning of medical services within the Greater Stockholm
area. Specific agreements were negotiated concerning children's diseases in 1958, maternity and women's (gynecologic)
care in 1963. In the same year, a hospital plan was processed by the County and the City for the Greater Stockholm
area. Simultaneously, the City and County organized the
Greater Stockholm Hospital Board (Stor-Stockholms Sjukvårds-
beredningen). Five representatives from the City and five
from the County serve on the board, which is assisted by a
committee of experts from the City and County staffs. Provision is also made for a managing office.

Continued cooperation of the City and the County was
directed towards the financing and construction of a collective
traffic system in Greater Stockholm, which materialized with
the signing of an Agreement on Principles (principöverenskommelse) in 1965. On the basis of this Agreement, an Association (kommunalförbund) was formed the same year (Kommunalförbundet för Stockholms stads och läns regionala frågor). A representative council with 40 representatives from
the City and 40 representatives from the County was established. An Executive Board of 17 with eight deputies became
the executive organ of the Association. To start the Association functioning, the Executive Board created two committees: Traffic, and Water and Sewage and Industrial Waste
Treatment and Disposal. The Association lacks taxing power
and must be financed by the City and County; however, it is
authorized to borrow up to 300 million kroner to meet expenditures until 1970. The first objective is collective traffic

including the underground network; next is regional water and
sewage and industrial waste treatment and disposal, and
thereafter cooperative work on other urgent matters of common interest, delegating to the Association the submission of
recommendations to the City and the County for final decisions.

Sewage treatment and disposal are provided by the
City of Stockholm for three suburbs to the north of Stockholm
and four suburbs to the south. In the northeastern portion of
Greater Stockholm, sewage treatment and disposal are provided by Kappalaförbundet, a "kommunalförbund," including
in its membership 11 suburbs. This communal association
was organized in 1957 and its installations were to be in full
operation by 1969-1970. Coordination is secured through the
Greater Stockholm Planning Board, in which Kappalaförbundet
as well as the City of Stockholm have representatives.

A committee of representatives from the cities of
Stockholm and Södertälj and three neighboring communes decided that a joint corporation was necessary to provide sewage treatment and disposal in the area covered by the afore-
mentioned cities and communes. The Southwest Greater
Stockholm Regional Waterworks Company (Sydvästra Stock-
holmsregionens Va-verks-aktiebolag) was established in 1964
and will be in operation in the early 1970s.

Water purification and distribution are provided by the
City of Stockholm to 13 suburbs immediately surrounding the
City. The northern suburbs with the exception of two which
are serviced by the City receive purified water through the
Greater Stockholm Water Works Association (Stockholmstrak-
tens Vattenverksförbund), one of the oldest "kommunalförbund" in Sweden. This communal association has 13 members. Of the total population in the Greater Stockholm Area,
95 per cent are now provided water purification and distribution service. Here also coordination is secured through the
Greater Stockholm Planning Board.

The corporate device is used for housing as well as
utility development. In 1961, the City of Stockholm and the
City of Nacka established a housing company to assume responsibility for the redevelopment of land which Stockholm
owns in Nacka. The actual planning, building and administration of the housing was assigned to "Hyrehus i Stockholm
Aktiebolag," a City of Stockholm corporation. The jointly-
owned dwelling units are divided between the Stockholm and

Nacka housing placement agencies. By 1966, eleven similar
housing agreements had been negotiated, involving 25,000
dwelling units whereof approximately 70 per cent have been
or are at the City of Stockholm's disposal. [16]

Following World War II, the future use of Järvafältet,
a military base in and immediately north of the City of Stockholm and bordering on four other communes, became a center of interest for the five communes with the hope that this
territory could be made available for housing development.
Through the Fifties, the five communes and the Greater
Stockholm Regional Planning Association were active in their
efforts to get a clarification on the question of the national
government's eventual disposition of Järvafältet. A plan for
Järvafältet was officially approved in November 1963 by the
Board of the Greater Stockholm Regional Planning Association.

A committee of the five communes was formed in 1964
to coordinate negotiations with the Crown and the programing of each communes' activities in this connection. In 1966,
an agreement was reached between the Crown and the five
communes concerning 4000 hectares in Järvafältet, representing a beginning of the proposed development. The Committee
for the Acquisition and Development of Järvafältet) has arranged for a competition among Scandinavian architectural
firms for the development, and will continue representing the
five communes as long as necessary. Two decades of deli-
cate negotiations concerning the military base, involving the
City of Stockholm, two other cities, two communes, the
Greater Stockholm Regional Planning Association and the national government have been managed successfully without
serious disagreement. In this instance, a simple committee
played a vital role.

With the exception of the communal association and the
corporate bases of cooperation, the varied cooperative arrangements have involved and continue to involve planning,
which leaves to each individual commune the implementation
of the plan within its own jurisdiction. The communal councils in these instances must make the decisions.

This increasing complexity of the many coordinating
devices and agencies and the increasing need for some overall coordination motivated Mr. Hjalmar Mehr, finansborgar-
rådet, to present and advocate the "Stor-Stockholm" proposal.
In an address before the Stockholm City Council on December
5, 1963, Mr. Hjalmar Mehr presented the rationale for the

proposal. [17] In this statement he commences with the observation that many of the basic problems of the city have become metropolitan; also that due to a scarcity of land and
dwellings in Stockholm, population is moving into the suburbs,
and this new suburban population are the children of Stockholm residents and consider themselves "Stockholmare" and
therefore they consider the public transportation system and
the social and cultural institutions of Stockholm as their institutions.

Debate over a metropolitan administrative reorganization has been in process since the beginning of the decade,
sometimes intensive, but, paradoxically and luckily, not politically inflamed.   The political parties are conscious of the
exceedingly difficult and highly involved character of the administrative problems involved, Mr. Mehr says, and have
therefore adopted a "wait and see" attitude.   He continued
with the observation that nowhere in the world have the large
and difficult problems of administrative reorganization in metropolitan areas been functionally resolved with satisfaction.
It is, therefore, necessary to proceed slowly and methodical-
ly.

With this introduction, he presented the "one government" alternative for metropolitan Stockholm and immediately
raised the danger to local self-government. [18]   Mr. Mehr
continued with the premise that certain common problems are
better resolved in the larger scale.   The question then is
whether one shall let these matters be handed to the state
apparatus, or whether one shall preserve representative self-
government in communal self-government reform. [19]

Mr. Mehr's "Greater Stockholm" proposal was in effect a proposal that the City of Stockholm and the Stockholm
County appoint delegates to a joint committee to facilitate the
formation of a Greater Stockholm County, which would include the City of Stockholm and the communes in the metropolitan area, leaving in the existing Stockholm County the
rural and non-metropolitan urban portions.   The City of Stockholm and the several communes within the Greater Stockholm County would remain separate communes and retain local self-governing powers over purely local matters.   Involved in the responsibilities of the Greater Stockholm County
Committee are the determination of the problems that are
metropolitan in character and for which the Greater Stockholm County should assume responsibility, the delineation of
the metropolitan area geographically, an examination of the

economic and financial aspects of the situation, the legal requirements for the change, and the necessary administrative
and personnel planning.

The City of Stockholm Executive Board approved the
formation of a joint committee with the Stockholm County on
December 21, 1963 and the Stockholm County Council Administrative Committee gave approval on January 23, 1964. The
"storlandstings" committee met on March 12, 1964, selecting
Hjalmar Mehr as chairman and Erik A. Lindh, "Landstings-
rådet," as vice-chairman, and commenced work on the proposal. On June 15, 1966, the Stockholm County Council approved the propsal and on the evening of June 20, 1966, the
Stockholm City Council gave its approval without debate. The
proposition was not a party issue.

The Greater Stockholm County Committee listed the
metropolitan problems as follows:

    1. Regional planning, also coordination and support
of municipal housing construction.
    2. Hospitals.
    3. Coordination of the planning for water purification
and distribution, also treatment and disposal of sewage and
industrial waste.
    4. Traffic administration.
    5. Coordinated planning of education above the ele-
mentary level.
    6. Recreation and leisure time (Fritidsfrågorna). [20]

In connection with the submission of the 1966 budget
before the Communal Association for the City and County of
Stockholm Regional Problems (Kommunalförbundet för Stockholm stads och läns regionala frågor), Mr. Mehr presented
the forthcoming heavy and expensive responsibilities that
faced the Communal Association. The responsibilities transferred to the Association, pending the creation of the Greater
Stockholm County, were:

    1. Regional planning.
    2. Coordination and support of municipal housing con-
        struction.
    3. Water purification and distribution, and treatment
        and disposal of sewage and industrial waste.
    4. Metropolitan area traffic.

Coordinated planning of education above the elementary

level was also transferred to the Communal Association for
the City and County of Stockholm Regional Problems. Responsibility for hospitals remained with the Greater Stockholm Hospital Board. Recreation and Leisure Time Problems remained unassigned.

The Greater Stockholm Planning Board continued to
function as a coordinating agency among the communes in the
metropolitan area. In 1971 the new Greater Stockholm County is to take over the responsibilities that had been delegated
to the Communal Association and Greater Stockholm Hospital
Board and the Leisure Time Problems as well. The Greater
Stockholm Planning Board will continue in existence as a coordinating agency among the communes.

The final paragraph of the 1966 budget address to the
Communal Association (Stor-Stockholm Address), Hjalmar
Mehr repeated his assurance to the Stockholm suburbs,

> And finally, let me emphasize the strength and the
> kernel of the principal approach, which we have
> chosen. "Storlandstinget," endowed with independ-
> ent taxing power, answerable to the people in di-
> rect elections--with the Communal Association as
> a transition arrangement--shall handle the common
> larger problems, which have broken through the
> communal boundaries. The primary communes
> shall assume and handle the vital problems, which
> they from the citizens' viewpoint can best solve
> themselves. We carry through a revision in ac-
> cordance with the requirements of the development
> situation, which implies a redivision of responsi-
> bilities between primary and secondary communes.
> But we stand fast on the ground of communal self
> government. [22]

This approach helped to minimize the concern of the
suburban communes about the "storlandsting" proposal. The
steps for the gradual formation of the storlandsting were
taken and due dates for the final actions established.

As has been indicated in this and other chapters,
there are various delineations of the metropolitan area, depending on the function involved and the specific purpose of
the delineation. Generally, there has been wide agreement
on the areas to be included. Twenty-nine communal blocks
and groups of communes extending from and including Norr-

tälje in the north to and including Nynäsham in the south are
planned for inclusion in the Greater Stockholm County. [23]
The professional planners in the Greater Stockholm Regional
Planning Office anticipate urbanization around Lake Mälaren.[24]
It would seem that a Greater Stockholm delineation would
need to include development in this direction even though this
delineation westwards would extend into other counties.   To
take this action, the national government would need to step
in.   Consideration has been given in Parliament to a redrawing of county boundaries in accordance with the needs of the
economy, traffic needs and population trends.   This may be
closer to reality than proposals for the establishment of a
federal system for Sweden. [25]   The Greater Stockholm County
proposal, however, is now materializing within the boundaries delineated in Map 3, which it was estimated has a population of approximately 1.5 million in 1970.

          Storlandstinget will have 149 representatives, elected
September 20, 1970 in 15 election districts, seven in the City
of Stockholm and eight in the remainder of Stor-Stockholm
Län.   Eight to 12 representatives will be elected from each
district for three-year periods of service. [26]   Recommendations for the drawing of the election district boundaries have
been submitted by the Communal Association for the City and
County of Stockholm Regional Problems to the Storlandstingskommitten. [27]

          When storlandstinget meets, an administrative commit-
tee will be selected to function as "the government," composed of 17 delegated as committee members and ten delegates as deputy members.   At least eight other committees
will be appointed with the following responsibilities: 1) Finance,   2) Personnel, 3) Long-term planning and development,
4) Hospitals,   5) Social questions,   6) Education and Culture,
7) Traffic, and 8) Real Estate.   These committees will have
policy-making responsibility within their respective functional
areas.

          Nine boards have been proposed to exercise direct ad-
ministrative reponsibility within their respective functional
areas:

          1) Personnel, with nine members and nine deputies.

          2) Traffic, with nine members and nine deputies.

          3) Health and Hospitals; 13 members and 13 deputies.

Map 3.   Metropolitan Stockholm; Greater Stockholm County,
         January 1, 1971.

1   NORRTÄLJE
2   DANDERYD
3   DJURSHOLM
4   SUNDBYBERG
5   SOLNA
6   SALTSJÖBADEN
7   NYNÄSHAMN

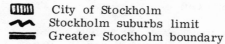

Ⅲ   City of Stockholm
∿∿∿   Stockholm suburbs limit
▬▬▬   Greater Stockholm boundary

Source: Storlandstingskommittens kansli och landstingets informationssektion, <u>Information om det nya landstinget</u> (Tiden-
Barnängen tryckerier ab 1970)

4) Dental Care; nine members and nine deputies.

5) Care and Education of the Psychologically Handicapped, with 11 members and 11 deputies.

6) Social, with 11 members, and 11 deputies, will have
responsibility for Children's Homes, Family Counseling, Vacation Home for Mothers Administration,
Care and Education of the Physically Handicapped
Children and Youth, and Care of Children and Youth
(to age 21) with Nervous Disorders having Neurotic
Tendencies.

7) Education, with 11 members and 11 deputies, will
have responsibility for education above the elementary level, including Trade Schools, People's Col-
leges and Agricultural Schools, and also responsibility to contribute proposals for overal cultural objectives.

8) Employment, with 11 members and 11 deputies, will
have responsibility for the training of handicapped
people for employment, job placement and arrangement for their transportation to the job if necessary.

9) Public Legal Counsel, with seven members and four
deputies, will have responsibility for the provision
free of charge of legal counsel and negotiation services to citizens in minor problem areas.

Central management offices, directly responsible to
the Administrative Committee, are proposed as follows:

1. Kansli, including a Secretariat, and Information,
Administrative, and Legal Divisions.

2. Finance Office.

3. Planning Office.

4. Negotiations Kansli providing assistance to the Administrative Committee and the Boards.

5. Building Office providing assistance to the Boards
in program planning.

The Planning Office, Negotiations Kansli and Building Office will function under one "landstings" committee, and will at a later date be merged into one office.

Administrative personnel problems and needs have been investigated by a special committee of eight delegates, representing both the City and the County of Stockholm, with Borgaråd William Forsberg of the City of Stockholm as chairman, since March 3, 1966.[28] It is estimated that the administrative staff for the Greater Stockholm County will total 25,000 to 30,000 employees. Likewise since 1966, the economic resources of the communes in the Greater Stockholm County area and the tax and budget requirements of the proposed Greater Stockholm County have been carefully investigated by the "storlandstingskommitte" kansli. A budget of approximately three billion kroner per annum is anticipated.

It is not the purpose of this study to enter into the minutiae of the preparations for the Greater Stockholm County installation. For those who can read Swedish, two informative publications will show the thoroughness of the preparations:

1. Storlandstingskommitten, Principbeslut om Storlandsting (Stockholm: Bröderna Siösteens, 1966).

2. Storlandstingskommittens kansli och landstingets informationssektion, Information om det nya landstinget (Stockholm: Tiden-Barängen, 1970).

Election districts have been officially delineated and all election preparations completed so that the Greater Stockholm County Council will be elected September 20, 1970; and during the calendar year 1970, all necessary preparations, legal, administrative, financial and personnel, as well as the headquarters for the Greater Stockholm County Council and administrative offices will be completed, so that the Greater Stockholm County will be officially installed January 1, 1971.

The national government has encouraged communal cooperation directly and through the County Governor's Office. In 1946, the Stockholm suburbs took the initiative by organizing the Cooperation Council of Stockholm Suburbs. Since that date, the City of Stockholm and the Stockholm suburbs have moved together in numerous and various cooperative endeavors until in 1963 Hjalmar Mehr stepped forth with the "Stor-Stockholm" proposal. In the meantime, the City of

Stockholm proceeded with caution so as not to cause undue
concern among the suburbs as regards the motives of the
core city.   The City of Stockholm has the technical staff to
provide services that the smaller communes cannot provide
and thus one city has not and cannot avoid playing a major
role.   It continues to be vital for the City of Stockholm to
be as helpful as possible, and it is important to have the
definite due date for the formation of an administrative metropolitan organization before the role of the City of Stockholm becomes too major.

This total development pattern since World War II has
provided the matrix of support from all parties concerned for
the Stor-Stockholmlandsting proposal.   Director Lennart Lyström correctly characterized the relations of the core city
and the suburbs in the Stockholm metropolitan area during
the second half of this century with one word: cooperation.

Sweden faces the same problem that other countries
with developed economies face: too many local jurisdictions
lacking the population and the resources to provide and maintain desired local services.   The Swedish government, however, has initiated action.

The Swedish Municipal Association and the Swedish
Communal Association, as specified earlier in this chapter,
have assisted all of the government levels in this effort to
reduce the number of small communes.   In addition, both associations provide numerous services to the member communes.

The Swedish Municipal Association maintains a computer service for its members.   The computer programing
languages best known in Europe are the Colbol and the Algol.
The latter is a European variant of Fortran, which is well
known in the U. S. A.   Secretary Skarström of the Swedish
Municipal Association, who is in charge of the computer service, considers the Cobol electronic data-processing the best
for administrative purposes.   This system has been installed
at the Swedish Municipal Association headquarters in Stockholm.   Five basic routines are performed: 1) children's allowances paid to mothers four times per year,   2) monthly
rents for municipally-owned apartments,   3) utility bills,   4)
salaries and wages, and 5) other bookkeeping routines.   Use
of the computer in city planning has been initiated with survey data.   Research is being conducted on more sophisticated
use of the computer in this field.   The Swedish Municipal As-

sociation has the equipment, but admits the need for more
investigation into the what and how as regards the use of the
computer in the field of municipal affairs.[29] Special services are also provided by the Municipal Association in the
following fields: 1) public health, 2) athletics and leisure
time activities, 3) municipal building problems, and 4) municipal history. For the above-mentioned and other services,
the City of Stockholm appropriated for 1966 the sum of
1,351,985 SKr, which is the equivalent of $230,397.[30] In
1966, 131 cities, 95 boroughs and 3 "municipalsamhällen"
were dues-paying members.[31]

       An organization of recent origin that has proven par-
ticularly helpful to the small communes but also to all municipalities, is the Local Government School, which was established at Sigtuna, located between Stockholm and Uppsala,
in 1956. Realizing the need for educating rural councilors
on the new responsibilities imposed by national law, correspondence courses and conferences were started in 1948 on
many aspects of local government. Now correspondence
courses are only a small part of the school's activities. The
Parliament voted an interest-free loan and amortization towards buildings. The Swedish Municipal Association and the
Swedish Communal Association each contributed financially.
A special committee was organized, the Local Government
School Foundation, consisting of three persons selected by
the Municipal Association, three by the Communal Association, and one by the national government, to manage the
school. The school director is appointed by and is responsible to this committee. There is no permanent faculty.
Lecturers and discussion leaders are drawn from the universities, the national administration, experienced local government officials, institutes and other recognized sources.
Stress is now laid on seminars. Between 90 and 100 partici-
pants come each week, totalling more than 4,500 each year,
including councilors, councilmanic appointees and career
staff. Cost of instruction and maintenance of buildings and
facilities are covered by fees, which are paid by the local
governments for the councilors and employees who are en-
rolled.[32]

       The interworkings of the Swedish Municipal Associa-
tion, the Swedish Communal Association, the Local Government School at Sigtuna and the Swedish governments, local
and national, have made possible an effective service to municipal government and have facilitated coordination of municipal governmental activities in Sweden.

The communal block arrangement is a slow but definitive move in the direction of bringing small communes together into larger governmental entities, capable of financing the needs of contemporary society. The preparations
now in process by the Greater Stockholm Committee constitute a relatively slow and deliberate but definitive move in
the direction of forming a government for the metropolitan
needs of metropolitan Stockholm, which will be a pattern
that can be used in the other two metropolitan areas in Sweden. Keeping within the boundaries of the existing Stockholm County in delineating the boundaries for the new Greater
Stockholm County postpones to a later date the probable necessity of changing the Greater Stockholm boundaries by action of the national government when the Stockholm MA has
grown westwards into adjoining counties around Lake Mälaren. The very thoroughness and deliberate nature of the
preparations for the formation of the Greater Stockholm
County and its government ensures its success.

Notes

1. Langenfelt, Per, Principles for a New Division of Swe-
    den's Municipalities (Stockholm: Swedish Institute,
    1962), p. 3.

2. Wallin, Gunnar; Anderson, Hans B. and Andren, Nils
    (editors), Gunnar Wallin, "Småkommunerna på Avs-
    krivning," Kommunerna i förvandling (Stockholm:
    Almquist and Wiksell, 1966), p. 27. Unless other-
    wise specified, the material in this chapter concern-
    ing the formation of communal blocks is taken from
    this source.

3. In 1965, the police administration was nationalized.

4. Langenfelt, Per, Op. cit., p. 7.

5. Sparrman, Bengt, Stockholm län--indelning i kommunal-
    block (Stockholm: Svenska Stadsförbundet Tidskrift,
    Dec. 1963).

6. Principoverenskommelse om Samordnung, Utbyggnad
    och Drift av Det Kollektiva Traffiksystemet i Stor-
    Stockholm, Dec. 14, 1964.

7. Larsson, Sixten, Riktlinier för Utvecklingsplanering

inom Kommunblock (Kristianstad: Kristianstads Boktryckeri Aktiebolag, 1965). Kommunförbundets' publication.

8. Interview with Mr. E. Wannfors, Division Director, National Building Board, June 28, 1966.

9. Kaijser, Fritz, Kommunallagarna, I. Kommunindelning
och Kommunalförbund (Kristianstad: Kristianstads
Boktryckeri Aktiebolag, 1959).

10. Ibid, "Lag om kommunalförbund den 31 maj 1957,"
p. 211-272.

11. Wallin, Gunnar; Anderson, Hans G. and Adren, Nils
(editors), Op. cit., Kanslichef Sten-Sture Landström
"Kommunförbunden," p. 200-201.

12. Interview with Lennart Lyström, Direktor, Storlandstingskommitten, May 13, 1966.

13. Interview with Mr. E. G. Westman, Stadjuristen, Stockholm, June 15, 1966.

14. Interview with Mr. Lyström.
    Unless qualified, the term "commune" refers gen-
    erally to city, borough and rural communes.

15. Storlandstingskommitten, Koncept Nr 2, April 28, 1966
    till Stockholms stadskollegium och Stockholms läns
    landtings forvaltningsutskott, p. 12.   And Stockholms
    stadskansli, Stockholms kommunalkalender, 1966, p.
    609 & 610.   Unless otherwise specified, material in
    the remainder of this chapter concerning contracts,
    associations and/or other cooperative arrangements
    are taken from one and/or the other of the two
    sources listed in this footnote.

16. Lundin, Folke, The Development of Greater Stockholm
    (mimeographed, 1965), p. 7.

17. Mehr, Hjalmar, Framsteg och Regional Samverkan
    (Stockholm: Utgiven av Stadskollegiets Reklamkom-
    mitte, 1963) pamphlet.

18. Ibid., p. 10-12.

19.   Ibid. , p. 26-27.

20.   Stockholms stadskansli, Stockholms kommunalkalender,
      1966, p. 620.

21.   Mehr, Hjalmar, Det regionala samarbetets utveckling i
      stor-stockholm (Stockholm: Wilhelmssons Boktryckeri,
      1966).

22.   Ibid. , p. 29.

23.   A list of the communal blocks and groups of communes
      to be included in the Greater Stockholm County is pro-
      vided in a Mimeographed Statement from storlandstings-
      kommittens kansli och landstingets informationssektion,
      February 24, 1970, p. 1 & 2.

24.   Interview with Mr. Gösta Carlestan, Architect, Stock-
      holmstraktens Regionplanekontor, May 12, 1966.

25.   Storlandstingskommitten, Op. cit. , p. 16-19.

26.   Kungl. Maj:ts proposition nr 112 år 1969, p. 109

27.   Storlandstingskommittens kansli och landstingets infor-
      mationssektion, Information om det nya landstinget
      (Tiden-Barnängen Tryckeri, 1970.

28.   Storlandstingskommitten, Principbeslut om Storlandsting
      (Stockholm: Bröderna Siösteens Boktryckeri AB,
      1966) p. 5.

29.   Interview with Secretary Skarström, Stadsförbundet,
      April 27, 1966.

30.   Stockholms stadskansli, Stockholms kommunalkalender,
      1966, p. 752.

31.   A "municipalsamhälle" is a relatively dense development
      within a rural commune, which has not been incorpo-
      rated into a borough or city, but needs more than
      rural communal services.   The "municipalsamhälle"
      has its own council, committees and administration,
      and the inhabitants pay a special rate to the "munici-
      palsamhälle" in addition to the rate they pay to the
      rural commune.   The number of these entities is
      steadily decreasing in number and it is anticipated that

they will disappear entirely, as other and better arrangements are made for these areas.

32.   Interview with Dr. Ingvar Hjelmquist, Director, Local Government School at Sigtuna, June 17, 1966; and Hjelmquist, Kommunskolan, a brief summary of a lecture delivered at Sigtuna by Mr. Hjelmquist, October 14, 1965 (mimeographed).

Chapter XIII

COMPARATIVE ANALYSIS

"Gemütlichkeit" and "Trivsel" have much in common.
Both words are value-loaded. Both are highly significant
within the value systems of their respective countries; Germany and Sweden. There is no English synonym. Both
words imply comfort, contentment, well-being, but more than
that: the amenities for good living; in brief, The Good Life.
Both the Germans and the Swedes are convinced that the
Good Life is possible in an urban setting, and proceed to
demonstrate it in their urban planning and city building. Cologne and Stockholm are good examples of this. More than
land-use is obviously involved. All municipal life needs to
be geared to a value system that give high priority to The
Good Life. Proper land-use can facilitate an approach to
this goal.

A non-quantitative typology, based on the major
"roles" of local government, classifies cities into four general types as those that: 1) promote economic growth, 2)
provide life's amenities, 3) maintain the usual services only,
and 4) arbitrate among conflicting interests.[1] All cities may
well claim to perform all four functions. Williams and Adrian in their use of this typology attempted to classify cities
according to the emphasis of their policy-making. Elaboration may be necessary on the fourth category. The emphasis here is on securing and maintaining a truce among conflicting pressure groups without moving forward with a definite program, an attempt to provide political peace with emphasis on the process rather than on the substance of a definite program for the city. This typology with four general
types is here presented because both Cologne and Stockholm
clearly give emphasis to the second category. Their interest in economic growth, in maintaining the usual services
and in arbitrating among conflicting interests are geared to
the major objective of providing for all citizens "life's amenities."

Luther H. Gulich stressed the vital importance of this
role of local government in the U. S. A. in his thesis that
America is lowered in the eyes of the world by the gap between our dreams and professed beliefs on the one hand and
our actual performances on the other, with the chasm being
widest and deepest in our metropolitan areas.[2]

Cologne and Stockholm have their problems. In both
cities, the housing shortage is problem number one. In Cologne the destruction of a goodly portion of the city in World
War II and the stupendous job of rebuilding following the war
makes the housing shortage no surprise. Stockholm experienced no war destruction; however, the heavy migration from
the farms and small towns has created a shortage. By stren-
uous efforts in residential building, both cities are now able
to see a solution on the horizon.

The requirement for high standards in construction,
particularly in Stockholm, may have slowed the process, but
the new construction will not have to be rebuilt, nor redeveloped, in the near future. The ideal of "high quality" in
everything in Sweden has reached the stage of reaction so as
to cause anecdotes to be exchanged about it in Stockholm. A
story circulated about the customer, who complained about
the high price of disposable plates, only to be told, "But
they are 'Hög kvalitet'."

There is a limited desire for single family homes in
both Cologne and Stockholm, which can be met in only a very
limited way. The Federal Government in the Bundesrepublik
is encouraging the building of single-family homes by liberal
loans. The Swedish Government is also providing housing
loans for the same purpose. Apartment dwelling, however,
is accepted in both countries as normal. In Stockholm it is
accepted practice for residents, even of modest means, to
rent an apartment in the city and own a "stuga" (vacation
cottage) on one of the lakes. Due to the housing shortage,
people who wish to move into Cologne or Stockholm are happy
to secure "housing" without specifications, except as to size
and facilities.

Prior to the 1850s, much of the land in Stockholm was
owned by the Crown or the City and leased for private use.
After the 1850s, the government began to sell land for private
development in accordance with private desires. At the turn
of the century, however, the City of Stockholm was convinced
that a mistake had been made, and proceeded to regain owner-

ship of the land in the city. By 1966, the City owned and
leased 36 per cent of the land in the Inner City and 83 per
cent in the Outer City, which totalled 74 per cent for the entire city; and it owned and leased twice as much land outside the city limits.

    Cologne commenced purchasing land under Conrad Ad-
enauer's administration in the 1920s. This policy was reactivated when Adenauer was re-elected mayor after World War
II, and was continued by his successor with Dr. Max Adenauer (his son) as City Manager. Due to financial limitations,
Cologne buys land, plans its use, and sells with contractual
requirements concerning the plan, in order to buy and plan
additional land. The principle is the same: effective planning of land use by a public agency and effective administration of the plan. No one can build anywhere or change the
use of a structure anywhere without approval from the official planning agency. In addition to the Implementation Division in the Cologne City Planning Agency, which checks on
legal compliance with the plan, the Inspection Office, which
is also placed under the City Planning Agency, has 170 employees, who check very thoroughly on every aspect of land
use and building construction. Retaining ownership and leasing as in Stockholm, however, gives added assurance of continued observance of the official plan and the building laws.

    Since every square foot of land, except forests and
military property, is in a commune in both West Germany
and Sweden, every square foot of land is under a plan and
building law, which is enforced. As a result, there is no
uncontrolled urban sprawl, or urban fringe, wherein private
enterprise can engage in cut-throat competition to mutual disadvantage. Furthermore, with effective urban planning,
strict and effective land and building use and inspection, neither residential nor commercial areas have been permitted
to deteriorate to the slum levels as are known in the United
States. [3]

    Due to the serious concern about the central business
districts and the blight surrounding them in American cities,
attention is promptly given in this comparative analysis to
experience in Cologne and Stockholm concerning the CBD. A
reduction of residential land use in downtown Stockholm commenced as commercial enterprise outbid residential enterprise for space, but this was quickly stopped in 1962 with
zoning controls to protect the still existing residential land
use in downtown Stockholm. This is the only instance of

zoning controls anywhere in Sweden or Germany. With the above mentioned exception, land use is not controlled that way. Cologne, in rebuilding after the bombing of World War II, deliberately provided residential construction inside the Ring, which is the CBD. There is thus no twilight zone between the downtown commercial and the residential neighborhoods. The one merges into the other. In Stockholm, residential land use was preserved even in the Old City Island (Gamla Stan).

In addition, in both Cologne and Stockholm the central business districts have entertainment and cultural facilities, excellent restaurants and small parks. Cologne has substantial public stretches along the Rhine and Stockholm has substantial public spaces along the waterways in the CBD. [4] All of this attracts people downtown. The downtown in neither city becomes empty after office hours. There are people on the streets in and around the central business district during and after working hours.

An added significance in the CBD of both cities is the preservation of the "historic," the reminders of a "past," evidences of a continuum through the centuries. Swedish citizens have their local patriotism recharged by "Gamla Stan" and by the Old City Hall, which is now a "showcase" of Stockholm's history. Likewise, the magnificent "Dom," the thirteenth-century walls and towers along the boulevards of the Ring, the remainders of the Roman wall in the central core of the CBD, and the City Hall, which has under one roof the remains of the ancient Roman Praetorium and the medieval "Rathaus," into the remains of which the new City Hall has been built, serve to revitalize the citizens' pride in Cologne's historic past.

An interesting contrast is evident in this comparison. Cologne is nearly two thousand years old, but the city has been destroyed many times over. In each rebuilding, the citizens of Cologne have carefully preserved what was left worth preserving for future generations to know that through the centuries from the First Century there has always been a Cologne. Stockholm, however, has a more recent origin, having been built in the Thirteenth Century, but has never been destroyed, except for fires in its first few centuries. Being first built on an island, it has been possible for the City of Stockholm successfully to preserve "Gamla Stan." One common characteristic of the two cities is that the "historic" preservations are not dead monuments to the past, but

are made serviceable for contemporary use. The fourteenth-,
fifteenth- and sixteenth-century structures in "Gamla Stan"
have modernized interiors and are used for residential and
commercial purposes. The shops are considered "ultra"
for specialty and exclusive shopping. The apartments are
considered choice for those who wish to be in the thick of
things where activity abounds, but for these apartments children are not recommended, because exterior play space is
very minimal. A very well known Swedish author (in America) and his equally well known wife (in Sweden), who reside
in Gamla Stan are Dr. and Mrs. Gunnar Myrdal.

        In Cologne exceptional ingenuity has been demonstrated
in the practical use of historic remains. Along the inside of
the thirteenth-century walls have been built contemporary a-
partments, which are not visible from the boulevards along
the Ring. The remains of the Roman walls edge parking
spaces. The merging of the "ancient," the "medieval" and
the "modern" in one structure--the new City Hall--was an
architectural tour de force, that is noteworthy. A full listing of historic preservations in the two cities is not given
here, merely a few to illustrate the principle. These are
not dead monuments.

        Dr. C. F. Ahlberg in a lecture at a study conference
arranged by the Royal Swedish Academy of Engineering Sciences in Stockholm in November 1963 developed the thesis
that everything man-made can be evaluated with reference to:
1) its practical usefulness, 2) its esthetic function, and 3)
its role as a symbol. He thereupon applies these criteria to
the urban core of cities. Having developed the practical
usefulness of the urban core and its esthetic function, Dr.
Ahlberg emphasizes its role as a symbol.

> The urban core, or certain elements of it, is also
> usually regarded as a symbol of the common inter-
> ests of the town. The urban core represents the
> town as a unit; it is the face. Consisting of or ly-
> ing within the oldest built-up area of the town, and
> therefore being more or less a tangible representa-
> tion of its historical development, it will often sym-
> bolize not only the common interests of the town
> today but also the community's link with the past. [5]

        Prime consideration obviously needs to be given to
people as social beings. This requires separation of people
as pedestrians from people as drivers of vehicles. Pedes-

trian-only streets have been introduced in several European
cities, and are in evidence in Cologne and Stockholm with
limitations on the use of the automobile in the urban core.
The most sophisticated development in this direction is Hötorget in Stockholm. Here the pedestrian has full, free and
complete use of the ground level and on the second level,
the terraces surrounding the central park, while all loading,
unloading and parking is underground.

    The unrestricted use of the automobile on the surface
streets in the urban core is also made unnecessary by the
construction of the underground rapid transit, which has been
merely started in Cologne, but has reached virtually full development in Stockholm with three systems spreading in 11
directions, connecting the new towns with the urban core,
making it easily accessible. Public transit in Cologne within the city pending the completion of the underground rapid
transit is greatly facilitated by having 60 per cent of the surface public transit separated from the street traffic so that
it can move swiftly. In the urban core in Stockholm, the underground, in addition to providing tubes for rapid-mass
transit, also has tubes for automobiles and pedestrians. Automobiles on the surface are being limited increasingly by the
prohibition of all parking on the streets and by the limitation
of the number of parking garages. A ring expressway a-
round the Stockholm CBD will be as close as most automobiles will get to the urban core on the surface. Stockholm
has built for the automobile age without permitting the automobile to be crowned "King." Cologne is moving in this direction. The purpose is to make the urban core a pleasant
place for people to meet and leisurely pursue their interests
without undue hindrance from motorized traffic, a place for
public concourse, not hectic maneuvering of traffic.

    The rapid transit connections of the urban core with
the Inner City, the Outer City, the "new towns" and the communes in the Stockholm metropolitan area provide essential
links between the heart of the metropolis and outlying areas.
With activities in the urban core in which the citizens of the
metropolitan area wish to participate, and events there which
the citizens of the metropolitan area wish to see and hear,
the rapid transit underground will keep the urban core alive.

    The lay of the land which for Stockholm has been a
distinct advantage in many respects, has had and continues
to have at least one disadvantage. The provision of adequate
circulation of men and material on three parts of the main-

land and 15 islands within the city limits has been a problem
of serious magnitude without taking into account travel
throughout the metropolitan area.   For circulation on the surface, this has meant the multiple construction of bridges in
all directions, which presents the double-edged problem of
construction and finance.   With underground construction of
rapid mass transit throughout granite, ignoring surface variations, this problem is partially eased. [6]

A serious problem in both cities in any redevelopment
in the CBD is the small size of parcels of land in the older
portions of the city that are not usable without change of parcel boundaries.   This is essentially a procedural problem.
Cologne after the war destruction coped with this by providing a special process whereby the owner, or owners, of parcels of property, or the official Planning Agency can appeal
to a committee of the City Council to arrange a redrawing of
property lines, but only the City Council has the authority to
change the property lines.   Property owners are compensated
for loss of property by such action.   Stockholm has no similar process; however, the City Council is authorized by special legislation to acquire parcels of property that are too
small for redevelopment.   In order to avoid paying inflated
prices for land that is to be redeveloped and to avoid permitting the property owners to profit from anticipated public
improvements, the legislation authorizes the City to acquire
the land at the existing market price on the basis of the City
Plan for the area in legal effect, and not make the redevelopment plans public until after the purchase.

Another procedural problem involves archaeologists,
antiquarians and organizations interested in cultural artifacts
from past centuries.   The National Swedish Institute for
Building Research recommends that the Planning Office check
with the County Antiquarians Office before preparing plans for
a development, or a redevelopment.   In Cologne, the excavations for the underground rapid transit have cause continuous disputes between the excavating firms and the antiquarians.   Due to the wealth of archaeological artifacts beneath
the surface of Cologne's downtown area, no satisfactory solution to the problem has been found.

Cologne also faces problems with the excavations for
the underground mass transit for other than archaeological
reasons.   The open-cut method is disruptive of normal traffic and commerce and is a public nuisance until completed.
The use of the Hamburg method of "shield tunnelling" avoids

the disruption of traffic and commerce, but is exceedingly
expensive, and any type of underground rapid mass transit
construction is a sufficient strain on the municipal budget.
Stockholm is more fortunate in that with the exception of
the gravel ridge (Brunkebergassen), all of the excavating for
the underground has been and any additional excavating will
be through granite, which can be performed without disturb-
ing the developments on the surface.   It is interesting to
note that the national government is providing Stockholm
grants to defray 95 per cent of the cost of building the underground mass transit system from the automobile tax.

        Transferring attention from the procedural to the sub-
stantive and to the larger scene, the plans and land-use controls in both cities provide ample open space. Cologne has
within its administrative boundaries 32. 6 per cent of the land
in agriculture and gardens, 12. 2 per cent in forests and 7. 3
per cent in parks, public greens, athletic fields and other
landscaped open spaces, totalling 52. 1 per cent in open space.
Stockholm has 32. 7 per cent in land reserves, 16 per cent in
planned open space and 5. 5 per cent in agricultural use, totalling 54. 2 per cent in open space.   Correlating "likes" in
the two classification systems of land use, a striking similarity appears:

Percentages of Total Area within the Administrative Boundaries

	Cologne	Stockholm
Developed (built-up) Areas	47. 9	45. 8
Land Reserves	32. 6	38. 2
Planned Open Space	19. 5	16. 0

        German federal law prohibits leaving land unused.
Undeveloped land in and around the built-up portions of Cologne is therefore devoted to gardening, if not agriculture
and forests.   In Stockholm, the City owns the overwhelming
proportion of the land surrounding the developed portions,
thus ensuring proper use of the land.

        Cologne is larger in population and area:

	Cologne	Stockholm
Population	854, 000	794, 000
Area in Square Kilometers	251	186

        Including the water areas, the two cities are virtually
equal in geographic coverage.   While population density is

computed in terms of population per unit of land, the reader
needs to be mindful of the water surface as open space, particularly in the Stockholm situation wherein the waters of
Lake Mälaren and the Baltic penetrate into and through the
city. Cologne has a population density of 7,116 persons per
square kilometer of developed land and Stockholm, 9,349.
The "point-house" and other high-rise apartment construction
on the hillsides along the waters of Stockholm has given the
city a greater population-land density.

Of increasing concern throughout the planet, particularly in the developed countries, is the continued deteriora-
tion of the environment. The ecological approach to the problem is all-inclusive, being concerned with all the resources,
their interrelationships and mutual dependencies. Conservation from this point of view means protecting the cycle of
life in nature, which is not something apart from and separate from human life, but very essential to it. It is therefore exceedingly dangerous to human life to permit urbanization to spread recklessly, uncontrolled by society.

In neither Cologne nor Stockholm is development permitted anywhere without adequate drainage and sewage disposal. In Cologne and even in the larger Rhine-Ruhr complex, water pollution is controlled, although air pollution
there is an admitted problem. In every square kilometer of
industrial development a testing box is installed and checked
monthly. An industry, that is found to be polluting the air
and does not take corrective action after notification, loses
its permit to operate. Steps are being taken, however, to
strengthen air pollution control. In Stockholm, on the contrary, air pollution has not been a problem, but the recent
findings of the International Meteorological Institute with headquarters in Stockholm has raised technical concern among
Stockholm scientists. Water pollution has been and is an admitted problem. All of Stockholm and a major portion of the
Stockholm metropolitan area is serviced by sewage pipe lines
and treatment plants, but the need for more effective controls over water pollution is one of the motivations for the
creation of the Greater Stockholm County, because the problem of water pollution extends beyond the boundaries of any
one city, or commune. Action by the national government
may be found to be necessary; and if this is the situation,
such action will be taken. Cologne and Stockholm are at
least aware of their environmental problems and are taking
action concerning them.

Stockholm has proceeded further than Cologne in the development of so-called "new towns." These "new towns" are actually new communities within the administrative boundaries of the city. At no time have the Stockholm or the Cologne planners claimed that these developments were "new towns" within the British concept thereof, where the new town movement started. As a matter of fact, they take special care to explain the differences. The pattern of development for these new communities is worthy of review. They are situated along the route of the underground rapid transit, except one that is being planned along a railway route, therefore they have a speedy connection with the urban core in Stockholm. The station is in the shopping center. An attempt has been made to provide ample parking space, and for those who leave in the morning for employment in the city core, the parking is ample. The shopping center in addition to providing space for shopping purposes also provides space for public non-commercial use: meeting halls, concert halls, spaces for the headquarters and conference rooms of citizen organizations, health centers and welfare centers. For five new towns, over half of the overall shopping center floor space is used, or is planned (if not constructed), for non-commercial public use.

Around the shopping center, multiple-story apartment buildings are built, followed by two or three story walk-up apartments, thereafter town houses, and finally single-family homes. There is no zoning, but the plan specifies the extent of each. As a result, a couple can remain in the same community as the need changes from a kitchenette apartment to a larger apartment and later to more spacious housing. Most of the neighborhoods within a new community have a few stores for "convenience shopping," which is made truly convenient. A multiplicity of surveys are made in existing new towns; and adaptations and modifications of land use are possible and are made, as surveys show the need. There is a serious effort to permit the desires and needs of the resident population, the consumer, to be the prime consideration, not the building or profit desires of the developers.

The bite must be taken out of land speculation in America . . . [7]

Land should be treated as the raw material for the fulfillment of human needs rather than as an article of merchandise. [8]

Since in Stockholm the City owns the land on which the
new towns are developed and leases the land to be developed,
the City can fulfill human needs.

Mr. H. J. Jensen, Director of Real Estate Special
Projects, the Pennsylvania Railway Company, points out the
need in the U.S.A. for large scale development in order to
provide the amenities, which are beyond the financial capacity
of ordinary subdividers. [9]

By planning and building a new development, or new
town, as a unit in its entirety, Stockholm is able to meet the
need specified by Mr. Jensen, and to avoid the difficulties
encountered in America, with efforts to bring in multiple-
story construction in an area already zoned for single-family
residences. Rezoning is necessary. The residents of the
area vigorously object, and in many instances with good reason, if the streets, sewers, school and other necessities were
not originally planned for such population increase. At the
same time, there is an increasing need for multiple-story
developments in the outskirts of many American cities.

Multiple-story development does not necessarily mean
inadequate open space. That depends entirely on the planning
of the land use, as Stockholm has so admirably demonstrated;
also demonstrated in Stockholm is the importance of the land-
scaping of the open space, so that people have, as Wolf von
Eckhart has effectively state, " . . . space to be alone in
and space to be social in."[10]

Wasteful of public space is the gridiron street pattern
and wasteful of privately owned space are the set-back requirements in U.S. zoning regulations, which provide front
lawns, which are in effect, neither public nor private. The
same space in the rear of the buildings can provide play
space and/or off-street parking space where needed.

A critical comment may well be made to the effect
that the public controls herein analyzed would stifle private
investment in land development in the United States. Dr.
Paul F. Wendt, Professor of Finance and Vice-Chairman of
the Business Administration Department, University of California, Berkeley, answers this critique in part with the observation,

> The experience of many European countries indi-
> cates that relatively high and stable levels of pri-

vate investment in land development can be maintained under a broadened system of public controls. [11]

Taking a broader view, Edward Durell Stone, a renowned American architect, made an observation in an interview in 1964, which describes a situation that is still too prevalent,

> Q: Mr. Stone, what did you have in mind when you said recently that we've made a 'colossal mess' of the face of this country?
>
> A: All you have to do is to look around you to see what I mean: Neon jungles. Catchpenny honkytonks. Noise. Clutter. Building without concern for the neighbors, for what is appropriate, for what is in good judgment and taste. All in all, I thought I made sense when I said that if you give a damn, you feel like committing suicide when you look around.
>
> Q: Are things really that bad in America generally?
>
> A: To my way of thinking, yes. We are the richest country in history, yet we surround ourselves with vulgar trash, clumsy symbols of the nouveau riche. [12]

In Stockholm and Cologne, strict regulation of permission to erect not only buildings, but billboards, signs, and exterior lighting, effectively prevents this type of "visual pollution." The choice is between more "public controls" or the current situation, which is well known to all observant people.

Throughout both Cologne and Stockholm, there is a surprisingly even distribution of income levels. Marienburg Community in the southern portion of Cologne and Oscars, Hedvig Lenora and Engelbrekt parishes in the eastern portion of Stockholm have concentrations of wealth. On the right bank of the Rhine and in other portions of eastern Cologne, also in Klara and Katarina parishes immediately north and south of Stockholm's "Gamla Stan," there is a higher proportion of low-income residents than elsewhere in the two cities. Yet there are no communities of extreme poverty, nor com-

munities of uniformly great wealth. In brief, there is no
community, or geographic, segregation of any type, economic or racial. Two contributing factors have to be borne in
mind. One is the absence of zoning in Cologne and in Stockholm the limitation of zoning to the CBD so that there are
no legal limitations by geographic classifications. Furthermore, the prevalence of apartment dwellings throughout the
two cities helps to maintain a relatively even distribution of
income levels. Another factor is the relative homogeneity of
the population both ethnically and racially.

In finding solutions to city planning and land-use problems, policy-making becomes vital. Who makes the decisions? In Cologne, the Christian Democratic Union (CDU)
has had a majority since World War II until the 1956 election, at which time the Social Democratic Party (SPD) gained
a plurality and in 1964 a clear majority. In Stockholm, the
Social Democratic Party has had a plurality since World War
II. With the multi-party system in Stockholm, government
in Stockholm requires coalition arrangements. Since 1966,
the government has been a coalition of the Liberal and Conservative Parties, which have 52 per cent of the council
seats.

A very wide range of vocational representation is
characteristic of the Cologne 67-member city council and the
Stockholm 100-member city council. Worthy of notice in Cologne are the 48 councilmanic committees, of which 21 have
relevance to some aspect of city planning and land-use control. In addition, 12 of the council committees have non-
council voting members, three of which have direct relevance
to city planning and land use.

Stockholm secures public participation in municipal
policy-making not through council committees, but by means
of the numerous administrative boards on which in addition
to council members, citizens who are not council members
serve. These administrative boards have responsibility for
administrative decision-making in their respective areas of
administration. Additional boards, which also have non-
council members, serve in an advisory capacity. Of significance is the operations of all of these boards in the role of
councilmanic committees in providing the council recommendations within their respective fields of competence. Thus
in Stockholm, non-council members have a voice at both
ends of the policy-making spectrum.

It is particularly significant that municipal government, which is "democratic" in the normally accepted usage of the term and concept, can plan and implement the plan in good form, contrary to the views of many critics.

Paul Ylvisaker, Director of the Public Affairs Program for the Ford Foundation, wrote in 1965,

> Urban beauty--at least as historical examples are cited to us--has been linked to concentrations of power and wealth seemingly necessary to produce it. [13]

Rolf Jensen, Dean of the Faculty of Architecture and Town Planning, University of Adelaide, goes further in his analysis,

> With both regret and envy, we are forced to conclude that however little we may wish to see an authoritarian form of government, these are the only conditions which have so far produced significant results in guiding physical development in any country on a basis of all-around community benefit. [14]

Both hypotheses are at least not proven, and Dr. Jensen's hypothesis is disproven by the Cologne and Stockholm findings in this study. Dr. Paul Ylvisaker's article entitled, "The Villains Are Greed, Indifference and You," in the special double issue of Life Magazine, entitled "The U. S. City, Its Greatness Is at Stake," December 24, 1965, is worthy of serious study for proposals concerning needed action.

A much needed reminder is presented by Dr. John D. Millett, Chairman, National Academy of Public Administration, in the following words,

> Ideals can be realized, goals can be reached, and policies can be fulfilled only when specific programs are put into effect at the ultimate point of performance. A requisite of an advancing democratic society is effective administration. [15]

In administration, Cologne is clearly and concisely organized with responsibility moving from bottom to top in an unmistakable line of progression. Having a council-manager system, well known in the U. S. A., the City Manager (Ober-

stadtdirektor) has final administrative responsibility and is
answerable to the City Council. Furthermore, the City Manager has means for providing leadership in city planning:
1) his own staff through which he has a) public relations responsibility and control, and b) the Division of Development
Planning, which was recently created and placed under the
City Manager's direct supervision for an indefinite period of
time; and 2) the Assistant City Manager's staff through which
he has direct responsibility and supervision of a) the Real
Estate Office, and b) the Statistical Office.

Another noteworthy characteristic is the concentration
of all major aspects of city planning and land use, including
billboard, sign and street lighting controls with the above-
mentioned exceptions in one department: Building Administration, which carries through from the initial planning to the
actual land-use control by means of the Implementation Division, the Inspection Office, the actual construction of all public improvements and with a few exceptions responsibility for
all publicly owned land and buildings.

The administrative organization in Stockholm is not as
"clear cut" as in Cologne.   There is a collegial administrative hierarchy from the numerous boards to the Board of Directors and to the Executive Board.   Decision-making is
sometimes a slow and tortuous process, but once a decision
is made, the policy is firm.   Conferences are continuously
in process between the various parts of the organization, providing coordination by consultation.   Thus a countervailing influence in Stockholm is the process which compensates
for the apparent lack of clarity in organization.   This makes
possible coordination of land use, transit, provision of utilities, parks, recreational facilities, schools and other necessities of good urban development.   This also helps in resolv-
ing the differences between the professional planners and the
professional politicians, who frequently have a different concept of urban needs and view differently that which is advisable in city planning.   Stockholm, however, does have in one
department the following divisions and bureaus: City Planning, City Surveyor, Building Permit and Building Inspection,
which is not as comprehensive as in Cologne, but is more inclusive than in American municipal administrative organization.   Observation needs to be made that in Stockholm also
strict controls are enforced over billboards, signs and street
embellishments.

One variation in Stockholm from practice in Cologne

and in American cities is the assignment of planners. In Cologne, planners are assigned to advance planning separately
from current planning. This is also true in cities in the
U. S. where advance planning is performed. In Stockholm,
planners are assigned to geographic areas within the city, who
provide both the so-called current planning and the advance
planning within their specified areas. The existing city plan,
guidelines and close supervision keep the total planning staff
functioning together in one consistent pattern. A distinction
is recognized between current planning and advance planning,
but the distinction is not made in terms of "who does the
planning" but in terms of "who makes the decisions," a difference in "process." Current planning proposals that require
official action above the Building Board go to the Executive
Board and if necessary to the City Council. Advance planning
proposals are processed through the Master Plan Commission,
which has in its membership the heads of all the relevant
agencies. These people can iron out the differences that have
in times past delayed controversial decisions in long-range
planning. When the Master Plan Commission makes a recommendation to the Executive Board, it is quite certain to be approved and forwarded to the City Council.

        The local level of government in both Germany and
Sweden has full freedom to plan. In Germany after the completion of planning the Land Government checks on compliance
with legal requirements. Likewise, in Sweden, after completion of planning, the county government checks and the national
government as well may check on compliance with legal requirements. The national government reviews all regional
plans, which must be approved before having legal effect.
The municipal master plan is carefully examined by the county government and may be examined by the national government. Approval by the county is necessary before having legal effect. The county checks the city plan for conformance
with the Master Plan and will raise questions concerning any
deviations therefrom. In both countries, however, the actual
planning is carried through locally without interruptions and
without the necessity of intermittent approvals from higher
levels.

        Coordination within the Stockholm metropolitan area has
materialized more in urban and regional planning than in any
other functional area. Land use and water pollution controls
are among the needs motivating the current action for a metropolitan governmental reorganization.

Since a metropolitan area is difficult to delineate geographically and varies with the function used as criterion, it is probably more realistic to view a metropolis as a system of interrelationships among organizations, institutions and people than an area wherein one government should have jurisdiction. It is undoubtedly helpful if one governmental institution has jurisdiction over a major portion of such an area; however, that is not necessary. What is necessary is that adequate coordination of governmental units be provided, and this coordination needs to be sufficiently clear so that it does not become a tangled skein of popularly unknown lines of responsibility and escape effective control by the elected representatives in the public interest. It should be noted that coordination within the two metropolitan areas of this study have been facilitated by higher levels of government. In Cologne the Land districts and the Land administration and in Stockholm the county administration and the national government have encouraged coordination. In the Stockholm MA the county and the national government have also initiated cooperative arrangements. Both Cologne and Stockholm have available devices for cooperation. In the Cologne MA the various types of special purpose districts, joint working association and the contract device are legally available, but actual use is largely limited to the "zweckverbände" (single-purpose districts). The Stockholm MA has a wider choice of cooperative devices and makes a substantially greater use of them: municipal associations, based both on private law and public law, contracts for cooperation concerning various municipal services, joint ownership of public corporations, cooperation under joint boards, and cooperation by communal committees.

The need for attention to a larger area than that within the city limits, the metropolitan area, and for certain purposes beyond the urbanized and developed metropolitan area is based not only on the interrelationships among people, who cross arbitrary municipal boundaries in their daily activities, but also on the interrelationships between that which is man-made and that which is natural. The notion that man conquers nature is a most destructive misconception, implied in much of the urban development that has taken place. Man can tame nature, but must learn to live with it and preserve it. We are very slowly and painfully learning this basic lesson. Without an ecological approach to conservation now, the time may come when future generations will be sad replicas of the human race, or the time may come when there will no longer be a human race on this planet.

Since human life still continues in urban concentrations with substantial satisfaction in some parts and with substantially less satisfaction in other parts of the planet, attention is directed again to the human and social situation. Generally throughout Europe, city-wide festivals (which have become metropolitan-wide) in which the entire metropolitan population participates, have been and are a vital part of the
civic life. These are festivals that are celebrated throughout
the metropolitan area, yet brings the metropolitan population
downtown into the core of the core city. The carnival season in Cologne begins after Christmas and reaches a climax
on Rosenmontag near the end of February. Parties are held
all over the metropolitan area. As the carnival season
moves into February, dinners, parties, dances and costumed
balls are held in the downtown area with a special costumed
ball in the Gürzenich, the historic festival hall, with several
dance orchestras and dancing throughout the famous Gürzenich. People appear on the streets in costumes during the
evening hours until on Rosenmontag everyone from the young-
est to the oldest appears in costume. Rosenmontag is the
day of the big parade with colorful and elaborate floats, some
of which have historic significance, others presenting carica-
tures of prominent public leaders and current public policies.
What is significant is that the entire population comes out to
celebrate a civic event, which has been celebrated annually
since the Middle Ages.

There is not the same gradual build-up for the Swedish historic festivities. The arrival of spring is an occasion
in the last weekend in April for a civic human explosion. In
Stockholm, the metropolitan population crowds into Skansen,
the island park east of Gamla Stan, for the traditional wel-
come to spring and a vigorous expression of historic patriotism. University students wear their traditional "student
caps," bands play, and at night tremendous bonfires burn on
the hillsides of the island. Likewise, Mid-Summer near the
end of June is the occasion for another mass celebration.
Folk dancing and dancing, similar to the American "Maypole
Dance," are symbolic of the Mid-Summer Festivity. At this
time of the year in the northland, the sun shines through the
night and the celebrations continue through the sunlit night.
The above-mentioned Swedish festivities are prehistoric in
origin, but they have been adapted through the centuries to
changing circumstances and the changing mores of the people.
On these two festival occasions, as in the Carnival Festivities in Cologne, the entire population comes out to join in the
traditional celebrations, which are given a civic expression.

These mass celebrations may be considered to be merely so much froth on the social surface and to have absolutely no relevance to urban planning or land use. If, however, the urban planning, land use and ecological conservation are such as to make possible "The Good Life" now and
in the future, the opportunity for "popular expression of
pleasure" facilitates "group life," which is an essential in
the urban setting.

        This gathering of the citizenry in Cologne and Stock-
holm is not limited to the festival periods nor is it limited
to the downtown. It is merely more highly concentrated and
reaches a higher intensity at these periods. Citizens in Cologne enjoy the pleasures of eating and drinking out-of-doors
during the spring, summer and fall in the plaza facing the
Dom, in the parks and at outdoor tables in other parts of
the city. Even in the northland during the spring, summer
and fall, the citizens of Stockholm enjoy eating and drinking
outside on the plazas of Hötorget, in Kungsträdgarden, a
downtown park, in other parks and public places and at outdoor tables elsewhere in the city. There are ample opportunities for the citizens of Cologne to meet with fellow-citi-
zens in the Biergartens, the Trade Union Halls, and at social events arranged by the numerous organizations in the
city. The citizens of Stockholm also have ample opportunities to gather at consumer cooperative meetings, study circles (Workers Education, Folk School and other adult education activities) and at social events of various types. Group
life is very much in evidence at all times throughout Cologne
and Stockholm.

        Barbara Ward Jackson, Albert Schweitzer professor
of international economic development at Columbia University,
at a meeting sponsored by the Chicago Council on Foreign
Relations, the English Speaking Union, and the Adlai Steven-
son Institute, recently delivered an address, entitled "Let Us
Choose Life," in which she urged the adoption of new priorities in the U. S. A. to win back the disaffected young, the
poor and the frightened and advocated that priority number
one should be: our cities. [16]

        The Demonstration Cities and Metropolitan Develop-
ment Act of 1966 specifies that "improving the quality of urban life is the most critical domestic problem facing the
U. S. " [17]

        An elaboration of this objective is given by the U. S.

Department of Housing and Urban Development in Urban and Regional Information Systems: Support for Planning in Metropolitan Areas as follows:

> Considerable resources, public and private, will be marshalled in the years ahead to meet that objective. The challenge to planning is for an orderly and coordinated program that will insure the optimal investment of these resources. [18]

The need is massive action now in this direction. May this study of Cologne and Stockholm provide constructive suggestions. The necessary financing of planned action is only a part of the total enterprise. In brief, the totality of our national life needs to be geared to a value system that gives priority to The Good Life for all of our citizens, who are increasingly residents of metropolitan areas.

Notes

1. Williams, Oliver P. and Adrian, Charles R. , Four Cities: A Study in Comparative Policy Making. (Philadelphia: University of Pennsylvania Press, 1963) Part III "A Typology of Civic Policies," p. 185-267.

2. Gulick, Luther Halsey, The Metropolitan Problem and American Ideas (N. Y.: Alfred A. Knopf, 1966), p. 6 and 7.

3. Surveying 47 cities throughout U. S. A. in the 1950s, the author gathered evidence establishing the following hypothesis:

> Blight is obviously not determined by the ages of a structure . . . The condition of the structure, if dilapidated, is symptomatic of something deeper.

> Multiple threads seem to be woven and interwoven into a complex pattern of causation. Basic to all of these factors, however, is land use. In brief, improper land use is the underlying cause. Blight may thus be defined as uneconomic land use, but uneconomic in terms of human considerations, human needs, human conveniences.

Hemdahl, Reuel G. , Urban Renewal (N. Y. : Scarecrow

Press, 1959), p. 31.

4.   Over 80 per cent of the Rhine shore throughout the city in Cologne and approximately two-thirds of the numerous lake and other waterfronts on the 15 islands and three parts of the mainland throughout the city in Stockholm are reserved for public use.

5.   Ahlberg, C. F., "Problems of the Urban Core," Lecture given at a study conference arranged by the Royal Swedish Academy of Engineering Sciences, Stockholm, November 7-8th 1963. (mimeographed) p. 4.

6.   Traffic regulation on city streets is a problem unto itself. The motorist who finds himself in the wrong lane for his destination, must either proceed over the wrong bridge to the wrong island and start over again, or jam traffic by forcing himself into the right lane. For the unsophisticated driver not accustomed to metropolitan driving nor sufficiently acqainted with Swedish signs, another possibility is to find himself in a lane that leads him onto either an elevated street or an underground street which then takes him way beyond his destination, when what he wanted was a surface street.

7.   Muirhead, Desmond, Green Days in Garden and Landscape (Los Angeles, California: Miramar Publishing Co., 1961) p. 256.

8.   Ibid., p. 257.   Quotation from Lewis Keeble.

9.   Jensen, H. J., Director of Real Estate Special Projects, The Pennsylvania Railway Co., Urban Land, Vol. 26, No. 10, November 1967. (Urban Land Institute).

10. Eckhart, Wolf von, "Toward a Better Community - Space in the City," American Home, September 1967, p. 12.

11. Wendt, Paul F., "Lessons from the Old World for America's City Builders," Appraisal Journal, Vol. 29, No. 3, July 1961, p. 389-398.

12. Stone, Edward Durell, "Are Most Cities Too Ugly to Save?" Interview with famed architect, U. S. News

and World Report, November 30, 1964, p. 82.

13. Ylvisaker, Paul, "The Villains are Greed, Indifference and You," Life: The U.S. City, Its Greatness Is at Stake, Special Double Issue, December 24, 1965, p. 93-94.

14. Jensen, Rolf, The Town Planning Review, edited by the Department of Civic Design, University of Liverpool, Quarterly, Vol. 38, No. 2, July 1967, p. 115.

15. Millett, John D., Chairman, National Academy of Public Administration, Second Annual Report of the Chairman (Washington, D.C.: American Society for Public Administration, July 1969), p. 3.

16. Jackson, Barbara Ward, "Let Us Choose Life," The Courier-Journal and Times Magazine, January 18, 1970, p. 8-11.

17. Public Law 89-754, Section 1. United States Code, 1964 Edition, Supplement II, Chapter 41, Section 3301.

18. U.S. Department of Housing and Urban Development, Urban and Regional Information Systems: Support for Planning in Metropolitan Areas, p. 13. (mimeographed)

Methodological Note

The purpose of this methodological note is to make observations and offer suggestions to the researcher for whom comparative urban studies is a new field.

There is an obvious lack of clarity concerning the term "urban" within the boundaries of this country. The problem increases in complexity when research crosses national boundaries. Chapter II of this book briefly analyzes the problem. Two useful sources on the problem prior to the initiation of research are:

1. The Office of International Population and Urban Research, The Institute of International Research, University of California, 2234 Piedmont Avenue, Berkeley, California 94720.

2. The United Nations Demographic Yearbooks.

Preliminary contacts with other institutions interested in urban research abroad, before drafting a research proposal, is advisable so as to avoid duplicating research in process and to receive valuable comments and suggestions:

1. The Atlantic Institute, 24 quai du 4 Septembre, 92 Boulogne-sur-Seine, France.

2. Section for Local Government, Public Administration Branch, Bureau of Technical Assistance Operations, United Nations, New York, New York.

3. The International Urban Studies Project, Institute of Public Administration, 55 West 44th Street, New York, New York 10026.

4. The International Union of Local Authorities, 5 Paleisstraat, The Hague, Netherlands. A visit to the library of this organization is highly worthwhile.

The outstanding urban research institution of West Germany and one of the outstanding urban research institutions in Europe is the Verein für Kommunalwissenschaften, 1 Berlin 12 (Charlottenburg) Strasse des 17, Juni 112. The concentration here is research on urban problems in the Federal Republic of Germany.

Specifically in the urban planning and housing field, the National Swedish Institute for Building Research is exceptional. While the institute focuses on city planning and housing problems in Sweden, the results of the research are of international significance. Address: Valhallavägen 191, Stockholm 27.

The above specifications are by no means intended to be a complete listing. Numerous other research institutes in West Germany and Sweden are relevant to specialized aspects of urban problems, the names and addresses of which can be secured from the Embassy or the nearest Consulate of the country concerned.

Both West Germany and Sweden have the equivalents of the American Municipal Association. In both countries, there are two organizations, one for cities and one for other communes:

I. Federal Republic of Germany
  1. Deutscher Städtetag, Köln-Marienburg, Lindenallee 11.
  2. Deutscher Gemeindetag, Bad Godesberg, Koblenzen Strasse 37-39.

II. Sweden
  1. Svenska Stadsförbundet, Hornsgatan 15, Stockholm SÖ.
  2. Kommunalförbundet, S:t. Paulsgatan 6, Stockholm SÖ.

Invaluable assistance is available from any one of these organizations in the arrangement of interviews, particularly with the agency's own staff and under certain circumstances with municipal officials of member cities or communes.

In the universities throughout much of Europe, that which we know as "Political Science" consists largely of Law and Theory. Systematic and scholarly study of Public Admin-

istration has been introduced in the institutions of higher
learning in Great Britain, France, the Scandinavian countries,
West Germany, and a few other European countries.   The
universities in Great Britain and the Scandinavian countries
are similar to the universities in the United States in the
recognition of Political Science as a separate discipline.

    The Political Science Departments of the five univer-
sities in Sweden initiated at the end of 1965 a joint five-year
research program on Swedish local government.   The program is organized into three parts:

> 1.   The Citizens' Influence in Local Government.
> This includes various investigations of communal
> elections, the activities of communal assemblies,
> the participation of elected representatives in com-
> munal administration, the position of communal of-
> ficials, etc.

> 2.   The State and Local Self-Government.   Under
> this heading are included studies of the state's gen-
> eral direction and supervision of communal activity,
> the actual degree of self-government in some ma-
> jor areas of communal activity, etc.

> 3.   Communal Units in Relation to Communal
> Functions.   The purpose is to study the relation
> between function and area (or population) and to
> shed light on the question of the proper size and
> type of commune for the performance of different
> communal functions. [1]

    The project has been financed by a fund created to
commemorate the founding of the Bank of Sweden in 1668.
To direct the research a committee was formed consisting of:

> 1.   Professor Jörgen Westerståhl, University of
> Goteborg.

> 2.   Professor Pär-Erik Back, University of Umeå.

> 3.   Docent Nils Elvander, University of Uppsala.

> 4.   Professor Nils Stjernquist, University of Lund.

> 5.   Docent Gunnar Wallin, University of Stockholm.

It is planned that the project will be finished in 1970.
For the benefit of American and British political scientiests
and the general reading public, this study should be published
in English, as well as Swedish.   The above is indicative of
the increasing research attention being given to urban problems by European researchers.

Since the basic problem in this study was to discover
what we in the U. S. A. can learn from West German and
Swedish experience, it was necessary to investigate their
planning objectives, planning procedures, and to investigate
how the planning processes fit into the total policy-making
and governmental process.   It was necessary to investigate
what legal support is provided the planning process and the
land-use regulation.   Since zoning, as we know it in the
United States, is nowhere to be found in West Germany and
is unused in Sweden with one exception in central Stockholm,
how do they control land use and what is the extent of this
control?   All of this is a matter of comprehension and analysis of a system.   Measurements with mass data through
computers will have to come later in separate studies.

Procedurally, major reliance was placed on legal interpretation, analysis of administrative reports and on interviews; therefore in terms of research method and techniques,
nothing new is contributed.

Note

1.   Westerståhl, Jörgen, Swedish Local Government, A
     Five-Year Research Project (mimeographed statement,
     April 1966), p. 2.

Appendix

(Tables 2-18; Charts 1-3)

Table 2. Cologne Metropolitan Area: Jurisdictions, Population, Area, and Density.

Jurisdiction and Type[1]		Pop. 1966	Area in sq. km.	Pop. per sq. km.
(Northeast of Cologne)				
Leverkusen	Kreisfrei Stadt	106,347	46.16	2,308.8
Rhein-Wupper	Landkreis			
Opladen	Stadt	43,187	16.61	2,600.0
Bg. Neukirch	Gemeinde	5,563	8.82	630.7
Leichlingen	Stadt	18,312	25.43	720.0
Witzhelden	Gemeinde	3,563	15.35	232.01
Burzscheid	Stadt	15,454	27.57	560.5
(East and Southeast of Cologne)				
Rheinisch Bergischer	Landkreis			
Bergischer-Gladbach	Stadt	47,586	32.10	1,482.4
Odenthal	Gemeinde	10,866	41.28	263.2
Bechen	Gemeinde	2,483	16.13	153.9
Kürten	Amt	11,563	79.77	144.9
Bensberg	Stadt	38,325	61.67	621.4
Rösrath	Gemeinde	17,570	40.18	437.2
Porz	Stadt	70,059	73.89	948.1

(Southwest and West of Cologne)

Köln	Landkreis	237,543	292.61	811.8
Euskirchen	Landkreis			
Liblar	Amt	13,866	29.40	471.6
Kierdorf	Gemeinde	2,308	4.60	501.7
Bergheim	Landkreis			
Türnich	Gemeinde	13,161	25.36	518.9

(Northwest of Cologne)

Grevenbroich	Landkreis			
Nettesheim-Butzh.	Gemeinde	1,233	9.38	131.4
Frixheim-Anstel	Gemeinde	1,316	9.22	142.7
Straberg	Gemeinde	1,604	10.20	157.2
Heckenbroich	Gemeinde	3,831	12.29	311.7
Dormagen	Amt	25,285	28.87	875.8
Total of Suburbs		691,025	906.89	761.9
Cologne-Kreisfreis	Stadt	859,830	251.38	3,420.4
Grand Total		1,550,855	1,158.27	1,338.9

1. The meaning of the jurisdictional terms is given in Chapter 6.
2. All of Köln Landkreis is in the Cologne metropolitan area; therefore there is no listing of jurisdictions therein. The other Landkreis is partially in the metropolian area, therefore the listing of those jurisdictions is included.

Sources: Deutscher Städtetag, Statistisches Jahrbuch Deutscher Gemeinden, 1964; and, letter from the Statistisches Amt der Stadt Köln, 1967.

Table 3.   Stockholm Metropolitan Area: Jurisdictions, Population, Area, and Density.

Jurisdiction[1] and Type[2]		Pop. 1965	Area in sq. km.	Pop. per sq. km.
(North and Northwest of Stockholm)				
Solna*[3]	Stad	54,715	19.51	2,804
Stocksund*	Köping	4,966	3.02	1,644
Djursholm*	Stad	7,637	10.44	731
Danderyd*	Köping	14,728	12.63	1,166
Syhdbyberg*	Stad	27,802	6.82	4,077
Färingsö	Landskommun	3,276	82.16	40
Järfälla*	Landskommun	34,534	55.75	619
Sollentuna*	Köping	32,361	51.97	622
Upplands-Väsby*	Landskommun	12,273	78.21	157
Täby*	Köping	28,078	60.41	465
Märsta*	Landskommun	12,598	168.68	75
Sigtuna	Stad	3,735	53.38	60
Vallentuna	Landskommun	6,700	153.77	44
Österåker	Landskommun	8,042	211.40	38
(East of Stockholm)				
Lidingö*	Stad	33,661	30.73	1,096
Nacka*	Stad	23,418	28.17	486
Boo*	Landskommun	7,630	35.25	217
Saltsjöbaden*	Köping	6,179	12.00	515
Vaxholm	Stad	4,231	16.09	263
Gustavsberg	Landskommun	6,195	102.03	61
Värmdö	Landskommun	2,191	160.33	14

		(South of Stockholm)		
Huddinge*	Landskommun	41,150	129.35	318
Tyresö*	Landskommun	13,769	68.90	200
Österhaninge*	Landskommun	14,605	292.82	50
Grödinge	Landskommun	2,307	110.95	21
Västerhaninge	Landskommun	9,608	161.15	60
Sorunda	Landskommun	2,712	168.55	16
Ösmo	Landskommun	2,415	160.12	15
Nynäshamn	Stad	10,217	27.82	367
		(West and Southwest of Stockholm)		
Botkyrka*	Landskommun	15,522	83.23	187
Ekerö	Landskommun	4,550	133.79	34
Salem	Landskommun	2,739	63.91	43
Södertälje	Stad	43,472	104.37	417
Total of Suburbs		498,016	2,877.71	173
City of Stockholm		793,714	186.03	4,267
Grand Total		1,291,730	3,063.74	

1. The total list of jurisdictions belongs to the Greater Stockholm Local Traffic Association. Source: Principöverenskommelse om Samordnung, Urbyggnad och Drift av Det Kollektiva Traffik-systemet i Stor-Stockholm, Dec. 14, 1964. All the jurisdictions are in Stockholm Län (province or county).

2. Stad = city; Köping = borough; Landskommun = rural commune. The so-called rural communes in this listing, however, are not rural.

3. The jurisdictions which are asterisked belong to the Greater Stockholm Planning District. Source: Statistiska Centralbyrån, Statistisk årsbok, 1965, Table 13. They are also considered to be "Inner Suburbs." All the others are considered to be "Outer Suburbs," except Nynäshamm, Sigtuna, Sorunda, Södertälje and Ösmo, which are not officially included in the suburb category.

Table 4.   Cologne: Communities and Districts showing Population, Area in Hectares, and Population Density.

District (Stadtbezirke) Community (Stadtteil)	Total Hectares	Population	Population Per Hectare	Industrial Hectares
Altstadt-Süd	510	81,500	174.5	25.0
Altstadt-Nord	597	63,835	114.0	-
Duetz	504	20,406	50.0	43.5
Altstadt/Duetz	1,611	165,741	115.5	68.5
Bayenthal	128	7,481	68.0	16.4
Marienburg	218	5,096	25.2	7.6
Raderberg	99	6,282	63.5	15.0
Raderthal	141	4,087	29.0	-
Zollstock	387	22,212	57.4	12.5
Bayenthal	973	45,158	48.1	51.5
Klettenberg	104	15,043	144.6	-
Sülz	354	41,359	116.8	14.9
Lindenthal	765	35,628	47.6	-
Braunsfeld	150	12,037	80.2	-
Mungersdorf	483	6,984	14.5	1.5
Lindenthal	1,856	111,051	60.4	16.4

Ehrenfeld	381	39,278	103.1	233.6
Neu-Ehrenfeld	302	25,445	85.1	22.6
Vogelsang	396	13,574	35.4	30.7
Bickendorf	200	12,797	64.0	84.4
Bocklemünd/Mengenich	422	2,133	5.1	16.7
Ossendorf	786	5,432	6.9	-
Ehrenfeld	2,487	98,659	40.0	388.0
Nippes	465	55,673	119.7	27.1
Mauenheim	51	7,814	153.2	-
Riehl	351	16,224	55.6	11.6
Niehl	771	18,411	29.6	368.6
Weidenpesch	917	20,349	22.3	249.6
Longerich	489	10,452	21.4	3.6
Nippes	3,044	128,923	45.5	660.5
Fühlingen	510	2,043	4.2	-
Roggendorf/Thenhoven	1,544	2,161	1.4	-
Worringen	1,177	9,892	9.0	191.6
Blumenberg	321	--	--	-
Chorweiler	140	--	--	-
Heimersdorf	285	8,473	29.7	-
Volkhoven/Weiler	450	1,308	2.9	-
Merkenich	1,164	4,976	4.8	40.2
Seeberg	181	465	2.6	-
Chorweiler	5,772	29,318	5.3	231.8

Stadtbezirke Stadtteil	Hectares	Population	Population Per Hectare	Industrial Hectares
Poll	519	9,938	22.2	49.1
Humboldt-Gremberg	283	15,209	53.7	6.9
Kalk	299	23,909	80.0	95.6
Vingst	115	15,622	135.8	–
Höhenberg	212	13,129	61.9	–
Ostheim	404	10,512	26.1	–
Merheim	497	6,485	13.2	16.0
Brück	731	8,040	11.0	–
Rath	1,097	5,581	5.1	3.0
Kalk	4,157	108,425	26.6	170.6
Mülheim	714	49,560	77.4	190.5
Buchforst	86	8,920	103.7	6.1
Buchheim	289	14,086	48.7	14.3
Holweide	404	15,595	38.6	8.2
Dellbrück	990	18,171	18.4	29.4
Höhenhaus	512	18,461	36.1	3.7
Dünnwald	1,087	10,794	9.9	5.4
Stammheim	378	9,130	28.4	4.5
Flittard	776	10,069	13.7	77.2
Mülheim	5,236	154,786	30.6	399.3

Total	25,136	842,061	34.8	1,926.6
West of Rhine	15,239	558,444	38.1	1,416.7
East of Rhine	9,897	283,617	29.7	509.9

Source: Statistischen Amt der Stadt Köln, Statistisches Jahrbuch der Stadt Köln, 1964.

Table 3 "Flächen der Stadtbezirke und Stadtteile"

Table 8 "Wohnbevölkerungnach Stadtbezirken und Stadtteilen"

Figures for industrial hectares were secured in a special report from the Statistisches Amt der Stadt Köln, prepared for the author upon request, as of January 1, 1967.

Table 5.   Cologne: Dwelling Units by Number of Rooms, classified by Communities.

Community	Number of Rooms in D. U.									
	1	2	3	4	5	6	7	8	9	10
Alstadt/Deutz	518	334	549	473	95	21	3	2	--	--
Bayenthal	108	43	126	177	52	3	1	1	--	--
Lindenthal	107	84	144	187	59	17	4	2	3	4
Ehrenfeld	100	143	249	264	109	44	19	5	--	2
Nippes	108	106	342	528	146	9	5	3	2	1
Chorweiler	6	38	65	309	206	327	66	2	2	--
Kalk	74	184	374	486	75	40	16	10	4	1
Mulheim	175	197	766	1326	452	42	37	10	1	1
Total	1196	1129	2615	3750	1194	503	151	35	12	9

Source: Statistischen Amt der Stadt Köln, Statistisches Jahrbuch der Stadt Köln
1964, Table 121, "Fertiggestellte Wohnungen nach Stadtteilen sowie nach
der Anzahl der Räums."

Table 6. Cologne: Church Membership by
Land Legislative Districts as of June 6, 1961

Land Legisla- tive Districts	Roman Catholic %	Evangelical %	Other %
14	66.4	28.0	5.6
15	64.6	29.6	5.8
16	68.2	26.4	5.4
17	66.1	28.0	5.9
18	66.5	28.3	5.2
19	66.5	28.4	5.1
20	63.8	30.6	5.6
TOTAL	66.0	28.5	5.5

Source: Statistiches Amt der Stadt Köln, Mitteilungen der Stadt Köln,
         1965, pp. 114-115.

Table 7.   Cologne: Election Returns for 1962,
1964 and 1965 by Land Legislative Districts.

Year	% of Eligible Electorate Voting	% of Vote for Political Parties[1]			
		SPD	CDU	FDP	Other
District 14					
1962	54. 0	48. 9	43. 1	5. 4	2. 6
1964	60. 7	61. 9	33. 4	4. 7	---
1965	69. 5	47. 2	43. 7	6. 3	2. 8
District 15					
1962	57. 5	41. 0	48. 6	7. 5	2. 9
1964	64. 1	55. 4	39. 1	5. 5	---
1965	69. 9	40. 7	48. 9	7. 6	2. 8
District 16					
1962	57. 7	45. 2	46. 0	5. 9	2. 9
1964	62. 4	57. 1	37. 9	5. 0	---
1965	70. 9	44. 0	46. 7	6. 5	2. 8
District 17					
1962	56. 2	44. 5	47. 2	5. 4	2. 9
1964	61. 4	58. 3	37. 0	4. 7	---
1965	69. 6	43. 6	47. 0	6. 5	2. 9
District 18					
1962	58. 2	44. 9	47. 8	4. 7	2. 6
1964	64. 6	56. 4	39. 9	3. 7	---
1965	73. 7	44. 4	47. 8	5. 5	2. 3
District 19					
1962	61. 6	48. 9	44. 1	4. 3	2. 7
1964	65. 6	58. 5	37. 8	3. 5	0. 2
1965	74. 7	48. 8	43. 8	4. 9	2. 5
District 20					
1962	59. 9	53. 2	39. 6	3. 9	3. 3
1964	64. 5	63. 4	32. 9	3. 7	---
1965	74. 2	51. 6	40. 7	4. 8	2. 9
Cologne - Total[2]					
1962	62. 4	45. 3	46. 5	5. 3	2. 9
1964	64. 8	57. 4	38. 1	4. 5	0. 0
1965	81. 0	44. 2	47. 0	6. 1	2. 7

1.   Election returns without absentee ballots.
2.   Election returns including absentee ballots.
Source: Statistisches Amt der Stadt Köln, Statistische Mitteilungen der Stadt Köln, 1965, p. 117-118.

Table 8. Cologne: Percentage of Persons in Each Occupational Classification (Soziale Stellung)[1] by Land Legislative Districts.

| | Land Legislative Districts | | | | | | | |
	14	15	16	17	18	19	20	Total
Self-Employed	9.2	11.1	9.7	9.8	6.4	6.1	5.5	8.3
Family Members Helping in Household	1.4	1.3	1.3	1.4	1.0	0.9	0.8	1.2
Officials	5.6	8.9	5.5	8.4	6.6	4.9	5.3	6.5
Employees	28.7	31.7	25.7	29.6	24.3	27.0	23.5	27.4
Labor	33.8	24.5	37.1	29.4	41.5	41.9	45.3	36.0
Pensioners	18.4	18.7	17.3	18.3	17.6	17.6	17.8	17.9
Other[2]	2.9	3.8	3.4	3.1	2.6	1.6	1.8	2.7

Source: Statistisches Amt der Stadt Köln, Mitteilungen der Stadt Köln, 1965, p. 114-115.

1. According to the predominant means of livelihood of the supporter, including the members of the family.

2. Apprentices, students and military personnel.

Table 9. Cologne: Committees and Subcommittees of the City Council, specifying Number of Councilmanic and Citizen Voting Members, and Party Affiliation of Members and Chairmen (September 1966).

Committees and Subcommittees	Councilmanic Members		Chairmen		Citizen Members	Total
	SPD	CDU	SPD	CDU		
1. General Administration	8	5	x		0	13
2. Retrenchment of Expenditures	3	2		x	0	5
3. Advisory Council for Questions on Building Design	3	2	x		3	8
4. Negotiations	4	3	x		0	7
5. Naming of Streets (Special)	3	2	x		0	5
6. Resolutions	3	2	x		1 SPD & 1 CDU	7
7. Federal Garden Appearance (Special)	8	5		x	0	13
8. Custody of Ancient Monuments and Natural Beauty	5	4	x		0	9
9. Design of the Cathedral Neighborhood (Special)	3	2	(not specified)		0	5

No.	Committee						
10.	Investigation of Expenditures (Special)	3	2		x	0	5
11.	Completed Construction (Special)	3	2		x	0	5
12.	Finance and Taxes	10	7	x		0	17
13.	Gardens, Green Spaces and Forests	8	5	x		0	13
14.	Foreign Workers in Cologne, Social and Cultural Care as well as Health	2	2	(not specified)	x	13	17
15.	Inns and Restaurants	3	2	x		0	5
16.	Health	8	5	x		0	13
17.	Industrial Developments, Neue Stadt, Worker Concern	4	3	(not specified)		0	7
18.	Reconstruction of the Hacketäuer Military Post (Special)	4	3		(not specified)	0	7
19.	Chief Committee	10	7	x		0	17
20.	Multiple-Story Structures	8	5		x	0	13
21.	Youth Welfare	5	4		x	15	24
	a) Youth Hostels	(1)	(1)			(4)	
	b) Youth Homes	(2)	(0)			(6)	
	c) Youth Care	(1)	(1)			(6)	
	d) Child Care	(1)	(1)			(3)	

	Councilmanic Members		Chairmen		Citizen Members	Total
	SPD	CDU	SPD	CDU		
22. Jurists	4	2	x		0	6
23. Holweide Hospital (Special)	4	3	x		0	7
24. Art and Culture	9	6	x		0	15
a) Small Committee for the Hänneschen-Theater	3	2	x		0	5
b) Museums	4	3		x	0	7
c) Theater and Music	4	3		x	2	9
d) Adult Education	4	3		x	0	7
25. Real Estate	8	5		x	0	13
26. Neue Stadt (Special)	5	4		x	0	9
27. Public Facilities	8	5		x	0	13
28. City Hall New Construction	4	3	x		0	7
29. Auditing	8	5		x	0	13
30. Law and Security	5	4		x	0	9
31. Schools	9	6	x		4 w/vote 3 no vote	19 w/vote
32. Social	8	5	x		6	19
33. Sports	10	7		x	0	17
34. Stadtautobahn (Special)	5	4	x		0	9
35. City Planning	9	6	x		3	18
36. Underground Construction	8	5	x		0	13
37. Transfer	1	1	(not specified)			
38. Subway (Special)	5	4		x	0	9
39. Expenditure for General Matters (Incidentals)	3	2	x		0	5

No.	Committee/Subcommittee						
41.	Traffic Safety	8	5		x	8 w/vote 1 no vote 3 police 3 admin.	21 w/vote
42.	Traffic Signs	3	2		x		11
43.	Defense	5	4		x	0	5
44.	Cooperation with the Displaced Persons and Organizations	3	2		x	0	5
45.	Water and Bridge Construction	5	4		x	0	9
46.	Domestic Economy and Harbors	8	5	x		0	13
47.	Residential Construction	8	5		x	0	13
48.	Regulation of Hardship Cases in accordance with sec. 6, para. 5 of the Law on the Increase of Fees for the Use of the Public Municipal Facilities for Waste Disposal (Special)	3	2		x	0	5

The Committees and Subcommittees are listed in the order given by the Office of the Oberstadtdirektor, which is alphabetical in the German original.

Table 10. Cologne Landkreis: Jurisdictions, Population, Area, and Density.

Jurisdiction and Type		Pop. 1961	Area in sq. km.	Pop. per sq. km.
Brühl	Stadt	35,302	36.09	978
Frechen	Stadt	26,613	32.68	814
Brauweiher	Gemeinde	6,742	23.73	284
Hürth	Gemeinde	45,695	56.83	804
Lövenich	Gemeinde	18,754	17.25	1087
Rodenkirchen	Gemeinde	29,141	43.68	667
Stommeln	Gemeinde	3,811	25.26	151
Wesseling	Gemeinde	20,000	16.35	1223
Fulheim	Gemeinde	6,148	14.84	414
Sinnersdorf	Gemeinde	3,666	19.00	193
Total		196,655	292.61	675.4
Increase in Population 1961-1966:		18,845		
Total 1966		215,500	292.61	811.8

Source: Statistische Rundschau 1965 für den Regierungsbezirk Köln, published
by Statistisches Landesamt Nordrhein-Westfalen.

Table 11. Stockholm: Dwelling Units by Number of Rooms, Classified by Inner and Outer City, as of 1965.

Dwelling Unit Classification	Inner City	Outer City	Total City
1 room kitchenette	33,437	17,606	51,043
2 or more rooms, kitchenette	10,993	5,090	16,083
1 room & kitchen	45,723	19,344	65,067
2 rooms & kitchen	37,710	53,306	91,016
3 rooms & kitchen	16,906	43,291	60,197
4 rooms & kitchen	8,300	16,341	24,641
5 rooms & kitchen	4,909	7,234	12,143
6 rooms & kitchen	2,258	2,657	4,915
7 rooms & kitchen	816	930	1,746
8 rooms & kitchen	347	404	751
9 or more rooms & kitchen	248	194	442
Data not available	324	228	552
Total dwelling units	161,971	166,625	328,596
Total rooms	311,541	414,382	725,923
Total kitchens	117,922	143,710	260,932
Total rooms & kitchen	428,763	558,092	986,855
Average rooms & kitchen per dwelling unit	2.6	3.3	3.0

Source: Stockholm Office of Statistics, Monthly Statistical Review, 1967, No. 6, Table 1, p. 8*.

Table 12.   Stockholm: Inner and Outer City Parishes showing Population, Area in Hectares, and Population Density, as of 1968.

Parish	Area, hectares			Population	Pop. per hectare
	Land	Water	Total		
Inner City	3440	5	3445	301,221	88
Nikolai	42	-	42	6,281	150
Klara	65	-	65	1,900	29
Kungsholm	108	-	108	19,778	183
St Göran	284	-	284	34,183	120
Adolf Fredrik	51	-	51	8,724	171
Gustav Vasa	78	-	78	13,400	172
Matteus	133	-	133	31,215	235
Jakob	63	-	63	1,735	28
Johannes	77	-	77	12,408	161
Engelbrekt	885	5	890	19,190	22
Hedvig Eleonora	59	-	59	12,727	216
Oscar	849	-	849	37,744	44
Katarina	169	-	169	35,812	212
Sofia	256	-	256	18,395	72
Maria	62	-	62	14,999	242
Högalid	259	-	259	32,730	126

Outer City					
Hägersten	15158	478	15,636	470,703	31
Brännkyrka	1972	13	1,985	79,795	40
Vantör	1333	15	1,348	42,953	32
Enskede	1020	10	1,030	59,627	58
Skarpnäck	875	-	875	41,762	48
Farsta	1568	224	1,792	40,685	26
Bromma	1538	184	1,722	65,232	42
Västerled	1563	17	1,580	38,756	25
Essinge	932	10	942	26,411	28
Spånga	95	-	95	8,048	85
Hässelby	3491	5	3,496	39,738	11
	771	-	771	27,696	36
Entire City	18598	483	19,081	771,924	42

Source: Svante Fornö, Stockholms Stads Statistiska Kontor, March 10, 1969.

Table 13. Stockholm Metropolitan Area: Community Shopping Centers in New Towns.

Name of Community and Direction from	CBD	Floor Area for Shops		Floor Area for Community Services		Car Spaces
		sq. meters	sq. feet	sq. meters	sq. feet	
Vällingby	W	18,000	193,752	37,000	301,392	2,500
Farsta	S	28,000	302,000	57,000	613,548	2,300
Jacobsberg	NW	20,000	215,280	40,000	430,560	2,000
Täby	N	23,000	248,500	7,500	20,730	2,500
Märsta	N	40,000	430,560	140,000	1,506,860	5,280
Total		129,000	1,388,592	281,500	2,933,190	14,580

Source: Ahlberg, C. F., Shopping Centers and Satellite Towns in the Stockholm Region, Duplicated by Kungliga Tekniska Högskolan, Institutionen för Stadsbyggnad, 1965. Floor area for community service was not available on Skärholmen or Järvafältet Community Shopping Centers.

Table 14. Stockholm: Numbers of Establishments, Employees, and Median Incomes by Occupational Groupings, as of 1965.

Occupational Group	Number of Establishments	Number of Employees	Median Incomes per Establishment	Median Income per Employee
Agriculture[1]	211	1,677	27,114	20,662
Building Trade	1,195	30,599	28,050	24,630
Industry and Handicrafts	3,987	106,201	21,682	20,740
Communications	2,037	42,145	26,391	20,208
Business	9,770	146,616	27,502	18,012
Professions	2,608	16,235	32,845	18,164
Public Administration	---	87,780	---	20,000
House Work	---	2,380	---	6,758
Other	58	572	33,121	11,837
Total	19,866	434,205		
Median Income			26,967	19,707

1. Including related occupations.

Source: Stockholm Office of Statistics, Monthly Statistical Review, Volume 62, 1967 Number 1, p. 24* Table III and p. 25* Table V.

Table 15. Stockholm Metropolitan Area: Population and Employment in 1960.

Jurisdiction	Population	Resident and Employed	Working Places	Column 4 as %-age of Col. 3
Stor-Stockholm	1,148,916	550,819	536,758	97
Planning District	1,108,980	533,877	522,833	98
City of Stockholm	808,591	394,943	430,930	109
Inner City	342,466	178,652	320,326	179
Outer City	459,987	215,327	97,247	45
Inner Suburbs	300,389	138,934	91,903	66
Sundbyberg	26,987	14,075	10,718	76
Solna	50,863	25,532	25,465	100
Stocksund	5,027	2,053	733	36
Danderyd	11,641	5,205	2,999	58
Djursholm	7,436	2,787	1,664	60
Lidingö	29,330	12,575	7,754	62
Järfälla	19,034	8,652	4,247	49
Sollentuna	25,090	10,885	4,228	39
Täby	21,146	9,247	3,697	40
Uppl.-Väsby	8,826	4,179	3,060	73
Märsta	6,228	2,621	1,942	74
Boo	6,680	3,162	1,240	39
Nacka	20,737	9,840	10,701	109
Saltsjöbaden	55,302	2,175	1,325	61

Tyresö	5,977	2,786	1,263	45
Österhaninge	9,269	4,031	2,123	53
Huddinge	29,086	13,839	5,441	39
Botkyrka	11,730	5,290	3,303	62
Outer Suburbs	39,936	16,942	12,688	75
Vallentuna	5,424	2,224	1,189	53
Österåker	5,957	2,364	1,430	60
Vaxholm	3,788	1,577	1,417	90
Värmdö	1,925	767	569	74
Gustavsberg	5,154	2,553	2,177	85
Västerhaninge	6,405	2,731	2,304	84
Grödinge	1,980	744	363	49
Salem	2,302	982	589	60
Ekerö	3,869	1,654	1,675	101
Färingsö	3,132	1,346	975	72

Source: Stadskollegiets Utlåtanden och Memorial, 1965. Bihang Nr. 85, Tunnelbaneplan for Stor-Stockholm. Förslag avgivet av Generalplaneberedningens Tunnelbane-kommitte, p. 19.

Not included in the above tabulation are the following jurisdictions, which are included in Table 3: 1. Nynäshamn, 2. Ösmo, 3. Sorunda, 4. Södertälj.

316   Cologne and Stockholm

Table 16.   Stockholm: Voting Participation (by Per Cent of
Eligible Voters) in All Elections since World War II.

Year	Council Elections	Elections to the Second Chamber of the Riksdag
1946	74. 5	
1948		84. 2
1950	81. 4	
1952		80. 7
1954	79. 8	
1956		80. 8
1958	78. 7	76. 6
1960		85. 0
1962	78. 5	
1964		82. 6
1966	80. 4	
1968		87. 4

Source: Stockholm Office of Statistics by correspondence
through Mr. Svante Fornö, Secretary, March 10,
1969.

Table 17.   Stockholm: Median Income per Male Income
Earner, by Parish (1967).

Parish	Numer of Male Income Earners	Median Income in SKr
Inner City	112,678	20,577
Nikolai	2,273	20,792
Klara	727	17,575
Kungsholm	7,467	21,172
St. Göran	12,975	20,455
Adolf Fredrick	3,440	20,069
Gustav Vasa	4,881	20,640
Matteus	11,834	19,639
Jacob	981	19,879
Johannes	4,775	20,335
Engebrecht	7,116	22,828
Hedvig Eleanora	4,410	23,085
Oscar	13,048	26,377
Katarina	14,658	18,419
Sofia	6,742	19,345
Maria	5,886	19,516
Högalid	11,465	19,538
Outer City	159,219	23,331
Hägerstens	22,563	21,652
Bränkyrka	15,299	23,172
Vantörs	19,313	24,848
Enskede	16,149	22,346
Skarpnäcks	15,163	22,426
Farsta	21,262	23,682
Bromma	14,793	23,089
Västerleds	9,514	25,344
Essinge	3,327	21,450
Spånga	12,933	24,486
Hässelby	8,903	25,210
Total for City	278,704	21,971

Source: Stockholm Office of Statistics, Monthly Statistical Review, Vol. 62, 1967 No. 1, Table XI, p. 42*-46*. This report includes separate data on males and females and has a breakdown showing the percentage of income earners per 1000 SKr, in addition to the data given in this table.   The parishes are listed in the above table in the same sequence as they are given in the official report.

Table 18. Communal Blocs by Election Districts for the Proposed Stor-Stockholm
Landsting, showing the Population in 1963 and the Estimated Population for 1975.

| Communal Blocs | Population | |
	Dec. 31, 1963	1975 Estimate
District I		
Märsta	14,955	27,100
Vallentuna	8,266	10,000
Åkerberga	8,721	11,200
Vaxholm	4,094	6,000
Upplands-Väsby	11,690	15,000
Sollentuna	31,060	35,000
Jacobsberg	30,745	60,000
Roslags-Näsby	26,121	40,000
Danderyd	26,274	31,800
Lidingö	32,956	45,000
Solna-Sundyberg	81,675	121,000
Träkvista-Tappström	7,408	8,500
Total	283,964	405,500
District II		
Östhammar	9,064	8,000
Hallstavik	10,952	10,500
Norrtälje	18,210	19,300
Rimbo	7,879	8,200
Total	46,105	46,000

District III

Nacka	36,338	70,500
Bollmora	11,514	15,000
Gustavsberg	9,375	10,000
Huddinge	37,731	75,000
Handen	21,778	32,000
Tumba	16,806	28,500
Total	133,532	231,00

District IV

Nynäshamn	15,175	20,000
Södertälje	66,439	87,000
Total	81,614	107,000

Grand Total (not including the City of Stockholm)	544,945	789,500

Source: Calmfors, Rabinovitz and Alesch, Urban Government for Greater Stockholm, (New York: Frederick A. Praeger, Publishers, 1968), p. 70. Table 17. The listing of Communal blocs is rearranged in accordance with the listing and grouping by the Storlandtingskommitten in its recommendations for election districts for the proposed Stockholms Storlandsting.

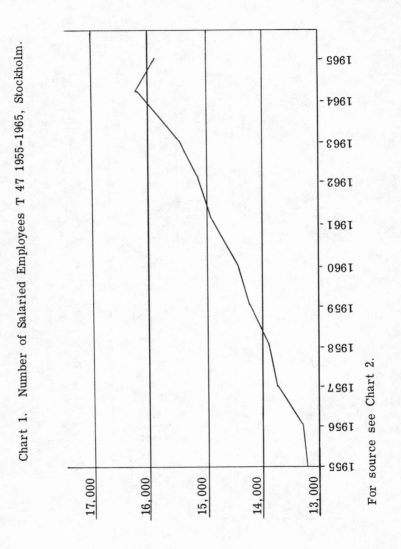

Chart 1. Number of Salaried Employees T 47 1955–1965, Stockholm.

For source see Chart 2.

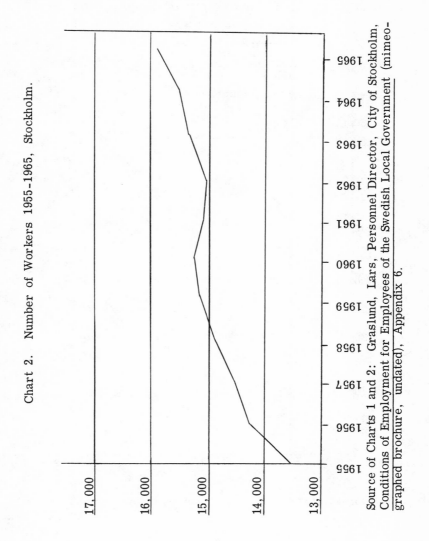

Chart 2.   Number of Workers 1955-1965, Stockholm.

Source of Charts 1 and 2: Graslund, Lars, Personnel Director, City of Stockholm, Conditions of Employment for Employees of the Swedish Local Government (mimeo-graphed brochure, undated), Appendix 6.

Chart 3.
Development of Salaries and Wages in Stockholm 1955-1964.

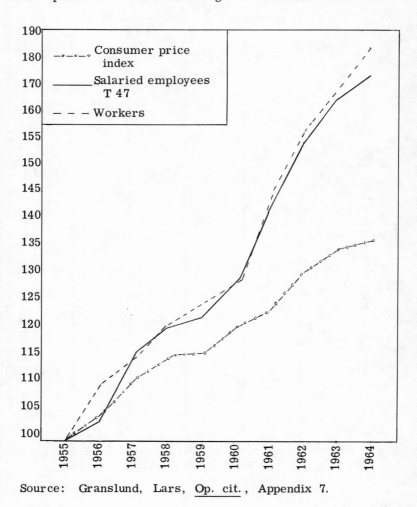

Source: Granslund, Lars, Op. cit. , Appendix 7.

Index

Academy of Administrative Sciences, Speyer, West Germany, 135

Administration,
    Cologne, central management headquarters, 116
        over-all administrative organization, 114-115
        Office for the Examination of the Records of the City, 118
        respect for professional education and experience, 88
        supervision and coordination, 120, 124
    Stockholm, central management headquarters, 224
        over-all administrative organization, 224-225
        boards, 179-180
        respect for professional education and experience, 192
        role of permanent, expert staff in policy determination,
            192-193
        sharing of common values, 194-195
        supervision and coordination, 237
    Comparative, 277-279

Ahlberg, C. F., Director of Regional Planning, Stockholm,
    153, 154, 155-156, 158, 162, 218, 268

Almström, Lars, Stockholm Chamber of Commerce, 214

Atmer, Thomas, Arkitekt S.A.R., Stadsbyggnadsekreterare,
    Building Office, Stockholm, 140, 218

Berlin, 15, 32-33, 61, 65

Billboards and exterior advertising,
    West Germany, 64-65
    Sweden, 165-166
    Comparative, 275

Bonn, 33-35, 66, 129

Bridges, effect on development,
    Cologne, 53-54
    Stockholm, 269, 270

Building Administration, Department of,
     Cologne, administrative headquarters, 93
          City Planning Office, 94-96
          Building Inspection Office, 97-98
          Office for Residential Housing Promotion, 100
          Office for Above-Ground Construction and
               Maintenance, 102-103
          Office for Below-Ground Construction and
               Maintenance, 103-104
          Garden and Cemeteries Office, 105
          over-all responsibility for urban development, 106
     Stockholm, Building Board, Department of Greater
          Stockholm, 201-202
          Building Office, 201-204
          City Planning Office, 204-205
          City Surveyors Division, 204
          Building Permit Bureau, 204, 209
          Building Inspection Bureau, 210

Byström, Olof, Stockholm University and Senior Keeper,
     City Museum of Stockholm, 143

Calmfors, Hans, Chief Clerk, City of Stockholm, 179

Cathedral of Cologne, 48-49

Center for Local Government Studies, Berlin, 134

Central Business District,
     Cologne, 51-53
     Stockholm, 160, 166-168

Circulation of men and material,
     Cologne, motor traffic, 63-64
          subways, 65-67
     Stockholm, motor traffic, 165
          subways, 162-165
     Comparative, 269-270

Citizen access to government,
     Cologne, 85-86
     Stockholm, 197, 236-237

City Council,
     Cologne, 76-79
          committees, 83-87
          control of administration, 88

    non-council representation on committees, 85-86
    sessions, 89
    vocations of members, 83
  Stockholm, 178-179
    committees, 189-190
    concern of apathy of citizens, 195-196
    control of administration, 178
    influence of proportional representation system of
      elections, 193
    non-council membership on boards, serving as
      council committees, 180
    sessions, 191-192
    sharing of common values, 194-195
    vocations of members, 188-189
  Comparative, 276

Communes, Sweden, efforts to reduce the number of small
    rural communes, 241-242
  communal blocks and collaboration councils, 242-245
  metropolitan area communal blocks, 244
  provision for guide lines for planning within communal
    block, 244
  difference between communal associations and commune
    associations, 245

Communities and neighborhoods,
  Cologne, 60-61
  Stockholm, 152-153, 217-219

Conservation Office, Cologne, 93, 110

Council for the Preservation of the City's Beauty, Depart-
    ment of Greater Stockholm, 203-204

County of Stockholm, 38, 248, 252

Demonstration Cities and Metropolitan Development Act of
    1966, U.S., 282-283

Deutschen Städtetag, West Germany, 15, 134

Development procedure, Stockholm, 210-211

Division for municipal development planning, Cologne, 93, 107

Dusseldorf, Rhine-Ruhr metropolitan region, 33-35, 66, 129

Economic and social pattern,
    Cologne, 79-80
    Stockholm, 185-186
    Comparative, 275-276

Elections,
    Cologne, 76-79
    Stockholm, 181-185, 193, 196-197

Essen, Rhine-Ruhr metropolitan region, 33-34

Finance,
    Cologne, budget procedure, 121
        budget totals, 120
        income including taxes, 121-122
        audits, 122
    Stockholm, budget procedure, 225-226
        budget totals, 228-229
        income including taxes, 227
        surpluses during the 1960s, 226
        audits, 230

Garpe, Joakim, former Commissioner for City Planning,
    Stockholm, 145

Godlund, Sven, University of Gothenburg, Sweden, 27

Gothenburg, Sweden, 16, 42-43, 244

Gottman, Jean, University of Paris, 27

Gräslund, Lars, Personnel Director, City of Stockholm,
    232-233, 235

Greater Stockholm County,
    proposal, 250-254
    government, 254-257

Hall, Peter, Birkbeck College, London, 33, 35, 38

Hamburg, 15, 61, 65, 67

Hanson, Bertil, Joint Center for Urban Studies of the M.I.T.

and Harvard University, 192-193

Heckscher, August, Commissioner of Parks and Administrator of Recreation and Cultural Affairs, City of New York, 152

Hellden, David, Arkitekt S.A.R., Stockholm, 166-167

Historical origin,
Cologne, 15, 53
Stockholm, 141

Holland, Laurence B., 218-219

Holm, Lennart, Director, National Swedish Institute for Building Research, 140

Holm, Per, Editor, Plan Tidskrift, 211

Housing,
Cologne, shortage, 56
size of households, 57-58
social housing, 100-101
land and stadt loans and grants, 100
home-owned dwellings, 101
Stockholm, shortage, 144-147
construction, 145, 149
size of households, 146
standards for residential construction, 149-151
"social approach" housing, 215
"general approach" housing, 215-216
national loans and grants, 216
Comparative, shortage, 265
apartment dwellings accepted as normal, 265

Human and social implications of the environment, 281-282

Hötorget, Stockholm, 166-167

Industrial development,
Cologne, 61-63
Stockholm, 161-162

Inter-communal relations between Stockholm and suburbs, three stages, 246

327

Jensen, Rolf, University of Adelaide, 277

Land-use,
   Cologne, development policy, 110
      Federal Space Ordering Law, 68-69
      Land law prohibiting unused land, 55, 69
      land-use determination of municipally owned property,
         109
      open spaces, 53-55, 105-106
      outside city limits, 68-69
      over-all, 54-55
      problems, 52, 67-68
   Stockholm, land-use determination of municipally owned
      property, 211
      National Building Act, 205
      National planning policy, 206-207
      over-all 151, 154
      parks, 151-152
      regional plans, 207
      Vallingby, 158-159
   Comparative
      open spaces, 271-272
      outside city limits, 266
      problems, 270-271
      supervision and assistance from higher levels of gov-
        ernment, 279-280

Langenfelt, Per, Swedish Association of Rural Municipalities,
   23

Lehman, President, Cologne Deutsche Gewerkschaft Bund, 82

Leverkusen, Cologne M.A., 34-37, 61, 129

Local Government School, Sigtuna, Sweden, 232, 259

Local political and administration subdivisions
   West Germany, amt (North Rhine-Westphalia), 126, 132
      gemeinde, 126-127, 132
      landkreis, 127-128, 132-133
      kreisfreie stadt, 134
      landschaftsverband (North Rhine-Westphalia), 129-131
      regierungsbezirke (North Rhine-Westphalia), 128-129
   Sweden, communes, 241-245
      län (county), 176, 205, 228, 241-244

Local self-government,
  West Germany, historical background, 73
    after World War II, 73-74
    Basic Law of the Federal Republic of Germany, 74-76
  Sweden, historical background, 175-176
    after the 1920s, 176-178
    Communal Law for Stockholm, 179

Lundh, Secretary, Swedish Association of Rural Municipalities, 23

Malmö, Sweden, 43, 244

Mehr, Hjalmar, former Commissioner of Finance, currently Commissioner of Real Estate, 250, 253

Metropolitan, coordination within area,
  Cologne, special purpose districts (zweckverbände), 131-132
    planning districts (planungsverbände), 132
    joint working associations (arbeitsgemeinschaft), 132
  Stockholm, contracts, 246
    joint corporations, 249-250
    communal cooperation by committee, 250
    Communal Association for the Stockholm Regional Problems, 248-249, 252-253
  Cooperation Council of Stockholm Suburbs, 246-247
  Greater Stockholm Delegation, Department of Greater Stockholm, 201, 203-204, 247
  Greater Stockholm Hospital Board, 248
  Greater Stockholm Local Traffic Association, 38-39
  Greater Stockholm Planning Board, 38-39, 249, 253
  Greater Stockholm Regional Planning Association, 247

Metropolitan, definitions,
  Bollens, John C., University of California, 29
  Boustedt, Olaf, Director, Statischen Landesamtes, Hamburg, 30
  Foley, Donald, University of California, 31
  International Research Urban, University of California, 28-29
  Robson, William A., University of London, 29-30
  U.S. Bureau of the Census, 29
  West Germany and Great Britain, 30

Metropolitan, geographic extent of area,
  Rhine-Ruhr Region, 32-38

Cologne, 34-37, 129, 133-144
Stockholm, 38-41, 253-255
Comparative, 280

Millett, John D., Chairman, National Academy of Public
   Administration, 277

Morstein Marx, Fritz, Academy of Administrative Sciences,
   Speyer, West Germany, 135

Mumford, Lewis, 48

Munich, 15, 61, 65-66

National Swedish Institute for Building Research, Stockholm,
   219

New towns,
   Cologne, Neu Stadt, 58-59
   Stockholm, 152, 154
      Vällingby, 154-156
      Farsta, 156-157
      comparison of Vällingby and Farsta, 156-158
      seven policites, 159-160
   Comparative, 273

Oelrich, Nils, Statsarkitekt in charge of the Building Inspection Bureau, Stockholm, 211

Parking facilities,
   Cologne, 64
   Stockholm, 166

Pedestrian streets,
   Cologne, 49
   Stockholm, 166-167, 214
   Comparative, 268-269

Personnel,
   Cologne, organization, 116-118
      classifications, 119
      number per classification, 118-119
      personnel policies, 116-119
   Stockholm, organization, 230

classifications, 230-231
number per classification, 231
selection of personnel, 231
induction training, 231-232
collective bargaining, 232-234
salaries and wages, 234-235
other personnel policies, 235-236

Planning,
Cologne, planning law, 68, 69, 96
process, 94-95
implementation, 96-99
shopping centers, 99
problems, 106-107
Stockholm, National Building Law, 205-207
process, 204-206, 208-209
Master Planning Commission, 205
regional plans, 207
town plans, 208
approval by higher levels of government, 209
implementation, 209-210
shopping centers, 153-159
problems, 217-218
urban renewal plans, 214-215
citizen participation, 209, 219
National Swedish Institute for Building Research, 219
Comparative, process, 278-279
citizen participation, 276
implementation, 266
supervision by higher levels of government, 279-280

Pliscke, Elmer, University of Maryland, 89

Political parties,
West Germany, 76-77
Cologne, 77-79
Stockholm, 180-185
Comparative, 276

Pollution, regulation of,
North Rhine-Westphalia, 63, 71-72 (footnote 30), 131
Stockholm, 216-217
Comparative, 272, 280

Population,
Cologne, density, 57
distribution, 129

Stockholm, density, 148
   distribution, 147
Comparative, density, 271-272

Preservation of the historic,
   Cologne, City Hall, 49-50
   Dionysius-Mosaic, 50
   Hohestrasse, 49
   Roman wall, 50
   Thirteenth Century Wall, 51
Stockholm, Gamla Stan (Old City), 16, 141-143
Comparative, 267-268

Pressure groups,
   Cologne, trade unions and Chamber of Commerce, 81-82
      issues, 82
      tactics, 83
      representation in the City Council, 83
      influence built into the council structure, 90
   Stockholm, trade union and other organizations, 186-187
      issues, 187-188
      tactics, 188
      representation in the City Council, 188
      influence built into the administrative structure, 180

Public ownership of land,
   Cologne, 109
   Stockholm, 148-151
   Comparative, 265-266

Randstad (Amsterdam, Rotterdam, the Hague, Leiden,
      Haarlem and Utrecht), 38

Real estate office,
   Cologne, 93, 107-108
      purchase and sale of land and buildings, 108-109
   Stockholm, 201-202
      purchase and sale of land and buildings, 202

Shepheard, Peter, English architect and landscape designer,
      151-152

Shopping centers,
   Cologne, 99
   Stockholm, 153-154

Vällingby, 155
Farsta, 156
Skärholmen, 158
comparative data on five shopping centers, 159

Siedenbladh, Göran, Stockholm Planning Director, 148, 153,
157, 165, 217-218

Sigtuna, Stockholm M.A., 39

Södertälj, Stockholm M.A., 39-41

Stone, Edward Durell, U.S. architect, 275

Swedish Commune Association, 232, 244, 258-259

Swedish County Council Association, 232

Swedish Municipal Association, 17, 232, 244, 258-259

Urban, definitions,
    France, 21
    Great Britain, 22
    Sweden, 22-23
    United States, 24
    West Germany, 21

Urban design, Stockholm, 218-219

Urban development, four periods, Stockholm, 140-141

Urban renewal, Stockholm, plans, 214-215
    zonal expropriation procedure, 212-214

Urbanization, extent of, Northeastern European countries and
    the United States, 25-27

U.S. Department of Housing and Urban Development, 283

Valuation of land and Buildings for purchase and sale,
    Cologne, 108-109
    Stockholm, 213-214

Wagener, Frido, Department Secretary, Association of
    Countries, 128
333

Wannfors, Erik, Division Director, National Building and
    Planning Board, Sweden, 206-207

Waterfront,
    Cologne, 51-52
    Stockholm, 151

Wendt, Paul F., University of California, 274-275

Ylvisaker, Paul, Director, Public Affairs Program,
    Ford Foundation, 277

Zoning, Stockholm, 208, 266-267, 274, 276

Zoo management, Cologne, 53-54